OTHER A TO Z GUIDES ... THE SCARECROW PRESS, INC.

The A to Z of
New Age Movements

Michael York

The A to Z Guide Series, No. 33

THE SCARECROW PRESS, INC.
Lanham • Toronto • Plymouth, UK
2009

Published by Scarecrow Press, Inc.
A wholly owned subsidary of
The Rowman & Littlefield Publishing Group, Inc.
4501 Forbes Boulevard, Suite 200, Lanham, Maryland 20706
http://www.scarecrowpress.com

Estover Road, Plymouth PL6 7PY, United Kingdom

British Library Cataloguing in Publication Information Available

Library of Congress Cataloging-in-Publication Data

The hardback version of this book was cataloged by the Library of Congress as follows:

York, Michael, 1939–
  Historical dictionary of New Age movements / Michael York.
    p. cm. — (Historical dictionaries of religions, philosophies, and movements ; no. 49)
  Includes bibliographical references and index.
  1. New Age movement—Dictionaries. I. Title. II. Series.
BP605.N48 Y675 2004
299'.93—dc21   2003012725

ISBN 978-0-8108-6816-8 (pbk. : alk. paper)
ISBN 978-0-8108-6332-3 (ebook)

♾™ The paper used in this publication meets the minimum requirements of American National Standard for Information Sciences—Permanence of Paper for Printed Library Materials, ANSI/NISO Z39.48-1992.

Printed in the United States of America

To my former teacher
Peter Bernard Clarke,
who championed my interest
in this area
and
taught me how to approach
its many dimensions
from a critical yet sympathetic perspective

Contents

Acknowledgments

The people to whom I am indebted for this work are legion and include all those who have contributed to my own interest in religion and spirituality from my grandparents, parents (Otto H. York and Myrth Brooks York), my ministers in the Morrow Memorial Methodist Church of Maplewood, New Jersey (Dr. Ralph Davis and Reverend William Burns), and my methodology mentor at San Francisco State College (Carlo L. Lastrucci), to other encounters that have ranged from Howard Fenton (Professor Emeritus, University of California at Santa Barbara) and Keith Ward (Oxford University's Regius Professor of Divinity), to such religious luminaries as Father Divine, Rev. Billy Graham, Alan Watts, Jiddu Krishnamurti, Stephen Gaskin, Anton LaVey, His Holiness the Dalai Lama, the Venerable Dharmawara (Bhante), Her Holiness Ma Jaya Sati Bhagavati, His Holiness Pope John XXIII, His Holiness Pope John Paul II, Benjamin Creme, Elizabeth Clare Prophet, Supreme Master Ching Hai, Burton Pretty On Top, John Twobirds, His Holiness Baba Virsa Singh and Dada J. P. Vaswani.

Particularly inspiring writings have been those of Joseph Campbell, Northrop Frye, Will Durant, Aldous Huxley and Charles Jencks. It is especially to Peter B. Clarke (King's College London), however, that I owe whatever ability I have developed to approach the study of religions from an objective and academic perspective. Peter refined my understanding of the scientific methodological approach in the light of sociological nuance. Particularly helpful exchanges have occurred with Eileen Barker (London School of Economics), Bryan Wilson (Oxford University), Massimo Introvigne (CESNUR), J. Gordon Melton

(ISAR), William H. Swatos, Jr. (ASR), James Richardson (University of Nevada Reno), Michael Hill (University of Auckland), Brian Bocking (SOAS), Ninian Smart (UCSB), Paul Heelas (University of Lancaster), Philip Hammond (University of California Santa Barbara), Arthur Larry Greil (Alfred University), George Chryssides (University of Wolverhampton) and Thomas Robbins.

Additional guiding inspirations have been James Beckford (University of Warwick), Peter Beyer (University of Ottawa), Karel Dobbelaere (Catholic University of Leuven), Rodney Stark (University of Washington), Catherine Wessinger (Loyola University), Patricia Wittberg (Indiana University), Helen Rose Ebaugh (University of Houston), Lutz Kaelber (Lyndon State College), Stuart Wright (Lamar University), Nancy Ammerman (Hartford Seminary), Otto Madura (Drew University), Mary Jo Neitz (University of Missouri), Anthoni Blasi (Tennessee State University), Brenda Basher (Mount Union College), Benjamin Beit-Hallahmi (University of Haifa), Christel Manning (Sacred Heart University), Wendy Young (University of Florida), Jeffrey Hadden (University of Virginia), Jean-François Mayer (University of Fribourg), Lori Beaman (University of Lethbridge), David Hackett (University of Florida), David Bromley (Virginia Commonwealth University), Roland Robertson (University of Pittsburgh), Luigi Tomasi (Universita degli Studi di Trento), Jim Spickard (University of Redlands), Melinda Bollar Wagner (Radford University), Rosalind Hackett (University of Tennessee), Nancy Nason-Clark (University of New Brunswick), Phillip Lucas (DeLand University), Edward Bailey (Middlesex University), Roger O'Toole (University of Toronto Scarborough), Rhys Williams (Southern Illinois University Carbondale), Michelle Dillon (Yale University), Meredith McGuire (Trinity University), Keishin Inaba (Centre de Recherche sur le Japon, Paris), Lorne Dawson (University of Waterloo), Grace Davie (University of Exeter), Ursula King (University of Bristol), Robert Ellwood (University of Southern California), Chas Clifton (University of Colorado), Timothy Miller (University of Kansas), Sarah Pike (University of California Chico), James Cavendish (University of South Florida), Robert Segal (University of Lancaster), Jenny Blain (Sheffield Hallam University), Kieran Flanagan (University of Bristol), Kim Knott (University of Leeds), Joanne Pearson (University of Bristol), Steve Bruce (University of Aberdeen), Tony Walter (University of Reading), Vivianne Crowley

(Heythrop College University of London), Peter Jupp (University of Bristol), Douglas Ezzy (University of Tasmania) and Mary Farrell Bednarowski (Institute for Ecumenical and Cultural Research/United Theological Seminary of the Twin Cities).

I would also like to cite in particular Susan Palmer (Dawson College), Helen Berger (West Chester University), Bron Taylor (University of Florida), Susan Kwilecki (Radford University), Wendy Griffin (Long Beach State University), Tanice Folz (Indiana University Northwest), Marion Bowman (Open University), Helen Waterhouse (Open University), Barbara McGraw (Saint Mary's College of California), Dana Fenton (City College of New York), Graham Harvey (King Alfred's College) and Kurt Anders Richardson (Gordon-Cornwell Theological Seminary) for much fruitfully intellectual time together that has on some occasions stretched into the wee hours of the morning. Nicholas Schors (Arcanum, Amsterdam) was instrumental at an early stage in my career in getting me to think more in terms of footnotes and bibliography. To be included in any list acknowledging those who have been important both for information freely given and in shaping my thought are my colleagues at Bath Spa University College in, respectively, the Department for the Study of Religions (Denise Cush, Catherine Robinson, Jo Backus, Richard Hoskins and Mahinda Deegalle) and the Sophia Centre for the Study of Cultural Astronomy and Astrology (Patrick Curry and Nicholas Campion). My thanks also to Rob Mears and Caroline New in the Department of Sociology, and to Fiona Montgomery and Jill Palmer, respectively, Head and Senior Administrator for the School of Historical and Cultural Studies.

Among the more helpful insights I have gained is the analysis from the dissertation of Hildegard Van Hove in which she differentiates between "true New Agers" (those who believe in the coming Age of Aquarius as an actuality), and "spiritual seekers," "alternativists" and "clients" (casual consumers) comprising a steadily expanding but less committed series of concentric circles (*De Weg naar Binnen: Spiritualiteit en Zelfontplooing*, Katholieke Universiteit Leuven, 1999). Another work I should like to mention here is that of Daren John Kemp, namely, *The Christaquarians? A Sociology of Christians in the New Age* (King's College, University of London, 2000). Helpful New Age leaders and/or active participants in the forms of alternative spirituality that can be identified as New Age to whom I remain grateful in one manner or another include William Bloom, Malcolm Stern, Sabrina Dearborn, Leonard and Willa Sleath, Serena Roney-Dougal, Donna Nunn-Sims, Elissa Rigzin Giles, Matthew Fox, James Jacob Hurtak, Starhawk, Gillian Barton, Magdalena Caland, Barbara Floyd Dauphin, Caroline Shaffer, Voyce Durling-Jones and Mary Pat Fisher.

In particular, I am indebted to Kenneth Jay Wilson for forever timely and instructive counsel. My thanks are also to be extended to the staff of Scarecrow Press for guidance and constant encouragement—especially to Jon Woronoff, Series Editor, Nicole Averill, Editorial Assistant, and Kim Tabor, Acquisitions Editor. In the preparation of the camera-ready manuscript, the assistance of Alice Ekrek, administrator of the Sophia Centre for the Study of Cultural Astronomy and Astrology at Bath Spa University College, has been invaluable; without her assistance this task would not have seen completion. Finally, my thanks to the unending support and inspiration from my friend and partner, Richard Lee Switzler, who has not only endured countless hours of proofreading but also remains my most steadfast and loyal champion.

Editor's Foreword

Although the New Age has manifestly dawned, it is hard to say precisely when and any attempt at fixing a date would be futile, for the process has been gradual. It already strongly affects millions of people in North America and Europe, and smaller contingents in some Asian countries, while its influence is rather tenuous elsewhere. Moreover, there is a tendency to pick and choose, so that only some aspects may penetrate deeply, for certain people, while others remain shallow or scarcely noticeable. Nonetheless, it is obvious that many features have already become part and parcel of "modern" life, such as alternative medicine, a new spirituality and the fusion of Western and Eastern (plus other) philosophies and religions or the spreading fads (and sometimes more) for yoga, feng shui and aromatherapy. Thus, it is definitely appreciated to have a *Historical Dictionary of New Age Movements*, with an emphasis on movements since this is not just one great river but many smaller streams.

This book provides useful insight into things that are going on around us we may not clearly perceive, or indeed, approve of. Consequently, without necessarily judging them, numerous movements and their founders and/or leaders, many varied and even contradictory concepts and practices, and some of the controversies and problematics are presented in specific entries in the dictionary section. These are the parts of the New Age. The sum of the parts can be glimpsed through the introduction. Meanwhile, a chronology shows how it has dawned and spread, most notably over the past half century, but much earlier as well and with every sign that it will progress well into the twenty-first century. For those interested in the whole, or certain of the parts, the bibliography suggests further and more detailed reading.

This latest historical dictionary in the series, and one which mixes religions, philosophies and movements, was written by Michael York. He has specialized in new age and new religious movements ever since he was a student. His thesis dealt with the sociology of the new age and neo-paganism, and he later authored *The Emerging Network: A Sociology of the New Age and Neo-Pagan Movements*. Dr. York is currently reader at the study of religions department and the Sophia Centre for the Study of Cultural Astronomy and Astrology at Bath Spa University College in Great Britain. He has also taught at the Himalayan Yogic Institute and, earlier on, studied at the School of Traditional Indian Yoga. He has a good firsthand knowledge of key features and considerable experience in explaining these variegated phenomena to the public. With this book as a handy guide, readers can obtain a far better understanding of the vast transformation we are all undergoing, in one way or another, to one extent or another.

Jon Woronoff
Series Editor

Preface

My interest in the New Age movement per se began in the late 1980s with a small front page article in the *International Herald Tribune* describing a new religious movement involving the likes of Shirley MacLaine and JZ Knight and calling itself "New Age." As a child of the 1960s counterculture, I had already been programmed to think in terms of the coming "Age of Aquarius" heralded in the musical *Hair*. All this was, in fact, a further development of my interests in both Spiritualism, first fostered by my grandmother, Gertrude Zeth Brooks, and continued in my attending the public séances conducted by Mrs. Becker at the Spiritualist Church of San Francisco, and in healthy diet, fostered by both my grandparents: my grandmother in her capacity as president of the Women's Health Federation of Southern California and my grandfather, George Schubel, who served as private secretary to food faddist Bernarr McFadden. Another seminal influence on my fascination with marginal spirituality and the occult came through my friendships in Los Angeles with the astrologer and naturopath Dale Sherwood, and in Laguna Beach with the astrologers and mediums Ray Unger and Jack Fontane.

Through both my wife, Nancy Williams York, and sister-in-law, Pat Wilbarger, and their professional careers as occupational therapists, I was introduced to the human potential movement in general and to the thoughts and works of Kurt Adler, Eric Berne and Fritz Perls, in particular. As the New Age came to coalesce, I began to see it as a spiritualization of the human potential movement itself. The difficulty in studying the New Age is that it is not a single coordinated and structured organization but at best a loose congeries of separate though frequently overlapping movements. Compounding its pluralistic composition is its range of multiple identities that arise in response to whether it is being seen by wary Christians, hostile anti-cultists, dismissive scientists, sensationalist-seeking journalists, dubious psychologists, value-neutral sociologists, embarrassed dabblers, environmental futurists or fervent believers.

There is no single New Age for everyone. There are instead many different New Ages and many, often incongruent, components within any single individual's understanding of the phenomenon/phenomena. Consequently, anyone's approach to this vague spirituality that just as often rejects the New Age label as it affirms it is by default individualistic and personal. One person's understanding will by necessity be different from the next, and this shifting perspective applies equally to how I myself view the New Age and seek to present it. As a result, this *Historical Dictionary of New Age Movements* can only provide an introduction to the reader, rather than an exhaustive compendium, but I hope one that might spur interest and further pursuit of knowledge on a range of topics. At best, this dictionary might serve as a handy reference source. It unavoidably contains lacunae and omissions not only due to the amorphous scope of the subject but also because, as a living and dynamically growing orientation, the New Age phenomenon itself is constantly changing and developing.

The ambiguity of the New Age extends through its own boundary-indeterminateness into its frequent confusion with various NRMS (new religious movements) from Scientology and ISKCON to Neo-paganism and Wicca. Nevertheless, what struck me most in the compilation of this book is the remarkable consistency and organic unity that is detectable in the many diversified elements, individuals and teachings that may be identified as part of this many-headed Hydra. New Age is important to understand in our times not only as a spiritual option in itself but also for how it challenges the other religious traditions to articulate themselves in the face of this confrontation and to reform to the degree that New Age's alternative spirituality is perceived to offer and/or possess something that is worthwhile. Perhaps more than any other religious tradition, New Age has come to exemplify the market-based consumerism, one that includes spiritual commodification, of the late twentieth/early twenty-first century. New Age, in fact, has transformed the global forum of religions into a competing marketplace that affects everyone and all religions. Through its spiritualization efforts directed toward all aspects of life, New Age has fused spirituality with capitalism to the degree that all religions must compete more openly and less discretely with others as commercial enterprises catering to the religious consumer's wants and needs, seeking to attract followers as purchasers of the goods and ideas on offer and to reduce the number of their own buyers who might turn to another product. For many established religions, the New Age movements are a threat—as revealed, for instance, by the preliminary document published by the Pontifical Council for Culture/Pontifical Council for Interreligious Dialogue, "Jesus Christ, the Bearer of the Water of Life: A Christian Reflection on the 'New Age'" (February 4, 2003) that states that the widespread New Age conviction "that one creates one's own reality is appealing, but illusory."

But whatever the criticisms and dismissals of New Age spirituality there may be, we are directly witnessing in our times the conversion of a once marginal orientation into something more integral to mainstream culture. A study of New Age speaks potential volumes on spirituality and seekership, but it also has much to say about contemporary religious markets, their distribution mechanisms and the present-day world arena of ideational exchange and competition. The New Age must be seen at the end of the day as part of the modern human's effort to break free of Max Weber's feared and lamented iron-cage he foresaw would result from a ubiquitous rationalized bureaucracy. It may not be the only current attempt there is to re-enchant the world, but it plays an important role in this overall process and one that is worthy of our attention whatever our particular positions.

Chronology

2697-2597 B.C.E.	Dates of Emperor Huang Ti, author of the acupuncture manual, the *Nei Ching*.
97 B.C.E.	First mention of Taoism.
1555	Initial publication of the prophecies of Nostradamus.
1710	Samuel Richter establishes the Golden Rosicrucians.
1772	The Church of the New Jerusalem systematizing Swedenborg's thought is founded in London.
1784	Anton Mesmer is denounced by the French Academy.
1848	American Spiritualism begins with the claims of the Fox sisters in Hydesville, New York.
1875	Helena Petrovna Blavatsky, Henry Steel Olcott and William Quan Judge found the Theosophical Society in New York.

1877   Blavatsky publishes *Isis Unveiled.*

1878   Edwin Dwight Babbitt publishes *The Prin-
                     ciples of Light and Color* on chromotherapy.

1882   Formation of the Society of Psychical Re-
                     search in London. The book, *Oahspe: A New
                     Age Bible*, channeled through automatic
                     writing, is published by John Ballou New-
                     brough. Modern interest in Atlantis begins
                     with the publication of Ignatius Donnelly's
                     Atlantis: The Antediluvian World.

1884   Formation of the American Society of Psy-
                     chical Research.

1885   Emma Curtis Hopkins breaks with Mary
                     Baker Eddy to begin what subsequently
                     emerges as New Thought.

1887-1888   William Wynn Westcott and Samuel Liddell
                     MacGregor Mathers found the Hermetic Or-
                     der of the Golden Dawn.

1888   Blavatsky publishes *The Secret Doctrine.*

1889   Charles and Myrtle Fillmore found what
                     eventually becomes the Unity School of
                     Christianity.

1891   With the death of Madame Blavatsky, Annie
                     Besant becomes the head of the Esoteric
                     Section of theosophical students.

1893   Organization of the Nationalist Spiritualist
                     Association of Churches in Washington,
                     D.C. The World's Parliament of Religions is
                     held in Chicago.

1894	Swami Vivekananda founds the Vedanta Society in New York. Daniel David Palmer discovers chiropractic. William Q. Judge organizes the American branch of the Theosophical Society as a separate order.
1902	Founding of the Naturopathic Society of America.
1907	Max Heindel founds the Rosicrucian Fellowship.
1908	Formation of the International Vegetarian Union. Levi Dowling publishes *The Aquarian Gospel of Jesus the Christ*.
1909	The Tantrik Order is established by Pierre Bernard in America.
1910	The Sufi Order founded in London by Hazrat Inayat Khan. Arthur Edward Waite's publication of *The Pictorial Guide to the Tarot*. Linking the cards to the Kabalah ensures their popularity throughout the English-speaking world of the twentieth century.
1913	Reflexology introduced to the United States by William Fitzgerald. Rudolf Steiner breaks from the Theosophical Movement to form anthroposophy.
1914	Formation of the International New Thought Alliance.
1915	Founding of the Astrological Lodge of London.

1916   Gurdjieff introduces the enneagram to his
                               students.

1919   Rudolf Steiner's Waldorf Schools are insti-
                               tuted. Hatha Yoga is introduced to the West
                               by Sri Yogendra.

1920   Paramahansa Yogananda begins the Self-
                               Realization Fellowship in Boston.

1922   The International Sufi Movement is inaugu-
                               rated in Geneva. Alice and Foster Bailey
                               found the Lucifer Trust, later renamed the
                               Lucis Trust.

1923   Founding of the American Astrological So-
                               ciety. Alice and Foster Bailey establish the
                               Arcane School.

1924   Dinshah Pestanji Ghadiali founds the Spec-
                               tro-Chrome Institute. The Yoga Institute is
                               established by Sri Yogendra in Bombay.

1925   Krishnamurti is recognized as Maitreya by
                               Annie Besant and Charles Leadbeater. Sufi
                               Leader Meher Baba permanently enters "the
                               Silence."

1926   Aurobindo experiences the descent of divine
                               consciousness into the physical. Pir Vilayat
                               Inayat Khan is named by his father as the
                               successor of the Sufi Order. Founding of the
                               American Academy of Kinesiology and
                               Physical Education in New York.

1928   Publication of Gattefosse's *Aromathérapie*
                               in France.

1929	Krishnamurti formally denies he is Maitreya.
1931	Edgar Cayce founds the Association for Research and Enlightenment. The Vegetarian Society of New York is established.
1932	Guy and Edna Ballard establish the Saint Germain Foundation and the Saint Germain Press to sponsor the "I AM" Religious Activity.
1934	The Philosophical Research Society is organized by Manly P. Hall in Hollywood, California. The White Eagle Lodge is founded in England.
1937	Kirlian photography is discovered as a means to record the body's aura.
1937	Founding of the American Federation of Astrology.
1939	The contemporary Western pagan movement and Wicca are inaugurated by Gerald B. Gardner in England.
1942	The Organic Gardening Experimental Farm is established by J. I. Rodale near Emmaus, Pennsylvania.
1943	Corinne Heline publishes *Healing and Regeneration through Color*.
1944	Aleister Crowley publishes *The Book of Thoth*, affirming de Gebélin's belief in the Tarot as repositories of Egyptian magical symbolism. The Vegan Society is founded in

	England. Alice Bailey publishes the first volume of *Discipleship in the New Age*.
1946	Paramahansa Yogananda publishes *Autobiography of a Yogi*.
1947	Norbert Wiener and Arturo Rosenbleuth establish the discipline of Cybernetics. Kenneth Arnold launches the flying saucer era with sightings near Mount Rainier.
1948	Alice Bailey publishes *The Reappearance of the Christ*.
1949	Buckminster Fuller conceives the geodesic dome.
1950	The Urantia Foundation is established.
1951	The founding of Astara.
1954	L. Ron Hubbard founds Scientology.
1955	The Japanese Ministry of Health and Welfare acknowledges the validity of Shiatsu. Founding of the Aetherius Society by George King.
1956	Founding of the Spiritual Frontiers Fellowship. Past-life exploration through hypnosis is introduced with the publication of *The Search for Bridey Murphy*.
1957	Revision of the International New Thought Alliance's Declaration of Principles. World Fellowship of Religions established by Kirpal Singh.

1958	Mark Prophet founds the Summit Lighthouse. Founding of the Astrological Association of Great Britain.
1959	Virginia Satir, Don Jackson, Jules Ruskin and Gregory Bateson begin the Mental Research Institute in Palo Alto, California, focusing on Family Therapy. Benjamin Creme breaks with George King.
1960	Formation of the American Vegan Society.
1961	Ohsawa Foundation, the first macrobiotics organization in the United States, is founded by Michio Kushi and Herman Aihara.
1962	Esalen Institute is founded by Michael Murphy and Richard Price. The Findhorn Community is established by Peter and Eileen Caddy and Dorothy Maclean.
1963	Richard Alpert and Timothy Leary are expelled from Harvard University. Ann Wigmore establishes the Hippocrates Health Institute. Jane Roberts begins to channel "Seth."
1964	Idries Shah publishes *The Sufis.* "Initiation of the Earth" according to the Aetherius Society. Marguerite Maury's English publication of *The Secrets of Youth and Life.* Corinne Heline publishes *Color and Music in the New Age.*
1965	Rescinding of the Asian Exclusion Act, thereby opening the United States to large-scale immigration. Dr. Helen Schucman begins transcription of *A Course in Miracles.*

1966   Guru Maharaj Ji succeeds his father as the
               head of the Divine Light Mission at the age
               of nine. Swami Satchidananda forms the In-
               tegral Yoga Institute.

1966-1967   Richard Alpert receives the name Baba Ram
               Dass from Neem Karoli Baba in India.

1967   Tassajara Zen Mountain Center near Big
               Sur, California, opens as the first Buddhist
               monastery outside Asia.

1968   Tarthang Tulku Rinpoche opens the Ny-
               ingma Institute in Berkeley, California, to
               provide for the study and practice of Bud-
               dhist teachings. Holy Order of MANS
               (HOOM) is founded in California by Earl
               Blighton as a New Age School of Christian
               Initiation. Auroville's foundation stone is
               laid in Pondicherry, India. Haridas Chaud-
               huri founds the California Institute for Inte-
               gral Studies in San Francisco. Oschar Ichazo
               founds Arica in Chile. Carlos Castaneda
               publishes *The Teachings of Don Juan*.

1969   Fritz Perls publishes *Gestalt Theory*. Eliza-
               beth Kübler-Ross publishes *On Death and
               Dying*. Tokujiro Namikoshi, founder of Shi-
               atsu, introduces his practice of body-work to
               the English-speaking world. The Krishna-
               murti Foundation is established in Ojai,
               California.

1970   Chögyam Trungpa Rinpoche founds the
               Karme Choling center, predecessor of the
               Vajradhatu Foundation. Sun Bear founds the
               Bear Tribe Medicine Society in Placerville,
               California. Yogi Amrit Desai discovers Ki-

palu Yoga. William and Gladys McGarey
found the A.R.E. Clinic in Phoenix, Arizona.
Ida P. Rolf establishes the Guild for Struc-
tural Integration (Rolf Institute). Stephan
Gaskin establishes The Farm in Tennessee.
David Spangler becomes a co-director of
Findhorn. Jane Roberts publishes *The Seth
Material.*

1971   Yogi Bhajan receives the authority from
              Amritsar's Golden Temple to initiate his fol-
              lowers directly into the Sikh faith. Sir
              George Trevelyan founds the Wrekin Trust
              in England. The Arica Institute is established
              in New York. Ram Dass publishes *Be Here
              Now.*

1972   President Nixon opens contact between the
              United States and China, allowing American
              investigation of Chinese medical practice.
              The Academy of Religion and Psychical Re-
              search is founded in Evanston, Illinois. Adi
              Da Samraj (Franklin Jones) opens his first
              ashram in Los Angeles. Benjamin Creme
              announces the imminent arrival of Mai-
              treya/Christ. Hyemeyohsts Storm publishes
              Seven Arrows, popularizing the Medicine
              Wheel.

1973   Chögyam Trungpa Rinpoche, in his 1973
              book *Cutting Through Spiritual Material-
              ism*, introduced the new phrase of "spiritual
              materialism" into New Age vocabulary.
              David Spangler leaves Findhorn to form the
              Lorian Association. Guru Maharaj Ji's disas-
              trous launch of the spiritual millennium in
              Houston, Texas. With the death of Mark
              Prophet, his wife renames the Summit

Lighthouse as the Church Universal and Triumphant. Ken Keyes opens the Living Love Center in Berkeley, California. *The American Journal of Chinese Medicine* begins publication. Kevin Ryerson begins to channel "John."

1974

Chögyam Trungpa Rinpoche establishes the Naropa Institute, subsequently to become the Naropa University. Leonard Orr completes his development of the process of Rebirthing. Rajneesh founds Poona ashram. H. Jay Dinshah organizes the North American Vegetarian Society. Maharaj Ji is deposed by his mother as leader of the Divine Light Mission. Leonard Orr opens the Theta House in San Francisco as a center for Rebirthing. Ram Dass founds the Hanuman Foundation. Werner Erhard invites Swami Muktananda to the United States. Benjamin Creme is "overshadowed" by Maitreya. Jach Pursel begins to channel "Lazaris." Patricia Hayes founds the Arthur Ford International Academy to award "Certificates of Mediumship."

1975

Publication of *A Course in Miracles*. Linda Clark publishes *The Ancient Art of Color Therapy*. The Siddha Yoga Dham Associates is founded.

1976

David Spangler publishes *Revelation: The Birth of a New Age*. Brad Steiger publishes *Gods of Aquarius*, introducing the concept of "Star People." Wayne Dyer publishes *Your Erroneous Zones*. Patrick Watson founds the School of T'ai Chi Chuan.

1977	Leonard Orr and Sondra Ray publish *Rebirthing in the New Age*. Avanta: The Virginia Satir Network is founded. Luc Jouret founds the Order of the Solar Temple. Ken Wilber publishes *The Spectrum of Consciousness*. Marianne Williamson encounters *A Course in Miracles*. Matthew Fox founds the Institute in Culture and Creation Spirituality in Chicago. Benjamin Creme announces that Maitreya has begun his descent from the Himalayas. JZ Knight begins to channel "Ramtha."
1978	Mass suicide/murder deaths of the People's Temple in Jonestown, Guyana. Bernie Siegel begins the Exceptional Cancer Patients program for individual and group therapy. Foundation of the American Holistic Medical Association. Foundation of the Sirius Community as a Findhorn spin-off. Foundation of Insight Transformational seminars by John-Roger Hinkins under the auspices of MSIA. *The Silva Mind Control Method* is published.
1979	Ruth Montgomery presents the concept of the "walk-in" in her book *Strangers Among Us*. Gary Zukav publishes *The Dancing Wu Li Masters*. James Lovelock develops his Gaia hypothesis that conceives the earth as a unified living organism. Thelma Moss publishes *The Body Electric*. Mark Satin publishes *New Age Politics*. Lyall Watson publishes *Lifetide* presenting the concept of the "Hundredth Monkey."
1980	Marilyn Ferguson publishes *The Aquarian Conspiracy*. Michael Harner publishes *The*

Way of the Shaman. The American-International Reiki Association is founded.

1981   Rajneeshpuram created in Oregon. John Lilly establishes the Human/Dolphin Foundation. Lynn Andrews publishes *Medicine Woman.*

1982   Frank Alper publishes *Exploring Atlantis,* stimulating New Age interest in crystals. Benjamin Creme announces through a worldwide newspaper campaign the imminent return of Maitreya the Christ.

1983   Barbara Weber Ray publishes *The Reiki Factor.* The countercultural commune, The Farm, is reorganized into a cooperative village. Constance Cumbrey attacks Benjamin Creme with her publication of *Hidden Dangers of the Rainbow.* Matthew Fox publishes *Original Blessing,* shifting away from the Christian doctrine of original sin. Shirley MacLaine publishes *Out On a Limb.*

1984   Werner Erhard modifies his controversial *est* program. Vicky Hall develops Aura-Soma.

1985   Terry Cole-Whittaker establishes Adventures in Enlightenment.

1986   The Unity School sponsors *A Course in Miracles* festival in Honolulu. Holy Order of MANS (HOOM) is disbanded. Jonathan Horwitz founds the Scandinavian Center for Shamanic Studies. Adi Da Samraj begins his divine self-"Emergence." Penny Torres-Rubin begins to channel "Mafu."

1987   Celebration of the Harmonic Convergence
               on August 16th and 17th. Rajneeshpuram is
               disbanded, and Rajneesh returns to India.
               Aum Shinrikyo is founded. The television
               version of Shirley MacLaine's *Out On a
               Limb* is aired. John Robbins publishes *Diet
               for a New America.*

1988   Jamie Sams produces *Medicine Cards.*
               Louise Hay publishes *You Can Heal Your
               Life.* William Bloom, Sabina Dearborne and
               Malcolm Stern found the Alternative Pro-
               gramme at London's St. James's Church,
               Piccadilly. JZ Knight founds Ramtha's
               School of Enlightenment. Matthew Fox is si-
               lenced by the Vatican for a year.

1989   Tarthang Tulku establishes the World Peace
               Ceremony at Bodh Gaya, India.

1990   Copies of *A Course in Miracles* sold reach a
               half million.

1993   The centenary celebration of the World's
               Parliament of Religions is held in Chicago.

1994   First mass deaths in the Order of the Solar
               Temple. Andrew Weil founds the Program
               in Integrative Medicine. Matthew Fox be-
               comes an Episcopal priest. Barbara Marx
               Hubbard proclaims that New Thought will
               become the most important movement on
               earth.

1995   Tokyo subway attack by Aum Shinrikyo.
               Deepak Chopra publishes *Journey Into
               Healing.*

1996   Wind Daughter becomes medicine chief of
                        the Bear Tribe.

1997   Findhorn is recognized by the United Na-
                        tions as an NGO. Leo Rutherford publishes
                        Principles of Shamanism.

1998   The United Nations Oslo Conference on
                        Religion and Belief accords the New Age
                        Movement equal status with established re-
                        ligions.

1999   The third gathering of the World's Parlia-
                        ment of Religions is held in Cape Town.
                        William Bloom founds Holistic Partner-
                        ships.

2001   Leo Rutherford publishes *Way of Shaman-
                        ism.*

2012, December 21st   Beginning of the Aquarian Age, according
                        to José Argüelles.

Introduction

The New Age movements that emerged chiefly in the second half of the twentieth century constitute together an expression of the personalization of religion that has characterized modern Western spirituality in the wake of an increasing decline of institutional religious influence on social concerns, the increase of secularization as a non-religious option and the growing search for individual solace in the face of cultural uncertainties and bureaucratic hegemonies. In the ever-expanding pluralism of the West in which the individual possesses multiple affiliations and social identities, many people are concerned with developing an identifiable empowerment of self to counter the confusions arising from a surfeit of choice as well as the expanding macro-contexts that continue to dwarf individual independence. The religio-spiritual often appears to offer a last domain in which a person retains the feeling that some freedom of self-determination is not only a possibility but is necessary to any viably sustainable location of value and meaning. Personalized religion takes many different forms (New Age, paganism, implicit religion, sectarian choice, evangelism, secular ideology, etc.), and part of this proliferation is the consequence of the "age of information" that has emerged and in which the individual is confronted by knowledge and awareness of other religious possibilities beyond that in which he/she has been born and acculturated.

In modern times, the West has been characterized by periodic religious revivals or "Great Awakenings." At the same time, an alternative and eclectic metaphysical tradition has always persisted in the West that has offered a range of contrasting possibilities to accepted ecclesiastical tradition. This occult potpourri or "cultic milieu" has provided a perennial source for Western alternative religious inspiration, including both contemporary Western paganism and New Age spiritualities.

Early American expression of counter-traditional spiritual interest appears with the rise of transcendentalism in the New England states of the late nineteenth century that promoted an interest in Eastern spirituality, especially Hinduism. Perhaps more of a literary development than a full-fledged religion, Transcendentalism became a leading instigator behind the American or Western metaphysical tradition with its concern for healing and its emphasis on the reality and immanence of the spiritual. As the alternative spirituality of the nineteenth century, the Metaphysical Tradition stressed not only the reality of the spiritual world and the importance of the mystical experience, but also the healing value of reputedly invisible forces that operate on the mind and body. Between them, such people as Emanuel Swedenborg (1688-1772), Franz Anton Mesmer (1734-1815), Phineas P. Quimby (1802-1866), Ralph Waldo Emerson (1803-1882) and Warren Felt Evans (1817-1887) created the common language of the transcendentalist and metaphysical traditions in America.

It was Swedenborg who first stressed for the modern West the importance of exploring the supernatural personally and directly rather than simply accepting the lackluster mediation offered by mainstream churches. His own alleged communication with angelic forces or beings, as well as his out-of-body experiences, laid the foundation for a revival of gnosticism's prioritization of spirit over matter and its consideration that spirit is ultimately the only reality. Emerson, in turn, was deeply influenced by Swedenborgian ideas, as well as by the spiritual notions embedded in the Hindu *Bhagavad Gita*. He advocated as a consequence an understanding of a unified world as an expression of mind or God. His philosophy's nature mysticism attracted such other thinkers as Henry Thoreau, Margaret Fuller and Amos Bronson Alcott. Beside stressing a Unitarian reaction to Calvinist doctrine, New England Transcendentalism promoted a reliance on intuition and a development of human potential that together became the hallmarks of the American metaphysical tradition and eventually the broad congeries of New Age movements that emerged in the twentieth century.

To understand New Age spirituality, it is also necessary to consider the developments of spiritualism, New Thought and theosophy that grew out of Swedenborgianism and transcendentalism. New Thought in particular owes much to Mesmer and his teachings concerning animal magnetism and, eventually, the dynamics of hypnosis. The power of the mind becomes the central affirmation, and illness, poverty and misfortune in general are considered illusions that a proper *gnosis* and mental acumen will dispel and eliminate. With Quimby, the spiritual orientation that led to New Thought focused on healing—whether physical, mental or spiritual—through the power of suggestion.

While spiritualism leads to such peripheral New Age emphases as channeling and other forms of discarnate guidance, and theosophy—itself an offshoot of spiritualism—provides another range of cosmetic additions such as the Eastern spiritual notions of karma, reincarnation and ascended masters, it is New Thought which lies at the core of New Age identity and its fundamental assumptions. Often working still within an essential Christian framework, Jesus is now seen as the Way-shower rather than a necessary cosmic Redeemer of original sin. He is instead the one who indicates the way toward personal regeneration *par excellence*: Jesus exemplifies the mind-in-action and its power to shape the world and life toward spiritual achievement and emancipation. Instead of atonement, the goal is now "at-one-ment" between God and humanity through which each person regains and unfolds his/her essential divine nature. New Age interprets its Christian heritage of biblical metaphysics metaphorically, while expanding its Christianity with various Eastern concepts. Reincarnation is now accepted as providing the steps that lead to eventual immortality. As an assisting practice that augments spiritual growth and progress, basic Hindu and Buddhist predilections toward vegetarianism are also frequently incorporated.

As a product of the cultic milieu that comprises transcendentalism, the metaphysical tradition, New Thought, spiritualism and theosophy, the New Age movement or collection of movements is a specific development of the 1960s counterculture that abandoned the notion of any set spiritual script that must be followed. Spiritual resources become available utilities rather than dogmatic injunctions. They may be sampled, experimented with and incorporated or rejected as their usefulness is demonstrated to the individual. But on the global as opposed to the personal level, the counterculture demands a restructuring of the world in conformity with its utopian potential rather than simply maintaining its dominant corporate and national divisions. As such, the legacy of the 1960s counterculture includes both contemporary Western paganism and New Age. The former wishes to restructure the world in line with environmental and ecological holistics. The latter would redesign the global polity to reflect a transcendental hegemony. The one reflects the immanent animism, pantheism and polytheism of ancient paganisms; the other is a recasting of heretical gnosticism commensurate with the spiritual consumer market of today.

Both New Age and contemporary Western paganism draw their adherents from the broader religious exchange market in which religions themselves, as well as their various artifacts, practices and beliefs become marketable commodities. Vis-à-vis mainstream canonical religions, New Age and paganism are natural allies. They represent essential democratizations of religion, but not only are they generally condemned as heresies, they also encourage individual exegesis that is anathema to doctrinally established forms of belief. Both also incorporate a pervasive fusion between the religious and the psychological.

The difference between New Age and Neo-paganism lies foremost in the realm of theology and the respective attitude toward the tangible, physical and/or natural world. Pagan ways of thinking understand the sacred as all-pervasive—including, if not beginning with, the material dimension. New Age, in contrast, and following its gnostic and transcendental heritage, posits the corporeal—whether consciously or implicitly—as an obstacle to spiritual progression. Nature is an illusion that must be sundered and bypassed. If it is considered a bona fide reality, it is nonetheless a secondary reality at best and ultimately worthless when placed into the grander scheme of things. The final spiritual goal is transcendence of the mundane, a transcendence of the impediment that the material presents to ethereal self-fulfillment and not the pagan aspiration to honor, cherish and celebrate the substantial as part of the pleasures of life. New Age seeks to regain an original state of gnostic grace and re-find the spark of divinity latent within each individual. Paganism avoids the ladder metaphor for that of the ascending spiral—cyclical but advancing. What lies ahead is not a return but an evolution.

Apart from their contrasting theologies, New Age and paganism differ also in their social compositions or expressions. New Age manifests chiefly through what sociologists Rodney Stark and William Sims Bainbridge understand as the audience and client cults, only occasionally as a full-fledged cult movement. The primary venue is the lecture theater—whether a borrowed church, hired hall or New Age center meeting space. Almost as important for New Age is the client consultation with a service provider—whether an astrologer, yoga teacher, therapist, psychophysical trainer, geomancer, mediumistic channel, etc. For contemporary pagans, by contrast, the venue is a private home or garden, a leased university hall, a summer camp, a private woods, a public park, a tavern or an ancient site depending on whether the occasion is social, initiatory, ritual or a festive fair. The pagan occasion is less that of an audience gathering with little that is characteristic in terms of the client-consultant relationship. While both movements have little in the way of hierarchical structure, let alone bureaucracy, and both movements are composed by relatively high numbers of solitary practitioners, the group coalescing that does occur and their subsequent trajectories as well as the *raisons d'être* behind them are different.

Another major difference between New Age and contemporary paganism concerns theodicy. While both orientations tend to dismiss the reality of sin and evil, they nevertheless take different positions on what the negative is. For New Agers, misfortune is a figment of the imagination. Unhappiness, disease, poverty and so forth are all mental aberrations. The purpose of spiritual progress is to acquire the *gnosis* or understanding that allows one to neutralize and/or eliminate the power of faulty thinking. For pagans, however, the negative is not a product of ignorance as much as it is one strictly of illness—whether an imbalance in the natural and organic equilibrium or the result of an invading pathogen. Rather than enlightenment, the emphasis is one that seeks to cure an imperfect situation. If New Age emphasizes the acquisition of knowledge or understanding, contemporary Western paganism is primarily concerned with the development and exercise of will.

But if paganism and New Age have many similarities and contrasts, in practice they often tend to fuse and incorporate mutual elements on an *ad hoc* basis that make any operative differentiation between them difficult at best. Many scholars of religion, in fact, see Neopaganism as a part of the wider New Age umbrella. From an outsider's perspective, New Age is often an eclectic amalgam of appropriated elements from across the full religious spectrum and frequently seemingly without rhyme or reason. The very issue of appropriation is greatly contentious according to New Age critics and has raised the question of integrity and respect within the global spiritual arena. What is at stake here is the problem of spiritual ownership. The mix-and-match conglomeration that often results can appear not only superficial but also an insult to those from whom various elements have been appropriated—especially if this involves a people such as Native Americans or Australian Aborigines—who perceive themselves under threat of losing their own self-identity.

But the appropriation issue aside, understanding New Age spirituality as essentially a continuation of New Thought, despite the many different cosmetic additions that have been fused to it—sometimes permanently—allows a realization that New Age is much more consistent than might otherwise appear the case. This detectable consistency beneath its many multifaceted individual forms allows one to approach New Age as a legitimate and distinct spirituality, permits a mutual recognition between adherents and provides a common language, a sort of New Age speak, of spiritual nuance and vertical metaphor. The focus is almost invariably on healing—healing the body of infirmity, healing the mind of doubt, confusion, uncertainty and anxiety and healing the spirit from separation and darkness. In this quest for the *higher* state of being, for the higher mind and higher self, it is *gnosis* that breaks apart the chains of ignorance for a greater, more holistic, more integrated, more dynamic and more effective and ascending state of being. The acquisition of *gnosis* is to achieve enlightenment, and along with the up/down framework in which New Age chiefly operates, there is also employment of a pervasive light-versus-darkness symbolism.

Some New Age critics deplore what they perceive as New Age's exclusive exaltation of light. Among these are Neo-pagans whose more pantheistic approach honors both luminescence and darkness. New Age's light-fixation can be decried as one that leads ultimately to the praise of nuclear oblivion. More typical, however, of a general anti-New Age consensus is an attitude that sees it, perhaps less threateningly, as simply lavender-scented and pastel-colored, a mishmash of incense and crystals and the ultimate in self-pampering. New Age narcissism is certainly a criticism that is often leveled against spiritual consumerism in general, and the "airy-fairy" proclivities of New Age are often fair game for ridicule and dismissal by outside viewers.

But New Age frequently refers to itself as, or part of, the Wisdom Tradition. Its essential thrust represents an attempt to uncover hidden, esoteric and occult knowledge that reputedly belonged to the mages, sorcerers and secret societies that have flourished beneath mainstream spiritual traditions. Along with these, New Age includes the spiritual truths believed embedded in the mythologies and practices of indigenous peoples. In fact, New Age seeks to discover the common denominators linking *all* religions—whether mainstream, endangered, extinct or esoteric. In its quest for a "new age," one that is generally associated with the astrological notion of an Age of Aquarius, New Age spirituality advances the idea that spiritual property is no longer an exclusive or private concern of any privileged elite but is now part of a public domain accessible and potentially usable by everyone. The Wisdom Tradition that formerly survived *sub rosa* is, in the Aquarian New Age or Information Age, increasingly manifest. And it is this very Wisdom Tradition that New Age believes transcends any and all religion.

But it is not only this innovative declaration of the sacrosanct and independent integrity of this tradition that distinguishes New Age, it is also the insistence that this tradition is directly accessible. From a New Age perspective, there is no need of a middle person to mediate between the individual and a sacred reality. Gurus and teachers are instead guides: helpers rather than indispensable agents, wayshowers rather than magical surrogates. Consequently, New Age repudiates priests, prophets and other institutional authorities who presuppose that they can tell others what to believe and what to do that is mandatory in obtaining spiritual grace. Instead, it is the individual himself/herself who becomes, if not a self-authority, the self-determiner in regard to spiritual matters. Mistakes that a person makes become learning experiences, and it is this very experiential approach that constitutes the *sine qua non* experimentation and discovery of New Age identity. Even in the case of more institutional New Age sects such as the Church Universal and Triumphant, the locus of final authority is still believed to rest with the individual adherent who chooses to subscribe to a particular regime and spiritual framework. To the degree that New Age can be identified as championing the absolute freedom of individual self-determination concerning spiritual matters, it includes contemporary Western paganism. It is instead when considering what is spiritual that the two orientations are to be differentiated.

Consequently, New Age reveals a long legacy that stretches from ancient gnosticism, the Masonic and Rosicrucian lodges from the middle ages, ceremonial magical pursuit of the Renaissance, New England transcendentalism, spiritualism, theosophy, New Thought and the

American metaphysical tradition. For the most part, it occupies a middle ground between such differing expressions as the Holy Order of MANS (HOOM) and Heaven's Gate. The former, originally a typical New Age liberal blend of various traditions, slowly transformed into a conservative Christian institution. Its women were forced to surrender their holy orders. Membership developed into village-like enclaves, and in 1988 its remaining 750 members underwent baptism and joined the Holy Orthodox Archdiocese of Queens, New York. The group assumed its new name of Christ the Savior Brotherhood. Along with most remaining parishes, the Brotherhood later joined the more mainstream Orthodox Church in America. It is now dedicated to converting the world to Eastern Orthodoxy, and the remnants of its former New Age expectation have been channeled into preparation for Christ's Second Coming.

Heaven's Gate developed from the nomadic spirituality of Marshall Herff Applewhite and Bonnie Lu Nettles—originally known to followers as Bo and Peep; later as Do and Ti. The two established a UFO cult in the American southwest that combined science fiction elements with biblical prophecy—seeking redemption in an extraterrestrial "Kingdom of Heaven" and accepting a gnostic theology in which human bodies are merely "shells" or "vehicles" antecedent to The Evolutionary Level Above Human (TELAH). The arrival of the Hale-Bopp comet was interpreted as a marker and arrival of a spacecraft from the higher state, and this culminated in the suicides of thirty-nine residents of Rancho Santa Fe in San Diego on the 26th of March, 1997, who believed that through the death of their mortal bodies, they would achieve TELAH. While the Heaven's Gate narrative is expressive of the extremes of New Age thought, it is not typical of the more moderate mix of ideas that constitute the bulk of the New Age movement. Both HOOM and Heaven's Gate are difficult-to-locate expressions within the more popular New Age spirituality that the present dictionary hopes to illustrate.

The Dictionary

-A-

A COURSE IN MIRACLES. The most complete presentation of **New Thought** metaphysics. It says in summary: "Nothing real can be threatened. Nothing unreal exists. Herein lies the peace of God." Miracle Experiences, Inc., was founded in 1976 to publish and distribute the three-volume work known as *A Course in Miracles.* Here the miracle image is used as the basic metaphor—the miracle being understood as an example of correct thinking which attunes an individual's perceptions to Truth. In other words, the miracle represents a shift in perception that allows one to relinquish guilt-based illusions. With regard to the appearance of the *Course,* the reception of the work—reputedly the words of the biblical Christ in first person—is more correctly understood as something that was **channeled**.

Between 1965 and 1973, Dr. Helen Schucman (?-1981), associate professor at Columbia University in medical psychology, responding to an inner mental voice that nevertheless dictated words clearly, transcribed a 622-page *Text,* a 478-page *Workbook* comprising 365 lessons, and an eighty-eight-page *Manual for Teachers*—together known as *A Course in Miracles.* This designation came from an early statement made by the inner voice to Schucman after she had experienced a series of intense dreams and fantastic visions, namely, "This is a course in miracles. Please take notes." Although personally skeptical and insisting on total anonymity, Schucman was encouraged by a colleague, and the manuscript was published by New York psychic-metaphysical community leader Judith Skutch in 1975. Skutch headed the Foundation for Parasensory Information. On the basis of her reading of Schucman's channeled materials, however, she founded the Foundation for Inner Peace—an organization that is now based in Tiburon, California. Miracle Experiences, Inc., the body which publishes the text as well as a newsletter, *Miracle News*, sponsors conferences and workshops and has promoted a network of study groups across the United States and abroad, is situated on Long Island, New York. By 1990, a half million copies of the text had been sold.

According to the Foundation for Inner Peace, the goal of the *Course* is to "remove the blocks to the awareness of love's presence, which is your natural inheritance." The central theme of the *Course* is that "nothing real can be threatened" and "nothing unreal exists." With typical New Thought emphasis, a distinction between truth and illusion is maintained. The self-study course aims to help one distinguish between the voice of the ego (recognized as fear) and the voice of inner wisdom (identified as love). The language of the *Course* is essentially biblical and **Christian**. Nevertheless, its appeal appears to be greatest among those who have become disillusioned with traditional Christianity—and this despite the text's dated language in which the three persons of the Trinity are invariably referred to as male, and humanity is understood as "Sonship."

The *Course* affirms that humanity deserves to be punished for its belief in its permanent separation from God. The *Course* maintains that the separation has indeed occurred because what one believes is true. Simply to deny the separation is "to use denial inappropriately" but "to concentrate on error is only a further error." Instead, the *Course* claims that separation requires "**healing**," and the most direct way for this to occur is through forgiveness based on the recognition that to attack and scapegoat is merely a product of self-condemnation and a need for love. "Ask not to be forgiven, for this has already been accomplished. Ask, rather, to learn how to forgive." Sin is, accordingly, an illusion—so God's forgiveness is not necessary. What is necessary, however, is that the individual awakes from the terror of his/her own making. Since salvation is a cooperative venture, human relationships become opportunities to recognize the projection of guilt onto others and to replace the need for fear-based reprisal with exculpation and love. The Holy Spirit is an intermediary in this process who helps one to perceive the reflection of heaven in the world of illusion of his or her making. The peace and joy of God become the only viable choice over the strife of the ego. A person's goal, according to the *Course*, is to extend divine love into the world in order to awaken and heal others.

Similar to Christian Science, *A Course in Miracles* is a complete digest of New Thought. It appears as a recasting of the New Testament at the same time as it is essentially a Christianization of Vedanta. It has long been advocated by the **Unity School** that sponsored *A Course in Miracles* festival in Honolulu in 1986. In the New Age milieu, especially its more Christian wing, the *Course* has emerged as a prominent focus—one that consistently promotes the New Thought side to New Age orientation.

ACUPUNCTURE. The world's oldest medical system in which fine needles are inserted into the body at specific energy nodes. Acupuncture is first presented in the *Nei Ching* of China (*The Yellow Emperor's Classic of Internal Medicine*). Attributed to the quasi-mythic Huang Ti (2697-2597 B.C.E.), this work describes the flow of *ch'i* or subtle energy through the body's fourteen meridian lines. Disease is considered a product of blockage that can occur in any of the energy fields' concentration points along the meridians. Thin needles unlock the acupuncture point and allow the energy flow to recommence for the body's **healing**. Acupuncture was introduced to the west in the first decade of the eighteenth century. From the 1930s, the practice spread throughout France. In the 1970s, acupuncture and its corollaries (acupressure and moxibustion) became popular in the holistic health movement. Acupressure replaces the needles used in acupuncture with hand pressure or massage of the acupuncture points. In moxibustion, heat is applied instead. Other methods involve electricity, chemicals, sound, laser beams or ointments. Despite the demonstration of healing results—especially as a form of anesthesia, western allopathic medicine has been reluctant to endorse the use of acupuncture which has instead become popular throughout New Age circuits involved with **alternative forms of medicine**. *See also* SHIATSU.

ADI DA SAMRAJ (1939-). Born Franklin Albert Jones, the Adi Da Samraj claims that his avataric birth is a conscious and intentional act of divine self-submission. As a Columbia University graduate, in 1964 he began his sadhana, or spiritual training, under Swami Rudrananda. Four years later he inaugurated study with Rudrananda's own guru, **Swami Muktananda**. The latter acknowledged Adi Da's yogic liberation. On his third visit to India during a pilgrimage to the grave of Muktananda's teacher, Swami Nityananda, Adi Da was instructed to submit directly to the Divine Goddess as guru. Returning to Los Angeles, he permanently re-awakened to the "Bright" as the "radiant form of love-bliss" he had known in his youth. This led to Adi Da's realization that "I *Am* the One Who *Is* Complete." In 1972, with the opening of his first ashram in Los Angeles, his formal teaching work began. From 1973 to 1979, he assumed the name of Bubba Free John. He next revealed his name as Da Free John as the "Divine Giver [Da] of Grace and Blessings."

A 1986 "yogic swoon" was the initial event of his divine self-"Emergence" as a "World-Teacher." As a "God-Realized being," in 1987 and 1988, he was known principally as Da Avadhoota. During 1990 and 1991, he took the name Da Kalki in reference to the tenth and last incarnation of the Hindu god Vishnu. In 1993, he revealed to his devotees that his birth as a "Divine Impulse to Manifest" represented a conjunction with and re-birth of the Vedantic master, Swami Vivekananda. Adi Da's "Revelation-Epoch" that began in 1972 came to a close in 1995. The names by which he is now addressed and referred to are Da, Da Loloma Vunirarama, Da Love-Ananda, Da Avabhasa, Adi Da, The Da Avatar, Adi Da Samraj, Ruchira Buddha and the Ruchira Avatar.

Since his "Emergence," Adi Da has shifted his focus from teaching to blessing. Foremost, his blessing work takes the form of a call to his devotees to recognize him as the "Divine Person" and live devotionally as a response to him—forgetting and transcending separate self-existence. In addition, he performs silent "Spiritual Blessing Work" to diminish the world's negative forces. In order for there to be spiritual contemplation and progress, the planetary environment's survival is mandatory. Adi Da achieves the bestowal of universal blessing by "Brightening" whoever or whatever particular is representative of the whole that is brought to him. The practitioners of Adidam maintain retreat centers in northern California, Hawaii and Fiji, which is where their avatar now chiefly resides. Devotees accept Avatar Adi Da as the promised "God-Man" of a new age or the New Age.

AETHERIUS SOCIETY. A "saucer cult," founded in 1955 by George King (1919-), that happily identifies as New Age, reveres a Cosmic Hierarchy, engages in a battle with evil forces and expects that everyone will eventually become a Master and continue to evolve. In 1980, King was consecrated as a bishop in the Liberal Catholic Church. As a regular practitioner of **yoga**, he claims to have attained *Samadhi*, in which he has gained access to many cosmic secrets. In 1954, the Venusian Cosmic Master, who had assumed the name "Aetherius," told King that he was to become the voice of the Interplanetary Parliament, and the following year the Aetherius Society was established in London. The Parliament is headquartered on the planet Saturn, and King receives "Cosmic transmissions" from Aetherius and other Cosmic Masters while in his yogic trance state.

In the **galactian** framework, the Aetherius Society is both gnostic and cosmic. It believes in **reincarnation** as well as the **Great White Brotherhood** of Ascended, or Cosmic Masters, that includes Jesus, Krishna, Buddha and others. Inasmuch as everyone will eventually become a Master, the Brotherhood consists of members from both genders. Like the **Church Universal and Triumphant** (CUT), the Society's belief system is essentially both **Christian** and **Buddhist** (both Jesus and Buddha come from Venus), but unlike CUT, which distrusts flying saucers as containing negative entities that are to be avoided, King teaches that saucers have saved the earth on several occasions from atmospheric damage caused by human civilization. In fact, space ships (in particular, Satellite Three) orbiting the earth distribute special Prayer Hours of spiritual energies, or *prana*, that members of the Society can then channel toward specific concerns through King's invention of spiritual energy radiators. The periods during which this distribution occurs, usually lasting three to four weeks, are called "spiritual pushes." One, designated Operation Bluewater, ended in 1976 and involved charging a specific spiritual energy battery, a "radionic" storing device that can be used in times of crisis. Another "spiritual push," Operation Starlight, lasted for just over three years (1958-1961), during which King and others climbed eighteen mountains around the world that had been selected through a vision of the Master Jesus. The purpose of this "push" was to charge these mountains permanently with spiritual power. Regular pilgrimages to these sites now allow members to use the holy energies for terrestrial benefit.

While the Interplanetary Parliament (or Cosmic Hierarchy) is responsible to the Lords of the Sun, each planet functions as a learning stage that must be completed before one progresses to the next. The planetary lesson requires, however, that many reincarnations are necessary before one learns to live according to God's Laws. Some Masters live on the earth, but the coming Master, whose magic powers exceed all military might, will appear in a flying saucer and launch a thousand years of terrestrial peace. Before this millennium arrives, the Great White Brotherhood remains engaged in a cosmic battle with a group of black magicians who seek to enslave humanity. The Society assists in this warfare by training its members to re-direct or channel *prana* through mantras and prayers. This is known as Operation Prayer Power and generally involves transferring energy in order to heal disease. Apart from spiritual healing and the use of yoga, the Aetherius Society is concerned with **alternative medicine**, dowsing and most of the practices characteristic of New Age and **human potential**. It has remained at the forefront of ecological anxieties relating to nuclear radiation pollution and industrial contamination. The initiation of the earth occurred on July 8, 1964, and occurred with the manipulation of cosmic energies by a gigantic flying saucer. This date, as well as the birth of Jesus, the birth of King and the end of the phase of Armageddon, known as Operation Karmalight, is celebrated annually.

AGE OF AQUARIUS. The astrological identity of the New Age (*see* **precession of the equinoxes**). In iconographic terms, the constellation of Aquarius is understood as Ganymede, the youth seized by Zeus/Jupiter to be cupbearer to the gods. In spiritual hermeneutics, this configuration has been reinterpreted to represent the servant of humanity pouring forth the water of knowledge to quench the world's thirst. The sign of Aquarius is ruled by the planet Uranus, which is said to preside over unexpected, dynamic and progressive change. By aligning the New Age vision with the astrological age of Aquarius, not only is the New Age grounded in a supposedly discernible astronomical event, it is also linked to Uranian newness and transformation. The major difficulty involved is the location of the actual astronomical date. Astrologer Nicholas Campion mentions at least seventy possibilities for the beginning of the Age of Aquarius covering a range of 1,500 years (*Book of World Horoscopes*). Some argue that the entrance into the new age is an inner rather than outer conversion. Within the broad spectrum of New Age movements, some expect the change to come through some kind of supernatural intervention (*see* **millennialism**). For others (e.g., **Ram Dass**), the entry is spiritual and depends on a sufficient number of individuals becoming aware of their "higher selves" and undergoing the requisite personal transformation for a quantum shift in planetary consciousness. Yet, thirdly, others stress (e.g., **Marilyn Ferguson**) for a New Age through ecological reform and consciousness, social work, education and the practical application of new ideas and innovations. From this last vantage point, the New Age of Aquarius is a social rather than supernatural or spiritual phenomenon. *See also* ASTROLOGY.

AKASHIC RECORDS. A reputed etheric compendium of pictorial records or "memories" of all events, thoughts and feelings that have occurred since the beginning of time. Spiritualists describe Akasha, or astral light, as a fluid ether inaccessible within the normal range of human senses but approachable by select individuals—including a spiritualist medium or channeler during a séance. Akasha is understood as a reservoir of occult power that transmits the energy waves of human willpower, thought, emotion and imagination. It is through this ocean of unconsciousness that allegedly links everyone that prophecy and clairvoyance are believed to become possible. **Edgar Cayce** referred to the Akashic Records as the skein of space and time that could also be called "God's Book of Remembrance."

ALCHEMY. The power or process of transforming or transmuting something of lesser value into something of greater value. As a medieval chemical science and speculative philosophy, alchemy was concerned with changing base metals into gold, with developing a universal cure for disease and with prolonging life indefinitely. Alchemy's "Great Work" focused on the reconciliation of opposites and the creation of divine harmony between heaven and earth. Its mythical founder is identified as Hermes Trismegistus, after whom are named the hermetic or occult arts of **magic**, **astrology** and alchemy. In alchemical drawings of Alchymya, the personification of alchemy, the figure is depicted holding the "Hermetic Vessel" that allegedly contains the key to all the mysteries and within which the "Great Work" is undertaken. Both the vessel and the tablet belonging to Hermes Trismegistus are, according to legend, composed of emerald. This indicates the subsequent identification between the Grail stories and processes of alchemy. Engraved on the emerald tablet is reputedly the occult dictum "as above, so below."

The objective of the alchemical quest is to isolate primary matter and separate it into its constituent reagents that could then be recombined into a miraculous new substance referred to as the elixir of life (*elixir vitae*), the Philosopher's Stone, the panacea, the secret of perpetual motion, etc. Alchemy holds that all objects possess spirits that are perfectible and transformable from lower to higher states. Moreover, working with an understanding that all substance is composed from four elements (earth, water, fire and air), alchemy holds that it is possible to change one substance into another (e.g., lead into gold). This physical transmutation depends on discovering the necessary but so far elusive miraculous agent. But inasmuch as the primary alchemical reagents, mercury and sulfur, are considered gendered, the male and female principles manifest in these minerals become linked to human sexual emissions, and sexual union, whether symbolic or concrete, becomes a central ritual effort. This required the male alchemist to have a female consort or assistant. Beyond the European tradition, similar alchemical practice is found in **Taoism**, **Hinduism** and **Buddhism**. For the Taoist, the inner alchemical union of *yang* (male) and *yin* (female) can be effected through a conjunction of male semen and female uterine blood. In **tantric** practices of Hinduism and Buddhism, transformation into invulnerable and perfected immortality is sometimes approached through sexual union.

Carl Jung transformed the medieval understanding of alchemy into a spiritual understanding that has come to permeate much of today's magical and New Age practice. Jung recognized alchemy as an elaborate system based on projection in which new meanings that arise from the unconscious psyche are understood when mirrored in outer reality. Consequently, he advocated the study of alchemy and astrology as a means of discovery of the human psyche's archetypal components. In other words, while alchemists and astrologers experience their projections as properties of matter or celestial body influence, they are actually experiencing symbolic processes within their own unconscious psyches. The resultant insight is part of a person's psychological and spiritual development that Jung referred to as individuation. In attempting to liberate gold from the *prima material* (primal substance) that Jung identified as the primal Self, the alchemist brings the Self to consciousness and differentiation from the *massa confusa* or unconscious. The making of gold is thus symbolic of bringing the Self to full realization and becoming as complete as possible. This perfection or transmutation of the soul is achieved by a total union or metamorphosis of opposites. For a different application of alchemy as a contemporary practice, *see* SHAMANISM.

ALEXANDER TECHNIQUE. A means of alternative **healing** developed by the Australian actor Frederick Matthias Alexander (1869-1955). The Alexander Technique is a method of re-educating the body for good posture, reduction of tension, relaxation and correction of speech defects through the elimination of non-conducive ingrained habits. This is achieved through working with a teacher, visualizing an image of healthy functioning, self-observation and conscious correction. The technique is particular popular with dancers, actors and musicians. It centers on the head and neck to achieve proper balance for the entire body. Alexander claimed that his technique is primarily educational rather than therapeutic, but it has nonetheless achieved noteworthy results for both healing and prevention.

ALTERNATIVE MEDICINE. Term used to designate various methods used for the prevention, diagnosis and/or treatment of disease not generally accepted by traditional or allopathic physicians. Alternative medicines include **acupuncture, ayurveda, chromotherapy**, herbal and ritual healing, **homeopathy, naturopathy**, magnetic therapy, psychic healing, chiropractic, osteopathy, diet (e.g., **vegetarianism**), **biofeedback**, guided imagery and therapeutic touch among a countless range of other techniques and practices.

AMERICAN METAPHYSICAL TRADITION. A nineteenth century movement that developed a concern for **healing** and an emphasis on the reality and immanence of the spiritual. As the alternative spirituality of its day, the tradition stressed the reality of the spiritual world, the importance of the mystical experience and the healing value of invisible forces operating on mind and body. In general, the movement holds to the idea of a divine spark within each individual, the power of the mind and the principle of spirit-matter correspondences between all aspects of the cosmos. Between them, **Emanuel Swedenborg, Franz Anton Mesmer, Phineas P. Quimby, Ralph Waldo Emerson** and **Warren Felt Evans** created the common language of the transcendentalist and metaphysical traditions in America. It is largely out of these traditions that the **spiritualist, New Thought** and **theosophical** movements each coalesced. These, in turn, are the primary antecedents of contemporary New Age movements.

ANDREWS, LYNN V. Former Beverly Hills socialite who became a self-described medicine woman shaman through apprenticeship to Agnes Whistling Elk and Ruby Plenty Chiefs, two Cree teachers. Little is known of Andrews' personal life, but through initiation into the secret Sisterhood of the Shields, she has become a prolific author of works that follow in the style of **Carlos Castaneda**. These include *Medicine Woman* (1981), *Flight of the Seventh Moon* (1984), *Jaguar Woman and the Wisdom of the Butterfly Tree* (1985), *Star Woman* (1986) and *Teachings Around the Sacred Wheel* (1990). Andrews also acknowledges Hyemeyohsts Storm and **Sun Bear** as principal teachers. She remains a controversial teacher of the "medicine way" and promotes use of the **medicine wheel**. This last, she argues, is the cosmic pattern the individual ought to employ in molding one's spiritual life. She conducts seminars, ceremonies and **meditations** for initiation, **healing** and personal growth, but following vociferous criticism from Native American circles concerning accuracy and fabrication, she has become increasingly reclusive. Nevertheless, she is frequently cited as having assisted many women in their own search for self-empowerment. *See also* SHAMANISM.

ANTI-SEMITISM. *See* CONTROVERSIES, NEW AGE.

APOCALYPTICISM. A type of late Judaic and early **Christian** thought that views the present age as evil and about to reach its dramatic conclusion. In the forthcoming battle between the forces of good and evil, the world will end—usually being consumed by fire—before reemerging, cleansed of the satanic, as the new abode for the righteous. The apocalypses include the biblical books of Daniel and Revelations as well as the non-canonical Enoch material.

In New Age, apocalypticism is largely a Christian-derived "end-times" situation that for some adherents describes the likely transition leading to the New Age. Inasmuch as New Age groups can possess this kind of **millenarian** expectation, they are vulnerable to the general scenario of which any doomsday religious movement is capable. Apocalyptic beliefs are characterized by dualism, the persecuted chosen, imminence, determinism and salvation through conflict. Its charismatic leadership tends to exert control over members with little sense of restraint. Suspicion of others arises and frequently leads to physical, social and psychological withdrawal. In such circumstances, the leader's power becomes intensified, and the group more unified and dependent. If this withdrawal is accompanied by an expectation of hostility and persecution, doomsday groups can feel that they must mobilize for the approaching "end-times" and secure weapons and other defenses. On the one hand, the group might go on the attack, as happened with **Aum Shinrikyo**. On the other hand, withdrawal may lead instead to suicide as with Heaven's Gate, or suicide and murder of unwilling members such as in the case of both the **Solar Temple** and the communal project of the People's Temple of Jonestown.

While the apocalyptic groups are illustrative of a possibility, they are not typical of the New Age movement in general. Much of the movement remains part of the current fashion in spiritual supermarket shopping. Gurus and religious leaders, sometimes charismatic, do appear but remain uncharacteristic of the religiosity in general which instead places more emphasis on personal autonomy and self-selection. Among the early warning signs presented by the Canadian Security Intelligence Service concerning doomsday religious movements, there can be found in New Age few illegal activities, little violent rhetoric, no real struggle for leadership and few circumstances that can be described as humiliating. Occasionally, one does find some relocation of New Age groups to rural areas, but without the other elements, but this cannot be taken as indicative of a threatening apocalypticism. While chiliastic expectation of earth-changes and end-times remains a part of the New Age "package" from **Ruth Montgomery** and **Edgar Cayce** to Elizabeth Clare Prophet (*see* **Church Universal and Triumphant**) and James Jacob Hurtak, the wider New Age anticipation does not draw upon the Christian heritage from the Book of Revelation but sees the **Age of Aquarius** as a natural progression of evolution. Here one might find the more prevalent New Age thought as embodied in the teachings of **Marilyn Ferguson, José Argüelles** or **William Bloom**.

ARCANE SCHOOL. *See* BAILEY, ALICE

ARCHETYPES. Prototypic phenomena, mythic elements and ancestral memories that compose the collective and individual unconscious. The concept of the archetype was put forward by Carl Gustav Jung

(1875-1961) as a transcultural component reflective of human behavior universally—transcending differences of gender, religion and culture. Typical archetypes might be the hero, the great mother, the trickster, the child and the wise old man or woman. Jungian analytic psychology claims that a person seeks wholeness and completion (individuation) and that dream analysis affords a major access to archetypal configurations and dynamics through which important creative development based on an organic synthesis can occur. Consequently, **dream-work**, along with the study of **myth**, constitutes a particular **therapy** that one encounters in both New Age and **Neo-pagan** circles. Both spiritualities stress efforts toward a holistic integration of the self in light of the complexities and depersonalizations that characterize much of postindustrial times. Apart from dreams, archetypal symbols are believed to be accessed through **clairvoyant** insight, psychic readings and **biofeedback** training.

ARGÜELLES, JOSÉ (1939-). New Age spokesperson and author of *The Mayan Factor* (1987) and *Surfers of the Zuvuya* (1989). In the earlier work, Argüelles lays the groundwork for an evolutionary timetable that culminates with the New Age. For Argüelles, the posthistorical world will be posttechnological. This rejection of the currently prevailing scientific-materialistic paradigm will allow the possibility of what Argüelles calls "the Armageddon by-pass." His spiritual outlook is **astral** and, rather than seeking contact with "past-life archetypes," he aims to "channel the stars directly." His **galactian** vision is grounded upon the sacred calendar of the Mayans, and he blames technological comfort and gadgetry for our current blindness to the collective bio-electromagnetic field and inability to recognize the sun as a living intelligence that resonates in attunement with Hunab Ku, the galactic core. In line with the Mayan "Great Cycle," Argüelles organized the worldwide celebration of the Harmonic Convergence, a "resonant frequency shift" that allegedly occurred on the sixteenth and seventeenth of August in 1987. While Sir **George Trevelyan** celebrated this at Glastonbury Tor in Great Britain as "the birth of the New Age," Argüelles locates the Aquarian age's inception with the culmination of the present Great Cycle on December 21, 2012 C.E. Influenced by Ouspensky, the **Naropa Institute** (Chögya Trungpa Rinpoche), Tony Shearer and **Sun Bear**, Argüelles pictures a shamanic future for humanity that flourishes in harmony with the greater natural harmony. *See also* AGE OF

AQUARIUS, SHAMANISM.

ARICA. A "School of Knowledge" founded by **Oscar Ichazo** in Chile in 1968 and incorporated in New York as the Arica Institute in 1971. There are approximately forty centers today in the United States, South America, Europe and Australia including branches in New York, Los Angeles and San Francisco. Broadly speaking, along with **Pir Vilayat Khan's Sufi Order** and **Meher Baba**'s Friends of Meher Baba, Arica is part of the Islamic tradition within New Age. It provides an integrated path to self-realization or what it terms the "True Essential Self." Its practice comprises a daily morning and evening exercise and **meditation** routine to provide immediate short-term benefits as well as attunement for achieving mystical transcendence. Like **Silva Mind Control**, Arica views meditation not as an end in itself but as a means to other ends. Eight members may form a social unit known as an Octagon that meets regularly and through group meditation offers energy to benefit an individual, social advance and/or human unity. In essence, Arica offers a psychological orientation that seeks to unlock the mysteries of one's sacred, inner powers. It provides a systematic progress to "the higher states of consciousness where enlightenment can be attained."

ARIOSOPHIE. Reputed "science of the Aryans" promoted by Guido von List (1848-1919) as an affirmation of racial superiority. It connects volkish thinking with occultism and **theosophy** and contains elements derived from **gnosticism**, hermeticism, **alchemy**, **kabalism**, **Rosicrucianism**, and Grail Legend. Ariosophie alleges further links with Celtic Druidry and the Mazdaism of ancient Persia. Employing the iconographic symbolism of Saints Michael and George subduing the dragon, Ariosophie interprets this as humanity defeating its lower principles— including unsublimated sexual power. While Ariosophie intersects with the German **Volktumsbewegung** that experimented with **vegetarianism**, **paganism**, freelove, nature religion and many other features associated with the later counterculture of the twentieth century, its theological and esoteric heritage fostered a principle of elite self-consciousness. Consequently, Ariosophie shares with New Age a pursuit of the "higher life" of spirit and mind. Its ideology ties in with notions of **karma**—especially group karma, as well as the acceptance that there are secret laws of the cosmos. Von List believed in **reincarnation** and "hereditary memory."

In 1908, through a follower of Von List (Jörg Lanz von Liebenfels), Ariosophie became a vehicle to justify and encourage the repression of the "lower races" and, in particular, to foster anti-Semitic resentment. He was here following ideas first formulated by **Helena Blavatsky** concerning the Aryans as the fifth "root-race." Ariosophie came to believe that children should be engendered consciously within the family structure and an awareness of **astrological** factors. Ariosophie survives today as the right-winged Gothic Armanenorden (The Arman Medal) that was created in 1976 by Adolf Schleipfer and his wife. *See also* CONTROVERSIES, NEW AGE.

AROMATHERAPY. The **therapy** based on use of aromatic oils derived from flowers, bark, spices, fruit, herbs and perfumes. Traditionally, crushed plant substances were held over the nose and mouth as a preventative (e.g., from the plague). In their New Age use, aromatic substances are produced in the form of essential oils which are often used in conjunction with other **healing** practices such as **yoga** and **massage** rather than sniffed directly. The therapeutic oils are employed to produce shampoos, massage oils, hair and skin conditioners, as well as cosmetics. The aromatherapy revival began with the publication in France of René-Maurice Gattefosse's *Aromathérapie* in 1928. In 1962, Marguerite Maury published her findings concerning new techniques for extracting and using oils (English version: *The Secrets of Youth and Life*, 1964). She stressed both the olfactory use of essential oils and their direct absorption through the skin. From France, Maury's methods spread to Great Britain and thence to North America. In the 1980s, aromatherapy became a main practice adopted by New Age.

ASAHARA, SHOKO (Chizuo Matsumoto) (1955-). Founder of the Japanese **Aum Shinrikyo**. Due to severely impaired vision, at the age of six, Asahara was sent to a special school for the blind. He graduated in 1975, but failing to gain admission into the schools of medicine of Kumamoto and Tokyo Universities, he began the study of **acupuncture** and pharmaceuticals. These studies culminated in his opening a pharmacy in Chiba that specialized in Chinese medicaments. Asahara was arrested in 1982 for the sale of fake remedies, and his business went bankrupt. His next venture was to launch a school for **yoga** and the sale of health drinks.

With the assistance of his wife, Asahara founded Aum Shinrikyo in 1987. He wrote several books that included predictions of Armageddon. This last was to begin with a gas cloud sent by the United States in 1997. The Tokyo Metropolitan government granted Aum Shinrikyo legal status as a religious organization in 1989. At this time, Asahara adopted the titles "Holy Pope," "Savior of the Country" and "Tokyo's Christ." He expressed admiration for Adolf Hitler and Mao Zedong and boasted that he could levitate and bestow super power on his disciples. Asahara honors Shiva, the Hindu god of destruction and regeneration. All in all, he teaches a mix of New Age notions and terminologies but in an application that differs from the various related movements in its predilection for subterfuge and violence. By the end of 1995, Shoko Asahara was in prison facing charges of having masterminded a series of crimes that included murder, kidnapping and manufacturing sarin, the poisonous nerve gas that caused thousands of casualties when it was released in a Tokyo subway. While he remains in prison, he has transferred power to relatives and disciples and would still appear to exercise an influence over his group.

ASSAGIOLI, ROBERTO. *See* PSYCHOSYNTHESIS.

ASTRAL ("belonging to the stars"). A supersensible substance that **theosophy** supposes to pervade all space and bodies. The astral plane is understood as the bridge between the spiritual and physical planes. It is the dimension in which **astral travel** occurs. It differs from the ordinary physical plane in that objects here possess a fluid form. They also emit light rather than being simply media that reflect luminosity. For human consciousness, the ability to concentrate becomes essential. Focusing on where one wants to be allows one to "travel" to the desired location. Shifting focus results in shifting direction.

As a "theological" term, astral and **gnostic** may both be **galactian**, but whereas gnostic is transcendental and understands the spiritual as *a priori*, astral is closer to **pagan** spirituality in recognizing the centrality and permanence of matter. However, it differs from the pagan in that generally paganism understands the mental, spiritual and supernatural as emergents that have ultimately a co-validity with the tangible. In the astral form of **Raëlianism**, however, there is no spiritual, and the universe has no beginning. Matter is purely mechanical. There is no *anima mundi* to the world or the cosmos.

ASTRAL RELIGION/ASTRALISM. *See* ASTRAL.

ASTRAL TRAVEL. Soul flight, exteriorization, or out-of-body-experience. A basic technique in **shamanism, dream-work** and **visualization**, astral travel refers to conscious experience of the self beyond the confines of the physical body. Astral traveling or projection is also referred to as OBE or "**out-of-body experience**." It is described as the experience of one's consciousness as appearing separate from the physical body. Similar experiences are recorded by people who have had **near-death** encounters.

In many religions, a core belief involves the idea that the human spirit detaches itself from the physical body at the time of death. In the concept of astral travel, this same possibility is said to occur on a temporary basis. Escape from the body is often interpreted as either an adventure or sign of spiritual growth. During astral travel, whether in sleep, controlled experiment or **meditation**, the traveler is alleged to be able to perceive things, places, events and/or people beyond his or her present location. Methods of inducing OBEs include lucid dreaming, visualization and self-imposed trance. To travel astrally at will requires a disciplined and focused mind. The optimum mental state is considered one that is quiet, completely passive and singlemindedly observant.

ASTROLOGY. An **astral** form of divination that is traced to the ancient Mesopotamians and Egyptians. Astrology flourished for irregular intervals under the Romans and was subsequently brought to Spain by the invading Moors in the ninth century. The legend of Faust in Germany portrays him as an astrologer as well as a sorcerer. During the reign of Catherine de Medici, astrology became popular in France, while in England it had been practiced by Bede, Alcuin, Roger Bacon and, in the seventeenth century, by William Lilly who employed the magical circle composed of astrological symbols for the evocation of spirits.

The current popularity of astrology finds its origins in the late 1930s with the emergence of daily horoscopes in newspapers. By far, it was the theosophist Alan Leo (William Frederick Allen, 1860-1917) who laid the foundations for the present-day understanding of this "science of the stars." As a professional astrologer, Leo founded the journal *Modern Astrology* and authored numerous books on the subject. In the course of the twentieth century, through its links with **theosophy**, astrology became the *lingua franca* of the 1960s counterculture as well as the New Age movements that have descended from it. Its use of the astronomical phenomenon of the **precession of the equinoxes** has become the seminal framework within which the New Age of Aquarius has been heralded. *See also* **Age of Aquarius**.

The key point of departure for the casting of an individual's horoscope is the person's place and time of birth. The natal horoscope presents a depiction of the positions of the planets and luminaries (sun and moon) relative to the person at the time of his or her birth. In other words, astrology is a geocentric understanding that takes a person's terrestrial nativity as the center of the entire cosmos. As a system of thought, astrology promotes an interdependent and interconnected picture of the universe as an organic and interrelated whole. Following the ancient principle "as above, so below," by which the microcosm is thought to mirror the macrocosm, astrology considers that understanding and prediction of earthly, personal and spiritual events are possible through a study of the stars. Astrology pursues this study through considering the placements of the planets and luminaries against the twelve astronomical signs (or constellations) of the zodiac and whether these solar system bodies form mutual conjunctions or significant angles vis-à-vis the earth namely, 90° squares or 180° oppositions as learning obstacles and 60° sextiles or 120° trines as harmonious and favorable influences for the individual or event concerned.

With the advent of the empirical sciences, astrology has received increased criticism and attack. Some astrologers maintain that the behavioral characteristics and eventual propensities predicted by the system have been acquired through years—even millennia—of observation. However, astrological interpretation appears instead to derive from an *a priori* matrix relationship between personality **archetypes** (e.g., mercurial, jovial and saturnine characteristics) and **numerology** or numerical symbolism. Science condemns this last as superstition, but New Age in turn tends to reject the restricted and narrow province of science as applicable to wisdom traditions with their corollary of mystical understanding. On the other hand, astrology must also face antagonism from traditional mainstream western religions. In particular, ca-

nonical **Christianity** considers that whatever of the supernatural is not
"of God" must, by default, be "of the Devil." Foremost among these
"satanic arts" is astrology. Nevertheless, New Age culture not only
seeks escape from the stranglehold of what it considers outmoded
thought forms, but it also establishes itself on astrological nuance,
metaphor and interpretation.

ATLANTIS. A part of Western cultural exchange ever since Plato first
mentioned the destruction of Atlantis in his *Timaeus* and *Critias*. Atlantis
tis echoes biblical **apocalypticism** and embodies both Hesiod's "golden
age" and the Book of Genesis' "garden of Eden" alike. The appeal of
the Atlantis story, therefore, is one that goes to the roots of Western
civilization: it depicts a glorious past that has been lost. As Francis Bacon
con in his *The New Atlantis* puts it, "the dream-like strength of this particular
ticular myth poses as an allegation of truth."

In 1969, Greek archaeologist Angelo Galanopoulos suggested that
Plato's Atlantis civilization had been that of Minoan Crete which was
destroyed by the volcanic eruption of the Aegean island of
Thera/Santorini around 1500 B.C.E. Dutch writer Joop Slagter has even
suggested that the Atlantean capital was not Herakleion on Crete but
Santorini itself—the very center of the explosion. Plato, however,
claims that Greece derived the story of Atlantis from Egypt when the
Athenian lawgiver Solon visited and first learned of it from priests of a
temple in Sais. Plato describes Atlantis as having been beyond the Pillars
lars of Heracles, that is, the Straits of Gibraltar and larger than Anatolia
and Libya together. Through military conquest, the Atlanteans reputedly
edly controlled much of the Mediterranean Basin but had been repulsed
by the Greeks. The destruction of Atlantis occurred at the height of its
power.

Despite lingering interest in the Atlantis story in the classical and
renaissance worlds, it was in the nineteenth century with the release of
Histoire philosophique du genre humain by Fabre d'Olivet and, more
particularly, with the 1882 publication of *Atlantis: The Antediluvian
World*, by Ignatius Donnelly, that modern fascination with the legend
begins. Donnelly collected all the known information on the island continent
tinent which he believed had been in the Atlantic Ocean and was where
civilization first developed and from where it was exported in the form
of colonies to the rest of the world. Among these colonies, Egypt was
the oldest. The end of Atlantis occurred through natural causes, and

only a few of its inhabitants managed to escape and bring the story to others where it has survived in the flood myths of various peoples around the world.

Donnelly's version of Atlantis was adopted by **Helena Blavatsky,** the founder of the **Theosophical Society.** For her, it became an essential part of her theory of root races in which Lemuria, a Pacific Ocean equivalent of Atlantis, was recognized as the home of the third root race, the inhabitants of Atlantis as the fourth, while the world is now occupied by the fifth root race. One unfortunate spin-off of Blavatsky's anti-Darwinian root race theory became the ideas of a "master race" developed by Germany's *Völkische* movement through the writings of Hermann Wirth, Karl Georg Zschaetzsch and Alfred Rosenberg which, in turn, led to a Third Reich Nazi obsession with Atlantis as the original Aryan homeland. But apart from this aberration, Blavatsky's student, **Rudolf Steiner,** claimed to be able psychically to access the "**akashic records,**" the traces of all events preserved on the **astral** plane, and thereby learn that the Atlanteans possessed telepathic powers, extraordinary memories and advanced technology. Not only did Steiner contribute to the currently popular understanding of Atlantis as a center of evolved civilization, but he also launched the New Age technique of **channeling** through which information concerning Atlantis and its history can allegedly be acquired.

The most important for the ongoing development of the Atlantis story has been the occultist and psychic **Edgar Cayce.** Cayce exalted Atlantis beyond being simply a place of advanced civilization into that possessing the highest degree of technical accomplishment. He also predicted the re-emergence of Atlantis near the end of the 1960s— thereby fueling the growing expectation of a "New Age." But there was also a new twist to the story that concerned the original demise of Atlantis. Whereas formerly the island continent had reached its end through the havoc caused by natural causes, in Cayce's version Atlantis was destroyed through its inhabitants' own hubris. The Atlanteans' downfall became a result of their own misuse of their engineering achievements. In other words, it became a punishment.

While not pictured this way by all New Agers, the Cayce comprehension of Atlantis is held in particular by those who feel the new era is to come about through apocalyptic earth changes and upheavals. This idea is found frequently within what might be designated as the "Christian wing" of New Age thought, but it also occurs among the "galactians" who follow the Enochic tale concerning the Watcher Angels of Genesis who had been sent by God to look after humanity but became lustful over the "daughters of men" and produced a lineage of evil offspring as a result. Within the New Age identity, various versions of the "angelic fall" are found ranging from James Jacob Hurtak's *The Keys of Enoch* to Elizabeth Clare Prophet's **Church Universal and Triumphant**. For Hurtak, Atlantis fell because its people had intermarried with the offspring of the fallen Lords of Light and had subsequently engaged in mixed genetic code experimentation. For Prophet, the descendants of the evil offspring now head the various governments throughout the world as well as the financial institutions, multinationals and underworld drug cartels.

Consequently, there are two different versions to explain the Atlantis catastrophe. The older and original understands the demise as a freak event of nature. It amounts to plain bad luck for the Atlanteans that they had their homeland and high level of civilization on a part of the earth that was cataclysmically vulnerable. In contrast, however, the theosophically-inspired New Age version sees the Atlantis story as a cautionary tale. Here, the consequence is no longer seen as an "accident of nature" or a random act of God but as the result of sinister and prideful behavior. However, if the older version supports what could be termed a "culture of nature" and feeds into today's **Neo-pagan** and earth-based religions movement, the newer version suggests a "culture of spirituality" or, more correctly perhaps, a "culture of transcendence" that reflects New Age's gnostic revival. *See also* PAGAN.

AUM SHINRIKYO (Aum Supreme Truth). A religious group founded by **Asahara Shoko** after a 1986 sojourn in the Himalayan mountains in search of enlightenment. It has been described as a high-tech and armed New Age movement. Aum's origins can be traced to Asahara's **acupuncture** business and **yoga** school. Headquartered at the foot of Mount Fuji, it became a blend of mystical **Buddhism**—especially **Tibetan Buddhism**, Hindu deities, Shivite yoga, esoteric spiritualism, the prophecies of **Nostradamus** and the Christian millenarian expectation of Armageddon. In its promise of enlightenment, community and supernatural power and use of such high-tech shortcuts to enlightenment as electrode caps, astral teleporters and magic DNA, Aum's basic sci-fi orientation would place it in the **galactian** wing of the New Age movement if its transcendental anti-materialism would not more decisively suggest an inherent gnostic theology. It has proved to be particularly attractive for postindustrial Japan's electronic communications-trained but disillusioned youth.

Asahara has claimed to have ten thousand followers in Japan and twenty thousand abroad—mainly in Russia, and regional offices in the United States, Germany and Sri Lanka. He attracted well-educated followers—many from prosperous families. His top leaders held degrees in such fields as law, biotechnology, medicine, chemistry, computer science and rocket technology. All members were expected to donate everything they owned to the group. Once or twice a day, they were served rice and stewed vegetables. Otherwise, they often fasted in Buddhist fashion. Yogic exercises were undertaken, and some acolytes at the Yamanashi training center wore special helmets equipped with electrodes that were expected to increase the wearer's alpha waves. Devoted worship would be rewarded with a drink of Asahara's bathwater.

At first, Aum's central mission was to reduce the number of victims of the coming Armageddon to only one-fourth of the world's population. If thirty thousand enlightened spiritual practitioners could be achieved, Asahara believed he could eradicate the world's negative karma to achieve a peaceful transition if not to a new age then to a spiritual paradise on earth. But in general, the means used by Aum toward this end have proven to be among the most contentious employed by any new religious movement: use of electric shock treatment on its followers and the collection of weapons of mass destruction. The guru's lieutenants have pursued a course of purchasing chemicals, obtaining licenses to fly Russian military helicopters, and negotiating to acquire aircraft and secondhand weaponry. Asahara's attempt to gain a voice in national politics failed when all twenty-five Aum Shinrikyo candidates lost in their 1990 bids for seats in the lower house of the Diet. He interpreted the Kobe earthquake of 1995 as proof of the approaching apocalypse. The sarin gas attack on the Tokyo subway two months later was, reputedly, an attempt by Aum to escalate the world into Armageddon and pave the way now for the survival of its followers alone. According to Asahara, his devotees will rise from the ashes of Armageddon as a race of superhumans. It was this premise that led the group toward wanting to hasten the arrival of the new order. But by the end of 1995, Asahara was charged with masterminding murder, kidnapping, manufacturing sarin and causing thousands of casualties in the Tokyo subway.

Aum Shinrikyo opposes Japan's this-worldly religious orientation. Asahara stresses the emptiness of this world and the necessity to live life ascetically. In its gnostic galactian interpretation, the world is understood as illusory and without real value. It becomes instead a place for suffering and ordeal—not one of enjoyment and satisfaction. Faced with the reality of death and the existence of hell for those who prefer the "lowly" this-worldly life, ascetic practice is emphasized as the means by which the soul progresses through stages of development toward "ultimate truth." Transmigration is still retained as an Aumist belief, but it is the otherworld that consists of various stages through which the soul achieves its real advance. The earthly plane is simply for clearing away bad **karma**. One chooses his or her life conditions. While healing is important, the real emphasis is placed on mystical experience and conscious spiritual elevation.

In Aum, this spiritual progression is combined with end-time prophecy and messianism. This last entails veneration of a **shamanistic** leader and/or living god who possesses special abilities in **healing** and divination and will ultimately function as a savior. Throughout Aumism, there is the urgency to proselytize. Inasmuch as Asahara teaches that one must meditate and involve oneself in body-transforming practice, Aum Shinrikyo retains a New Age preoccupation with mind-control through technological means: **meditation**, auto-suggestion and body-work, even though it does not expressly identify as New Age. More focused on the postapocalyptic earthly paradise than necessarily on a "golden age" of Aquarius, its **millennialism** is nevertheless couched in the same sort of expectation of end-times catastrophe that characterizes much of the expected transition to the "new age" of New Age—particularly its Christian wing. Abrahamic messianism is fused with eastern anticipation of the Lord Maitreya.

Even after the 1985 Tokyo debacle, however, Aum Shinrikyo continues to flourish by holding regular training sessions, recruiting new members and raising money. In Japan, some of its membership is monastic (ordained followers who live communally), and the movement maintains a presence in Russia, Ukraine, Byelorussia and Kazakhstan. The group is now led by a secretive six-member steering committee that increasingly focuses on two of Asahara's six children as spiritual symbols—his third daughter and his youngest son. However, unlike similar movements, Aum Shinrikyo is an extreme case—one that united world-denial, communalism, millennialism and messianic charisma into a particularly lethal combination. Despite its many similarities with doctrines and practices found throughout the wider New Age, the fragility of the movement due to unrealistic goals and increasing defections propelled the group into aggressive behavior in its expectation of a cataclysmic transition to the millennium. Through its gnostic inclination, Aum subscribed to an understanding of the world and itself as under attack by agents of evil.

AURA. In esoteric, occult and parapsychological studies, an essence or energy field believed to emanate from an individual, animal and/or object. Humans in particular are said to be enveloped by a glow or light field that only sensitives or psychics can "see." The colors, size and quality are interpreted by "aura-seers" as indications of the person's health, emotions and character. While dark red signifies passion and sensuality, bright red is an indicator of anger. Pink conveys affection, orange suggests selfishness, pride and ambition, and yellow designates intelligence and mental activity. On the other hand, brown is an indicator of greed, while gray indicates conventionalism and depression. Green may suggest a wide range of possibilities from augmentation to health, fresh growth and happiness. A blue aura generally relates to piety, devotion and religion; purple, to psychic powers. Gold is associated with reflection, protection and strength; silver, with rapidity and spirit guides. Black is another indicator of depression. It also represents negativity and problems and can appear as a hole in one's aura. White is its opposite and indicates health, goodness and complete spiritual balance. The aura conforms to the halo in Christian and Buddhist iconography. If it envelops the entire body, it is designated the "aureola."

AURA-SOMA. A "soul" **therapy** developed by Vicky Hall in 1984 following a series of meditative visions. Based on the use of bottled colored oils, special essences and pomanders composed of natural ingredients, it is a consultative practice in which the clients' color choice is said to reflect hidden needs within the self and the individual's possibility of communication with the soul. The resultant communication is known as "the Rainbow Bridge." The purpose behind this therapeutic choice and use of color is self-empowerment and the ability of the individual to become a co-creator of his or her future.

AUROBINDO, SRI (1872-1950). Indian independence activist and spiritual guide who taught a secularized or western version of eastern spirituality and insight. He has become equally seminal throughout much of the New Age movement along with its range of **theosophical** and eastern mysticism teachers. Aurobindo claimed to communicate with the likes of the deceased Swami Vivekananda. In 1926 he experienced "The Day of the Siddhi" as a descent of divine consciousness into the physical. Henceforth, he became a recluse and communicated only through Mira Richards (the Mother, 1878-1973). His practice is known as Integral Yoga, a right-hand tantric deep **meditation** based on quieting the mind in order to encounter the spaceless and timeless Brahman. The endeavor is to unite the polarities of spirit and matter. Instead of attempting to avoid life and matter, integral yoga aims to move into spirit so that one can then descend with its power and light and transform the ordinary and mundane.

Aurobindo's ideas have been highly influential not only throughout the New Age movement but also among European and American academics. Numerous centers were established in the 1960s and 1970s to promulgate his thought. In the United States, there is the Sri Aurobindo Association in High Falls, New York, Aurobindo International USA in Sacramento, California, and the Atmaniketan Ashram of Pomona, California. An Aurobindo Center is to be found in New York City, while in San Francisco, Aurobindo's student Haridas Chauduri founded the California Institute for Integral Studies. However, the key center has been the city of Auroville in Pondicherry—a planned community based on Aurobindo's vision of spiritual consciousness as manifested in social reconstruction. It has been called a "New Age planetary village," a place for Aurobindo's image of a new world, a new humanity and a new consciousness. In short, Auroville is a model—much like **Findhorn**—for the "planetary consciousness" of the New Age: the belief that is based on an understanding of humanity's interconnectedness and earthly dependence for survival, health and nourishment in which the needs of the planet supersede the claims of any nation, group or individual. The only obligation placed on the community's residents is the willingness to serve "Divine Consciousness." Human unity is stressed within the framework of progressive education.

Planetary consciousness focuses on the interconnection of human culture and, along with New Age visions of the future and concerns with holistic health, has established the guiding ideals seeking planetary transformation and **healing** in which loyalty is to the human community as a whole rather than to any subdivision of state or tribe. Key New Age spokespeople who back this impetus include **David Spangler** and **Barbara Marx Hubbard**. The concept of planetary consciousness itself has merged with the **Gaia hypothesis** that claims that all things are interdependent and constitute an ultimate single living organism. Seeing the Earth itself as a living being, the Gaia hypothesis advocates a deep reverence for life and conscious oneness with it.

Consequently, the shift in the Krishnamurti and Aurobindo inspired aspects of New Age, while fully fused with Hindu-Buddhist notions of spiritual oneness and growth, is away from the theosophical understandings of a cosmic or **divine hierarchy**. Both, however, share the belief in the oneness of humanity and the focus on human evolution, but while one branch is more concerned with canonical eastern concepts, the other—the theosophical—has developed a more magical and supernaturally colorful extension of the metaphysical and spiritual ideas of **Hinduism** and **Buddhism**. Nevertheless, the efforts of the Arcane School and Lucis Trust as well as **Benjamin Creme** are perhaps paradigmatic of theosophical mysticism that is nevertheless focused on the kind of social and consciousness transformations sought by someone like Sri Aurobindo.

AYURVEDA. Indigenous and holistic **healing** system of India, literally "Knowledge of Life." Ayurveda employs herbs and mineral concoctions along with dict, fasting, bathing, enemas and even bloodletting. Drawing authority from the ninth mandala of the *Rigveda*, it also promotes auto-urine **therapy** as a health-maintaining tonic and means to cure illness. Along with other forms of non-Western medicines and therapies, ayurveda has become part of the New Age portfolio of techniques concerning health and well-being. In India, its chief medical specialists are known as Vaidikas.

-B-

BAILEY, ALICE (1880-1949). Among the most instrumental figures in forming the present shape and range of New Age thought. Her spiritual career appeared to begin at the time she claimed to have received a visitation from a tall turbaned stranger that she subsequently identified as the Master Koot Hoomi. Foretelling future events in her life, Bailey was eventually led from her native England to the **Theosophical Society** in Pacific Groves, California. In 1919, she claimed to have been approached by Master Djwhal Khul or D.K. (the theosophist Djual Khool), wanting her to become his control. Through her, he is said to have dictated Bailey's first book, *Initiation, Human and Solar* as well as, subsequently, eighteen additional books. The Theosophical Society received this first work enthusiastically, but because of difficulties stemming from Annie Besant and subsequent marginalization of both Alice and her husband Foster, the Baileys broke with the Society and formed their own organizations in 1922, the Lucifer Trust—later renamed the Lucis Trust. Nevertheless, Alice Bailey's teachings are clearly theosophical and center on the divine hierarchy, the **seven rays** and evolution to higher levels. Bailey argued that by 1920 humans had evolved to a position in which a new age was possible and preparation was launched to welcome the coming schools of higher esoteric learning. In the 1930s, Bailey proclaimed that the new age and the reappearance of Christ were imminent. Combining loving service to humanity with the power of the divine hierarchy channeled through established **meditation** groups, followers of the Arcane School (founded in 1923) seek to bring about the "New Age."

Probably Bailey's most popular book is her 1948 *The Reappearance of the Christ*. She came to promote the term "New Age," and much of the very concept of the New Age can be traced to her writings. In 1944, the first volume of *Discipleship in the New Age* was published. The second volume appeared in 1955, while 1954 saw the release of *Education in the New Age*. Among Bailey's contributions to the New Age movement is the prayer known as the **Great Invocation** in which the power of the cosmic or **divine hierarchy** as it funnels down to earth is visualized.

In the understanding of the Arcane School, the spiritual energies are more strongly available during the time of the full moon—particularly the festival of Easter during the full moon of April, the festival of Wesak at the full moon of May, and the festival of Goodwill (now World Invocation Day) for the full moon of June. Combining Eastern and Western ideas into a new synthesis, Bailey believed that, successively, one actively celebrates the forces of Christ's restoration, the Buddha's forces of enlightenment, and the forces of reconstruction. Those forming the New Group of World Servers (founded in 1932) attempt to act as intermediaries between the spiritual hierarchy and humanity, while the Men of Goodwill (since 1950, World Goodwill) embark upon educational and political realignment programs. Since their formulation in 1937, the Triangles have developed as one of the basic units of the Lucis Trust. The Triangle is a group of three people who meditate for a short duration each day. These people may be in different parts of the world and may meditate at different times of the day, but their object is to link with each other through "creative meditation" to visualize the energies of light and goodwill flowing through themselves and onto the planet via the world's full Triangle network.

The Arcane School and the Lucis Trust continue the theosophical notions of **karma**, **reincarnation**, the divine plan and the spiritual hierarchy. Bailey's theosophical cosmology parallels the six **chakras** of the human body: (1) Shamballa/Sanat Kumara (the highest energy centre in which "the will of God is known"), (2) the spiritual Hierarchy, (3) "the Christ at the heart of Hierarchy," i.e., the heart chakra "where the love of God is known," (4) the new group of world servers, (5) men and women of goodwill everywhere, and (6) the physical centers of distribution: London, Darjeeling, New York, Geneva and Tokyo. As in theosophy, the three "Buddhas of Activity" in Shamballa are linked to the three "departmental Beings" in Hierarchy. Shamballa and Hierarchy are mediated by the Nirmanakayas as "the New Group of World Servers" connecting Hierarchy and humanity.

Following Bailey's teachings, there are two essential practices for group meditations: the Yoga of Synthesis and the Letting in the Light. In the former, the process begins with alignment followed by higher interlude, affirmation, meditation, precipitation, lower interlude and, finally, distribution. Letting in the Light starts with group fusion and proceeds through alignment, higher interlude, meditation, precipitation, lower interlude and distribution. This final sharing invariably involves the Group's chanting of the Great Invocation.

BEY, HAKIM. Pseudonym for an anarchist **Sufi** poet and grass-roots, small press essayist. He is an activist speaking for anti-authoritarian resistance and association-based community. Bey is particular known for his 1985/1991 polemical track, "The Temporary Autonomous Zone (TAZ)." According to the author, TAZ theory relates primarily to current and emerging situations rather than pure utopianism. One of its most important forms is the contemporary festival. Bey's ideas, however, have influenced the kind of Aquarian conspiracy thinking of someone like **Marilyn Ferguson**. The theory is applicable to villages, communes, communities, biospheres and other utopian-city form experimentation. This leads into Bey's understanding of the permanent TAZ or permament autonomous zone (PAZ) that relates to organic, natural and green Wild(er)ness and which he compares to Paul Goodman's Communitas and Ivan Illich's "cultural conviviality." Similar orientations include deep ecology, social ecology, permaculture and organic technology. What Bey calls for is "militant biophilism." He opposes the mind-body split of **gnosticism** and the more transcendental aspects of New Age.

BIOFEEDBACK. A 1960s extension of the "feedback" principle defined by mathematician Norbert Wiener (1894-1964) as controlling and/or augmenting a system's output by re-inserting part of the output as further input. The "feedback" is the return part of the original output. Biofeedback is the application of such regulatory systematic monitoring as a **therapeutic** technique. It employs visual or auditory feedback to the physiological processes of living organisms. Through the mechanical observation of bodily functions, such as galvanic skin response, and the concomitant development of breathing and relaxation techniques, patients are enabled to self-develop migraine relief, pain control, anxiety reduction, and phobia and hypertension management. In many respects, biofeedback is to be likened to **yoga** in slowing the heart rate and fostering altered states of consciousness. *See also* CYBERNETICS.

BLAVATSKY, HELENA PETROVNA (1831-1891). Founder of the **theosophical** movement. Blavatsky had mediumistic propensities and traveled from her native Russia to India and subsequently Great Britain and the United States where she became deeply involved with **spiritualism**. She claimed contact with the mahatmas, beings of great authority who had evolved into conscious co-workers for the universal divine plan. In 1875, with Henry Steele Olcott, she founded the Theosophical Society in New York. Later, they established the headquarters of theosophy in Adyar, India, and broke with spiritualism as Blavatsky came increasingly under the influence of **Hinduism** and **Buddhism**. Her two major books are *Isis Unveiled* (1877) and *The Secret Doctrine* (1888).

BLOOM, WILLIAM (1948-). British New Age and holistic perspective teacher and 1988 co-founder, along with Sabrina Dearborne and Malcolm Stern, of London's central New Age venue, the Alternatives Programme at St. James's Church, Piccadilly. With over fifteen thousand people attending annually, Alternatives sponsors seminars and workshops on tribal religions, new psychology, new science, spiritual ecology, **meditation**, metaphysics and chanting. Bloom began a two-year retreat in 1972 among the Saharan Berbers in the High Atlas Mountains. During this time period, he performed the medieval Abra-Melin ritual. Bloom received his Ph.D. from the London School of Economics (LSE) in political psychology and published his dissertation as *Personal Identity, National Identity and International Relations* (1989, 1992). After first teaching at LSE, he transferred to Southwark Community College where he worked for ten years with special needs adults and adolescents. In 1998, he persuaded the United Nations Oslo Conference on Religion and Belief to give the New Age and holistic approach an equal status alongside the established religions. A member of the faculty of the **Findhorn Foundation**, Bloom teaches internationally but especially in Denmark, Norway, Bulgaria and Slovenia. In 1999, he founded Holistic Partnerships to promote Core Energy Management (CEM). A prolific writer, among his works are *Psychic Protection* (1996), *Money, Heart and Mind: Financial Well-being for People and Planet* (1996), *Working with Angels, Fairies and Nature Spirits* (1999), *The Penguin Book of New Age and Holistic Writing* (2001) and *The Endorphin Effect* (2001).

CEM attempts to enable people to produce private sources of support and limitless access to benevolent energy. Its underlying premise is that the fundamental religious experience consisting of pleasure and connection with the *mysterium tremedum et fascinans* is biologically experienced through endorphins, roughly twenty different hormones or amino acids discovered in the nervous system and belonging to the family of neuro-peptides (information-carrying chemicals that circulate through the human body). Endorphins are endogenous forms of morphine—natural morphine produced by one's body. They block pain, eliminate stress, provide the basis of good health and produce the physical sensations of enjoyment—whether athletic euphoria, sexual climax, or countless other states of pleasure. As Bloom explains, "happiness and pleasure are built into the biological foundation of the human body." Building on his preoccupations with healthcare and personal development, Bloom's CEM teaches strategies to create localized feelings of pleasure and **healing** as well as the release of old tensions to encourage natural vitality to enter the body. He explains that the ongoing flow of endorphins through the body safeguards a state of biochemical fluidity which can maintain the immune system in optimum condition. Through his CEM program, Bloom is continuing his interest in physical health care, psychology, spiritual development and the energy medicine traditions (such as **yoga** and chi gung). The "Endorphin Effect" represents a set of strategies concerned with advancing the holistic approach to religion and spiritual experience. Combining an imminently amiable and gentle nature with a prodigiously inquisitive mind, Bloom has emerged as one of New Age's leading spokespersons.

BODY-WORK. A collective designation for those holistic practices that approach the body as the vehicle for changing and transforming the whole person through improved health, self-realization and spiritual enlightenment. Broadly, body-work techniques consist of manipulating the skeletal structure (e.g., **kinesiology**, chiropractic), massaging of skin and muscles (**massage therapy**, **Rolfing**) and applying pressure to acu-points (**acupressure**, **acupuncture**).

BUDDHISM. The religious practice that seeks to emulate the spiritual achievements of Prince Siddhartha Gautama or the Buddha ("Awakened One")(*c.*563-*c.*483 B.C.E.) based on the Four Noble Truths, namely, that all life is suffering, that the cause of suffering is desire, that only with the cessation of desire will suffering cease and that the Noble Eightfold Path will lead to the elimination of desire. The Buddha advocated the "Middle Way" between the extremes of asceticism and hedonism. This involves pursuing Right Views, Right Intent, Right Speech, Right Action, Right Livelihood, Right Effort, Right Mindfulness and Right Concentration, namely, the Noble Eightfold Path. Like **Hinduism**, Buddhism retains the concepts of **reincarnation** and **karma** and seeks to escape the perpetual round of rebirth through enlightenment (*nirvana*). Unlike Hinduism, Buddhism does not dismiss the tangible world as illusion (*māyā*), but inasmuch as it dismisses the material as without value, it conforms to a theological position of **gnosticism**. Formally, Buddhism comprises the "three jewels, baskets or refuges" on which its followers rely for support: the Buddha, the dharma or "truth" (the teachings) and the sangha or "community" of Buddhists (usually referring specifically to the monastic institution).

The central practice of Buddhism involves **meditation** and is essentially akin to **yoga**. For the New Age movements, Buddhism has been strongly influential through **theosophy** and its derivatives (e.g., **Alice Bailey**'s Arcane School and the Prophet's **Church Universal and Triumphant**) and through the forms of **Zen Buddhism** and **Tibetan Buddhism**. *See also* NAROPA INSTITUTE.

BUDDHISM, TIBETAN. *See* TIBETAN BUDDHISM.

BUDDHISM, ZEN. *See* ZEN BUDDHISM.

-C-

CASTANEDA, CARLOS (1925/31?-1998). A "father" of the New Age movement through his series of books detailing Yaqui Indian **shamanism**. Castaneda remained an enigmatic figure who avoided being photographed or recorded. His autobiographical information is also controversial with conflicts concerning his place of birth (Cajamarca, Peru or São Paulo, Brazil) and other details of his early life. In 1951, however, he moved to the United States and began studies in anthropology. He received his Ph.D. from the University of California, Los Angeles in 1973.

Castaneda met Don Juan Matus during a trip to Arizona in the early 1960s. He described Don Juan as a *nagual* or master sorcerer and claimed that he had been born in Yuma to a Yuma Indian mother and a Yaqui Indian father from Sonora, Mexico. When he was ten, Don Juan was taken to Mexico by his father who was subsequently killed in the Yaqui-Mexican wars. He then grew up with relatives in southern Mexico. According to Castaneda, at the age of twenty, Don Juan met Julian Osorio, a son of European immigrants, who had himself been initiated by *nagual* Elias Ulloa into a lineage of *brujos* (sorcerers) that reputedly went back twenty-five generations. Castaneda claimed that Don Juan bequeathed to him everything he knew about this lineage and its practice of a series of body movements that are described as "magical passes."

Toward the end of his life, Castaneda developed the "magical passes" of Don Juan into a New Age application dubbed "Tensegrity." In this blend of **meditation** and movement exercises, the individual is depicted as a "luminous egg" that contains about six hundred "assemblage points" or places where awareness shift can occur. As a process of depersonalization, Tensegrity seeks to break through the restrictions of ordinary cognition to understand the dynamics of pure energy. Fields of energy are conceived as luminous filaments that supersede the state of mundane consciousness. In typical New Age format, Tensegrity is taught through seminars and workshops.

Despite Castaneda's presentation of the Don Juan cycle as documentary fact, critics have insisted that the writings are essentially fictitious, and many have even doubted the historical reality of Don Juan. Nevertheless, Castaneda's first book about his alleged experiences with his Yaqui *nagual*, *The Teachings of Don Juan: A Yaqui Way of Knowl-*

edge (1968), proved to be an enormous success. He pursued his portrayals of "non-ordinary reality" with several additional works: *A Separate Reality: Further Conversations with Don Juan* (1971), *Journey to Ixtlan: The Lessons of Don Juan* (1972), etc. in which he promoted Don Juan's "stopping the world" as a replacement to belief without experience. The huge success of his books caused Castaneda to become increasingly reclusive. His death was not revealed for almost two months.

CAYCE, EDGAR (1877-1945). American psychic known as the "sleeping prophet" for his ability to enter a self-induced, hypnotic, sleep-like trance state to give "readings" for various individuals. He demonstrated an ability to prophesy the future, recall the past, describe distant events and, especially, diagnose and suggest treatments for illness that exceeded the medical knowledge of the time. Many of his readings extended into the areas of religion and **reincarnation**. Nevertheless, Cayce was an avid reader of the Bible and situated his teachings in a Protestant Christian framework. These teachings came to include acceptance of such ideas or doctrines as karmic implications of past lives, sojourns on other planets, the existence of **akashic records**, and the interpretive use of "signs" from **astrology**, **numerology**, dreams, vibrations from metallic stones, etc. Cayce's explanations have been pervasively influential on various New Age movements as well as on such figures as **Arthur Ford** and **Ruth Montgomery**. The record of his trance readings and the perpetuation of his ideas have been undertaken by the Association for Research and Enlightenment (ARE), founded by Cayce in 1931. Leadership of the ARE was continued under Hugh Lynn Cayce, Cayce's son, until his death in 1982.

Cayce himself has been termed by the *New York Times* "the most fascinating man in America." Apart from receiving visions, Cayce could perform extraordinary feats of memory. At the age of fourteen, he memorized a 110-page congressional speech in one night, purportedly by simply sleeping with the document under his pillow. As a psychic he was consulted by Thomas Edison, George Gershwin, Woodrow Wilson and Harry Truman, among others, and doctors, scholars and celebrities, including Houdini, along with hundreds of patients, gave testimony to Cayce's veracity in medical diagnosis. He predicted the onset of World Wars I and II, the 1929 stock market collapse and numerous individual events. The Cayce readings included a series on Jesus that elucidated details that were later confirmed with the discovery of the Dead Sea

Scrolls. Cayce claimed to remember nothing when he awoke from his
trances, but the streams of often cryptic information derived from what
he termed "The Source" were recorded by others during the sleeping
state. Several organizations now work with the material of Cayce's
readings: the Edgar Cayce Foundation and the Atlantic University,
which was reactivated in 1985 after closing in 1931 and offers today a
master's degree in transpersonal studies. There is also the Health and
Rejuvenation Research Center that analyzes the medical information
contained in the readings and incorporates findings into contemporary
medical research.

CHAKRAS (Sanskrit "wheel"). Seven, sometimes eight, ascending
points on the spinal column corresponding to steps or stages on the path
to enlightenment. Body chakras are likened to lotus petals or whirling
spoked wheels that are supposed to process the subtle energies in the
body. Their descriptions appear in the yogic literature of **Hinduism** and
Buddhism. While there are some differences between Hindu and Buddhist accounts, there are further variations often to be found in Western
descriptions. Ascending the chakra steps is known as "raising the Kundalini." At the same time, each step is equated to a stage of initiatory
teaching within a circle in a manner that is suggestive of the **Sufi** process involving the "halka" or "magic circle" in which arcane doctrine is
passed on by a teacher in the center to initiates circled around.

As the chakras are not visible to the naked eye, they can only be
"seen" clairvoyantly or "felt" through the hands when they are held just
above the skin surface. Through such supersensory means, some people
are supposed to be able to diagnose energy flow imbalances within the
body. Various alternative **therapies** such as **massage**, **shiatsu** or the
laying on of hands may be employed to heal "blocked" chakras or pathways.

The chakras are connected one to the other through thousands of
subtle energy channels known as "nadis." There are three chief nadis:
the "sushumna" which runs from the base of the spine to the medulla
oblongata at the base of the brain; and the "ida" and "pingala" which
spiral around each other as well as the sushumna from the base of the
spine—terminating respectively at the right and left nostrils. Each
chakra is associated with one or more colors. The associations understood in the west are simpler and correspond to the colors of the rainbow. Each chakra is believed to influence a particular somatic gland as

well as governing particular body parts. Apart from the occasional inclusion of the spleen chakra which influences the spleen and "rules" the liver, pancreas and digestive system, starting with the lowest, the seven chakras, their associations and behavioral and developmental functions are as follows:

The root chakra (Sanskrit *mwadhara*) influences the adrenals and governs the legs, feet, genitals, anus, coccyx and kidneys. In western systems it is associated with the color red; in eastern, with orange-red. The hara or navel chakra (*swadisthana*) connects with the gonads, genital area, sacrum, lumbar vertebrae and reproductive system. The east links it to red; the west, to orange. The solar plexus or *manipura* chakra affects the pancreas and controls the liver, gall bladder, diaphragm and nervous system and, in some understandings, the lumbar vertebrae. In the east, the color associations are green and gold; in the west, it is yellow.

The central chakra is the heart or *anahata* chakra. It connects with the thymus as well as the heart, lower lungs, chest, breasts, thoracic vertebrae and circulatory system. In the east, its aura is understood as gold; in the west, as green. The throat chakra (*vishuddha*) links to the thyroid, hands and arms, mouth, throat and voice, lungs, cervical vertebrae and the respiratory system. The east has it as silvery-blue; the west as blue. The brow chakra (*ajna*) corresponds to the "third eye." It influences the pituitary as well as the forehead, ears, nose, left eye, base of skull, medulla and nervous system. While in the west it is thought of as indigo, in the east it is half yellow-rose and half blue and purple.

The uppermost nexus is the crown chakra (*sahasrara*) that directs the pineal gland and is associated with the cranium, cerebral cortex and right eye. It is also considered responsible for the psychic function. The eastern color association is glowing purple. In the west it is related to violet and corresponds in the theosophical understanding of the **seven rays** to the important "violet ray." This last is invoked in particular by adherents to the **Church Universal and Triumphant**.

CHANNELING. A form of **mediumship**, inspirational thought, **clairvoyance** and/or **telepathic** communication with beings who are not of this world. In the early 1970s, author Jane Roberts (1929-1984) began publishing a series of books "received" from an entity known as Seth. *The Seth Material* (1970) essentially launched the New Age phenomenon known as "channeling." The term "channel" has largely replaced that of "medium"—possibly because of the attributions of fraud and fakery that have consistently been laid against the spiritualist movement.

Apart from the spiritualist works of John Newbrough and Levi Dowling, much of the literature that is now associated with New Age has been "received" by people in an extraordinary state of consciousness: via telepathy, automatic writing or directly through the vocal chords of a medium or channel. This includes the works of **Helena Blavatsky, Alice Bailey, Rudolf Steiner, Edgar Cayce**, and both the *Urantia Book* and *A Course in Miracles*. But whereas **spiritualism** draws its materials largely from voices claiming to be those of deceased relatives and friends, New Age has shifted its source to advanced discarnates and extraterrestrials. These may include historic figures, even groups, angels, classical gods and goddesses, nature spirits or *devas*, fairies, or entities from other planes of reality ("space brethren," etc.) Blavatsky, Bailey, Guy and Edna Ballard, and Mark and Elizabeth Clare Prophet claim contact with the Ascended Masters of the **Great White Brotherhood**. Dowling and Cayce both channeled from a cosmic information bank known as the **akashic record**. Dowling used Visel, the goddess of wisdom, as an intermediary; Cayce, in contrast, channeled directly from the akashic realm. Some contemporary channels, such as Mrs. Prophet and **Ruth Montgomery**, are fully awake and aware of what messages they are delivering. Others, however, go into trance—whether a light trance, such as Virginia Essene, or a deep trance, such as Cayce, Mrs. **JZ Knight** and the receiver of the *Urantia* material.

In the wake of Jane Roberts, popular New Age channels include Ken Carey (Raphael, Christ), Pat Rodegast (Emmanuel), Mary-Margaret Moore (Bartholomew), Virginia Essene (Christ, the Archangels Michael, Gabriel, Uriel, etc.), JZ Knight (Ramtha), Penny Torres (Mafu), and Jach Pursel (Lazaris). A collective group of discarnates known as "Michael" are channeled by various people. Some of the channeling interest has also been sparked by the UFO contactee groups. Consequently, Ken Carey's Raphael is identified as an extraterrestrial. Likewise, the variety of space entities channeled by Tuella (Thelma B. Terrell) fall into this category.

While some commentators understand channeling as a form of mystical experience, critics see it as a dangerous form of self-delusion. Nevertheless, there is a surprising consistency throughout much of the channeled material. Foremost, perhaps, is the **New Thought** doctrine that matter is created by mind. Invariably, New Age continues the spiritualist notion that the cosmos is essentially friendly and the obstacles to love are illusions that a developed mental-spiritual insight can remove. The overall thrust of New Age channeled messages is that humanity is on the brink of transition into a higher consciousness. This collective consciousness *is* the New Age—one that is predicated on an astrological framework and has been prophesized by numerous traditions.

CHIDVILASANANDA. *See* MUKTANANDA, SWAMI.

CHINESE ASTROLOGICAL YEAR. The classification of the year by the twelve signs of the Chinese zodiac along with the cycle consisting of the classical five elements: wood, fire, earth, metal and water. The twelve-year cycle follows the sequence of rat, ox, tiger, rabbit/hare, dragon, snake, horse, goat/sheep/ram, monkey, rooster/cock, dog and boar/pig. Combining the two cycles allows that sixty years elapse before there is duplication (e.g., water horse, iron/metal dragon, fire dog). As with any calendrical system based on **astrology**, the nature of the year being known by combining the specific animal and agent designations from the two sequences reputedly determines the character of those born during it. This Chinese divinatory year has become a part of the New Age portfolio of popular spiritual exotica adopted from different cultures. *See also* FENG SHUI.

CHOPRA, DEEPAK. Popular New Age author and director of educational programs at the Chopra Center for Well Being in La Jolla, California. Among more than two dozen books, Chopra's works include *Quantum Healing* (1989) and *Journey into Healing* (1995). A student of **Maharishi Mahesh Yogi**, Chopra employs a series of transcendental meditation mental techniques as central to his own teachings. He argues that **healing** is primarily a mental process since, following traditional **Hindu** thought, "the body is created out of consciousness." In the deep interconnection between physical/mental health and spiritual health, the first stage in bringing the physical system back into balance is relaxation. Only by relaxing, Chopra insists, can the body's capacity to heal be restored. This in turn allows a quantum shift in awareness through which the patient can direct his or her healing process. On their own, **visualization** or simply thinking oneself well is ineffective unless the individual can gain access to the "blue print of intelligence." Since disease and health both lie at the very depths of our being, the capricious intellect on its own is insufficient, and we must instead reach the "silent witness inside us." Through this contact, the ghost or memory of disease can then be confronted and vanquished.

Chopra's metaphysics speak of an almost invisible division or "gap" that actually separates the body and mind despite their interconnection. Within this chasm are to be found all of life's mysteries and possibilities—including the symphonies of Mozart. It is necessary, therefore, for the patient to journey across this "field of intelligence"—a one-way door that is "silent, has no thickness, and exists everywhere" in order to locate mind-body unity.

CHRISTIANITY. Religion that professes belief in Jesus as Christ or is based on his teachings. In general, Christianity has had less influence on New Age thought than such faiths as **Buddhism, Hinduism, Sufism** and **paganism** but has instead been frequently influenced by it. Nevertheless, such Christian developments as **spiritualism, New Thought** and even **theosophy** have played seminal roles in the formation of a New Age perspective. The chief difference between canonical Christianity and New Age Christianity (or what New Age scholar Daren Kemp refers to as Christaquarianism) concerns the role of Christ: divine redeemer for the one; supreme role model for the other. Through its New Thought legacy, New Age denies the reality of sin, evil and the negative. These are recognized as illusions of the mind, and Jesus is accepted as the person who most achieved the requisite mental control over reality in being the consummate miracle-worker of all times. The consequences of this position are twofold: illness as a negative is only a result of faulty thinking, and Jesus' teachings and example constitute the route to **healing** par excellence, on the one hand. On the other, the binary understanding of a world divided between good and evil is replaced by one between wisdom and ignorance. Reputing the whole notion of Satan as a theological entity, New Age Christianity has no need of a sacrificial redemption through a "personal Savior."

While conventional Christianity reveres a God that is transcendent and separate from the world and humanity, New Age tends to adopt a stance that is essentially pagan in that its deity (God/Goddess/All That Is) is understood as immanent in both nature and each individual. There is also more gender play in New Age Christianity that either reinterprets the Trinity or bypasses it altogether. The notion of a God who punishes and exacts retribution is virtually absent from New Age. The angry figure of the Old Testament is recast as a figure of "sweetness and light."

Nevertheless, there are some remarkable parallels between New Age and evangelical Christianity. Several scholars have noticed that both seek direct experience of the sacred. Pentecostal glossolalia or speaking-in-tongues is compared to New Age **channeling**, and spiritual guidance is the purpose for both. Moreover, an element of New Age entertains the very notion of the coming **apocalypse** of Revelations. New Age figures such as **Ruth Montgomery** and **Edgar Cayce** have adopted a millenarian outlook to frame the New Age expectation of the world on the edge of radical spiritual transformation. The Christian millennium becomes the **Age of Aquarius** (*see* **millennialism**). On the level of more immediate concern, like Christian evangelicals, New Agers center on spiritual and physical healing that is beyond the remit of mainstream allopathic medicine.

Moreover, and especially, being beyond the mainline churches, there is an anti-institutional emphasis that characterizes both orientations in which an overriding distrust of established institutions becomes the foundation for a deliberate spiritual emancipation from conventional norms, goals and practices. In contemporary parlance, this is frequently expressed as being "spiritual" rather than "religious." In the case of New Age, its Christian/New Thought emphasis would appear to represent a return to the latent **Gnostic** fundamentals that underlie much of Christianity's theological inclination—a general bias that was officially eliminated through the ecumenical councils but has remained largely present only in a *sub rosa* sense until the twentieth century flowering of the New Age spiritualities. New Age, though largely inspired by traditions outside Christianity, has in turn been a noticeable influence on contemporary churches themselves. *See* **Techno Cosmic Mass**.

In the United States, foremost fusers of Christian and New Age ideas include **Matthew Fox** and the Catholic monk Thomas Berry. Behind both, there are the insights and teachings of the German mystic Meister Eckhart (*c.*1260-*c.*1327) and the Jesuit **Pierre Teilhard de Chardin**. Blending **feminism** and **environmentalism** with Christian mysticism, Fox's "creation spirituality" is a decisive influence behind such projects as the Alternatives Programme of London's St. James

Piccadilly and the Omega Order and Trust in England. *See also* KARMA.

CHRISTIAN SCIENCE. *See* EDDY, MARY BAKER; HEALING; NEW THOUGHT.

CHROMOTHERAPY. Healing with color. As a form of **alternative medicine** treatment, chromotherapy derives from **Eastern mysticism** ideas of color-**chakra** associations, Western occult-**magical** color correspondences between macrocosmic/microcosmic or celestial/terrestrial realities, and study of color and behavioral reaction by modern physicists and psychologists. Early modern chromotherapists who operated in the late nineteenth century are Augustus James Pleasanton and Edwin Dwight Babbit. The former instigated the "blue glass craze," and the latter published in 1878 *The Principles of Light and Color.* Dinshah Pestanji Ghadiali (1873-1966) continued Babbit's work of "charging" water by placing it under direct sunlight in a colored glass. In the 1920s, Ghadiali developed in the United States spectro-chrome **therapy** based on his belief that basic colors stimulated glandular activity: red-liver, orange-thyroid/mammary glands, yellow-choroid, lemon-pancreas/thymus, green-pituitary, blue-pineal, indigo-parathyroid, violet-spleen, magenta-suprarenals/prostate, and scarlet-testicles/ovaries. He founded the Spectro-Chrome Institute in Malaga, New Jersey.

Other important investigators into healing through color include Ivah Bergh Whitten who explored chromotherapy from a **theosophical** perspective and organized the Amica Master Institute of Colour Awareness in the late 1920s, Roland T. Hunt who published *The Seven Keys to Colour Healing* in 1940, and **Rosicrucianist**/theosophist Corinne Dunklee Heline (1875-?) who was one of the first to employ the term "New Age" in the sense it is used by the movement today. Heline published *Healing and Regeneration through Color* (1943) and *Color and Music in the New Age* (1964). She is especially known for correlating colors with the **astrological** signs of the zodiac.

The more contemporary developments in chromotherapeutic understanding stem from health journalist Linda Clark's publishing of *The Ancient Art of Color Therapy* (1975) and *Health, Youth and Beauty through Color Breathing* (1976). She linked color treatment to use of crystals and gem stones, recognition of **auras** and a scientific understanding of vitamins and psychology. From a uniquely spiritual/pragmatic perspective, the ideas of color healing were also advocated by popular Cambodian **Buddhist** monk, the Venerable **Dharmawara**— particularly the creation of green environments for calming and healing effects. In Dharmawara's system the use of colored oils is also promoted—again green but also blue and yellow, whereas the color red is almost always avoided. In all, chromotherapists recommend a variety of techniques ranging from short sun baths in the nude, application of specific colors to the body, drinking water from colored glasses subjected to strong light, use of machines to direct colored light onto the patient's skin, and the wearing of colored filters over eye glasses to a form of **meditation** known as color breathing in which one concentrates on a particular imagined color and directs it to the areas of bodily affliction. *See also* AURA-SOMA and SEVEN RAYS.

CHURCH UNIVERSAL AND TRIUMPHANT (CUT). A New Age movement. With the death of Guy Ballard in 1939 and the infrequent reception of divine messages by his wife Edna, a renewed direct contact was sought elsewhere and beyond the orbit of the **"I AM" Religious Activity**. Probably the most successful of the new messengers was Mark Prophet (1918-1973) who, in 1958, began the Summit Lighthouse but was earlier associated with two "I AM" splinter groups: the Lighthouse of Freedom, and the Bridge to Freedom (now known as the New Age Church of the Truth). Prophet has come to be surpassed as a messenger by his widow, Elizabeth Clare Prophet (1939-), who renamed the Summit Lighthouse the Church Universal and Triumphant and amplified her own position with new titles (e.g., the Vicar of Christ, Mother Elizabeth, Guru Ma, etc.) Although I AM and the Prophets' Church claim no connection, the beliefs and iconography of the latter bear striking similarity to that of the Ballards' teachings. Both groups employ the saying of decrees, both invoke the "I AM Presence" and Ascended Masters, both assign a special importance to Saint Germain and Jesus, both consider Guy Ballard as himself an Ascended Master, and both display (at least within the United States) a prominent, conservative national patriotism. While Mark Prophet was certainly familiar with the teachings of previous Messengers, in 1958 he allegedly received the mandate from the Ascended Master El Morya to become the new Messenger of the **Great White Brotherhood**.

In Church Universal and Triumphant's teachings, an Ascended Master is one who has assumed the "Mind who was in Christ Jesus" and, accordingly, transmuted at least 51 percent of his or her karma in order to inhabit the spirit planes rather than the lower material worlds of the physical, emotional, mental and etheric. Once again the same figures have appeared in **theosophy** and I AM—though here with some further elaborations. Mark Prophet is now the Ascended Master Lanello—the Ever-Present Guru. Mrs. Prophet has, in previous lives, been Nefertiti, the biblical Martha, King Arthur's wife Guinevere, and Marie Antoinette. But among the Ascended Masters themselves, one encounters El Moraya Khan (formerly the patriarch Abraham, Melchior one of the three Wise Men of the East, King Arthur, St. Thomas à Beckett, St. Thomas Moore and the Mogul Emperor Akbar.) KH or Kuthumi (formerly St. Francis) is recognized along with El Moraya (Master M) and Madame **Blavatsky** as the founders of the Theosophical Society. Beside Gautama Buddha, Jesus Christ and Lord Maitreya, Saint Germain appears prominently. In fact, CUT explains that as Jesus was the cosmic teacher for the Piscean Age, Saint Germain is to be the same for the **Age of Aquarius**. Saint Germain's previous incarnations include the biblical prophet Samuel, St. Joseph, St. Alban, Merlin the magician as the teacher of Proclus, Roger Bacon, Christopher Columbus, and Francis Bacon. Another Ascended Master is Serapis Bey— formerly a high priest in the temple of the ascension on **Atlantis** who has also been Amenhotep III and the Spartan King Leonidas.

CUT's cosmic hierarchy follows suit with its predecessors (*see* **Divine Hierarchy**). Not only does it include the Ascended Masters of the Great White Brotherhood, but it centers on the I AM THAT I AM along with the Solar Logoi, the twelve solar hierarchies, angels and archangels, the Sons and Daughters of God including humanity, the elementals or nature spirits, and the Elohim who include the Graeco-Roman deities Hercules and Apollo. Each day of the week corresponds to a light ray emanation of the Godhead and is presided over by a chohan (e.g., Saint Germain, Hilarion, Paul the Venetian), a male-female pair of archangels (e.g., Michael and Faith) and a male-female pair of Elohim (e.g., Peace and Aloha). For the Aquarian Age, Saint Germain, the incarnation of the Word as Vishnu or the Son of God, also has a twin flame or *shakti* counterpart—namely, the goddess of justice or opportunity, Portia. While the Virgin Mary is venerated as a foremost embodiment of the Divine Mother, CUT sees itself as the true church of Jesus Christ *and* Gautama Buddha. Once again, there is also encountered the understanding that the godly part of each individual is a spark from the Great Central Sun, The Source of Life and Being, the "I AM" Presence. Distinct from this is the Real Self of each person, an individualized aspect of the universal Christ consciousness, that mediates the soul's return and eventual union with the "I AM" Presence. The goal of human existence is to wed the divine spark together with the Real Self as a unified, single soul. This was the accomplishment of the historical Jesus of Nazareth who, upon the termination of his earthly existence, was able to ascend immediately. Nevertheless, in our times, the first task of the individual is to develop one's feminine aspect before wedding the soul to the Universal Christ consciousness. This is known in CUT terminology as balancing the Alpha (spirit) with the Omega (matter), and it is thought to parallel the energy fusion of God, who is both Father and Mother.

In achieving the goal of self-mastery, Church members use the typical "I AM" Religious Activity tools of prayers, affirmations, decrees and mantras—collectively known as "the science of the spoken word." Light is invoked in order to expose evil and illuminate God's people. CUT discipleship aims not only to understand the karmic laws of reincarnation but also to regain the lost arts of **healing**. Nevertheless, the practice of decreeing, a modified version of **New Thought** affirmations, has been highly controversial—bringing sustained charges of brainwashing against the movement. While the decree goes beyond the affirmation in that it *demands* the spiritual powers to bring about the condition affirmed, CUT has increased the rate at which the decrees are spoken to a level that makes them unintelligible to an outsider. Church members often decree for hours at a time wearing headphones and accompanied by audio recordings.

Because, until relatively recently, of the central leadership role of Mrs. Prophet, unlike New Age in general, the Church Universal and Triumphant has been doctrinal and clearly boundary determinant. It possesses (or possessed) little of the laissez-faire and sexual fluidity of a more typical New Age center such as **Findhorn** on the north coast of Scotland. In fact, CUT's open denunciations of fluoride use, sucrose, tobacco, marijuana, liquor, heroin, cocaine and other drugs, **voodoo** and black magic as well as suicide, vigilantism, insanity, sado-masochism, rock'n-roll music, gambling, vanity, gossip, masturbation, homosexuality and lesbianism, and both the gay rights and women's movements make it appear closer to Christian fundamentalism. Nevertheless, the

Church has played an active role in the New Age movement, and Mrs. Prophet was formerly a regular speaker at New Age gatherings.

CLAIRAUDIENCE. The ability to hear voices—particularly of spirits. Like **telepathy**, clairaudience may be another source of information retrieval for New Age **channeling**.

CLAIRVOYANCE. Psychic or visionary sight. Clairvoyance refers to the ability to see into other dimensions of reality or at least to see things without the use of physical eyesight. It may involve reading a person's **auras**, psychically encountering living or deceased persons or animals, or having visions of past, present, future, other worlds, extraterrestrial or discarnate beings. Clairvoyance is described as extrasensory perception without the aid of any other mind or physical tool. It may constitute part of the shaman's soul-flight experience (*see* **shamanism**). It also figures largely in the mediumship practices of **spiritualism**. For an example of clairvoyance in the Bible, see John 4:16-29.

Clairvoyance has often been termed the "sixth sense" and sometimes as "high sense perception" (HSP)—described as a form of "seeing" or perceiving mental pictures without the use of normal vision. It is associated with the "third eye" and, as such, connects to the right side of the brain that governs the feminine, creative and intuitive aspects of human existence. Clairvoyance is a gift that often comes naturally—especially to children. For others, it may develop through a life-changing event or **near-death** experience. In some cases, it is a faculty that one may acquire through **meditation** or some other form of spiritual concentration. Psychic Barbara Brennan describes "clairvoyant time" as a shift out of linear time in which the clairvoyant becomes capable of witnessing a sequence of events that is not generally available through normal perception. For some, this "gift" is one of random access and a cause of distress. For those, on the other hand, who through practice and self-control come to master the tool, a command over the faculty may develop into an "art" in which they can see, hear, touch, taste, smell and perceive things that are outside the normal range of perception. A typical New Age expectation holds that clairvoyant gifts will belong to everyone once the full **Aquarian Age** is manifest.

COLE-WHITTAKER, TERRY. A much married and popular New Age writer and teacher. As a former Miss California, she became a minister in the United Church of **Religious Science** in the 1970s and developed the small La Jolla congregation under her pastorship into one of Religious Science's largest congregations. Most of this congregation followed her when she broke with the Church in the early 1980s and began her own organization called the Terry Cole Whittaker Ministries in San Diego. She also began at this time a television ministry. However, by 1985, her organization disbanded due to huge debts it had accumulated. A smaller foundation was then established and called Adventures in Enlightenment, and it is through this organization that Cole-Whittaker has continued to be a popular speaker in **New Thought** and New Age circles. In 1985, she published both *How to Have More in a Have-Not World* and *What You Think of Me Is None of My Business.* The following year, she wrote *The Inner Path from Where You Are to Where You Want to Be.* As a major advocate of **prosperity consciousness**, she argues that one can live out of an acceptance of God's abundance and possess everything one wants in life. Her basic teachings are that for humanity to advance, people must develop a deep love for each other despite the obvious differences; people create their own reality through thoughts, feelings, visions and actions; and as the God within is recognized, individuals are able to surrender to the will of the One and live in paradise as ascended Gods in Heaven on Earth.

CONTROVERSIES, NEW AGE. Apart from the common criticisms of New Age concerning narcissism, shallowness, consumerism and appropriation, there is a more controversial aspect of its underlying **theosophical** teachings concerning the New Age or New World Order as expressed in the writings of **Helena Blavatsky** and **Alice Bailey**. In the doctrine of the evolution of humanity toward godhood along with reliance on contact with spirit guides to engineer the new age, a racial element is introduced in the alleged connection of the Aryan peoples with the **Atlantis** myth. The new species that will constitute the new age is designated *homo noeticus.* This new humanity results, at least in part, through a "global cleansing action" that will eliminate the world of those not destined for inclusion.

This expectation in theosophy has frequently assumed an anti-Semitic tone. In *Isis Unveiled* II (1972:434), Blavatsky refers to the Semites as "the least spiritual of the human family." She continues that the Jewish people's "literature has left nothing original, nothing that was not borrowed from Aryan thought, . . . [in short] whose science and

philosophy are utterly wanting in those noble features which characterize the highly spiritual and metaphysical systems of the Indo-European
(Japhetic) races." Later (pp. 492f), she considers the national traits and
idiosyncratic failings that characterize the Jew to the present-day as
"rough realism, selfishness and sensuality." Judaism for her has become
something solely based on "Phallus service." This intense dislike for
anything Jewish, Old Testament and, ultimately, Christian was part of a
wider German milieu in Blavatsky's time that found expression as **Ariosophie** and the **Volktumsbewegung**.

   Blavatsky's anti-Jewish statements ought, at least in part, to be
seen against this *Völkisch* movement background. Even more controversial in this direction are various sentiments expressed in the writings
of Alice Bailey, and one of the reasons given for her expulsion from the
Theosophical Society is cited as Bailey's open anti-Semitism. This is
often tied to an anti-Christian sentiment as well. For instance, the original name of Bailey Lucis Publishing Company was the Lucifer Publishing Company—reflecting her intense opposition to canonical Judaeo-
Christian thought. But Blavatsky (1889:243) shared this opposition and
made similar comments such as seeing Satan as the real benefactor and
spiritual father of humanity and not simply the automaton created by
Jehovah. This Luciferian terminology is found even with more contemporary New Age figures such as **David Spangler** (1981:37, 44f) who
sees Lucifer as the angel of humanity's evolution into the new age.
Spangler, in fact, refers to the Luciferic initiation into the New Age. In
1983, Constance Cumbrey published her Christian evangelical bestseller, *Hidden Dangers of the Rainbow*, seeking to expose the New Age
movement—and **Benjamin Creme** along with the **Maitreya** in particular—as a sinister satanic conspiracy.

   In the framework of this persistent polarization between conservative forms of **Christianity** and a Christian formulation of New Age,
Bailey (1957:558n) claimed that there is no need for anyone to join the
Christian Church in order to be affiliated with Christ. She maintained
that the requirements are to love humanity, lead a disciplined life, and
rule one's daily life with love. Although Bailey attacked the Church of
Rome for its political actions and did not exempt it as a possible target
by the atomic bomb, she called for the recognition of divinity behind all
faiths and peoples. Bailey's symbolism of pure light and her "end-time"
scenario containing overtones of an approaching nuclear apocalypse
have rung alarm bells in people as diverse as eco-feminist Monica Sjoo

and Margaret Brearley of the Centre for Judaism and Jewish-Christian Relations (Selly Oaks Colleges). But it is Bailey's condemnation of the Jews for being separate and placing primary emphasis upon material well-being that is perhaps the most difficult to reconcile with planetary consciousness and the equality and respect for all peoples. For a seminal New Age thinker, these are strange and controversial declarations. She defines cosmic evil as materialistic selfishness and a hubristic isolation and attributes these same qualities to the Hebrew nation.

The defense of Bailey and Blatvatsky tends to argue that they were not attacking the Jewish peoples or the religion of Judaism but rather the latter's institutionalized ethnocentrism. Whether this is a sufficient argument remains an open question. Certainly, Bailey's feeling that the Jews are **reincarnations** of spiritual failures or "residues from another planet" sits uncomfortably with the essential thrust of the contemporary New Age movement. One unconvincing contention is that the mystical movement of theosophy is not all that influential on New Age and not to understand contemporary New Age as largely an updating of theosophy. Nevertheless, what is certainly true is that relatively few New Age adherents are aware—or would approve—of the anti-Semitic undercurrents running through the theosophical aspects of New Age. However, what theosophy, the **"I AM" Religious Activity**, the **Church Universal and Triumphant** and other related expressions have encouraged for the New Age movements is both a framework that incorporates a mystical westernized version of the Bodhisattvas as a collective repository of evolutionary wisdom and also an opening for the west to **Hindu, Buddhist**, San Mat, Sikh and even **Sufi**/Islamic understandings and movements. The question remains open whether New Age can move forward with its theosophical legacy while shedding its more controversial and sinister aspects.

CORE ENERGY MANAGEMENT (CEM). *See* BLOOM, WILLIAM.

CRANIOSACRAL THERAPY. An osteopathy laying-on-of-hands **therapy** used for relief of pain, fatigue, anxiety, digestive discomfort and repetitive stress injuries. Sometimes referred to as craniosacral release, this approach depends on hands-on light touch techniques that allow the practitioner an ability to evaluate the patient's body and correct physical imbalances. Through the development of light-touch pal-

pation skills, the therapist attunes to the subtle movements in the craniosacral system. The emphasis is to promote the body's ability to heal
itself through release of deeply held trauma and to restore balance and
mobility to the body as a whole. Widely used by New Age practitioners, craniosacral therapy postulates a "subtle body" that underlies the
physical, emotional, psychological and spiritual layers of the human
body and manifests as the subtle body pulse that results from the
movement of the cerebrospinal fluid.

Often combined with myofascial release that deals with attempts to
soften and free restrictions that have accumulated within the body's
connective tissues, craniosacral treatment itself is focused on the dural
tube—the connective tissue that lines the inside of the skull, separates
the lobes of the brain, encases the spinal cord as it descends through the
foramen magnum or hole in the base of the cranium and attaches to the
distal end of the vertebrae (sacrum/tailbone). The theory behind this
technique is that any dysfunction of the sacrum or dural tube will lead
to disability in the shoulders, neck and/or cranium, and vice versa.
Trauma results from strains or deformities that develop through injury,
surgery or incorrect posture. Craniosacral therapy attempts, therefore,
to deal with the entire body—both the dural tube and the fascia (the
three-dimensional web of connective tissue that holds the entire body
together).

Frequently combined with special muscle stretching exercises (op-
timally in warm water) and relaxation adjunct techniques, craniosacral
therapy and myofascial release do not constitute cures but instead attempts to relieve the body from persistent pain and assist it to work
smoothly. As a gentle, non-invasive method of enhancing the craniosacral system, the emphasis is placed upon the body-mind connection in
order to reduce stress and increase energy. Craniosacral Therapy (CST)
was developed by osteopathic physician John E. Upledger through research conducted at Michigan State University between 1975 and
1983—based on William Sutherland's theories of osteopathy at the start
of the twentieth century. The Upledger Institute at Palm Beach Gar-
dens, Florida, sponsors workshops and clinical services that combine
CST with Visceral Manipulation, Mechanical Link and Lymph Drain-
age Therapy. Other craniosacral centers include Michael J. Shea's International School for Biodynamic Craniosacral Therapy in North Palm
Beach, Florida, the Karuna Institute in England, and the Milne Institute
of Big Sur, California. There is a Craniosacral Therapy Association of

North America that licenses instructors in the technique. Craniosacral therapists are to be found across the globe.

CREME, BENJAMIN. (1922-). A New Age teacher who follows in the understandings of **Blavatsky**, the Ballards and the Prophets. This may be all the more ironic in that Creme had once been involved with the **Aetherius Society**, a UFO contactee group founded by George King. After breaking with King, in 1959, Creme began to receive inner messages foretelling the imminent reappearance of **Maitreya**, the head of the **Great White Brotherhood**.

Although there was an interruption, Creme has since embarked on affirming the coming of Maitreya to the world. In 1974, he was "over-shadowed" by Maitreya as the Master dictated messages concerning the preparation of a *mayavirupa* or body of manifestation through which Maitreya would then visit the earth. Henceforth, Creme began giving talks on the "Reappearance of the Christ." He claims not to be a channel but rather a mediator. Through further messages, Creme learned that the *mayavirupa* had been assumed on the 7th of July in 1977 and that the following day Maitreya began his descent from his Himalayan spiritual retreat where his body of light remains. Although the head of the spiritual hierarchy did not appear to the world in 1982 as had been predicted, Creme has continued to insist in public talks that Maitreya is at present living among the Indian community of London and will manifest himself shortly to the world as a whole.

In the **theosophical** tradition, Creme follows most closely in the teachings of **Alice Bailey**. The ageless wisdom teachings that have been given by the custodians of the spiritual hierarchy from the beginning of time (reputedly 18.5 million years ago) are centered on the "One Most Holy God." Both Blavatsky and Bailey have produced an intermediate phase of the teachings of the Great White Brotherhood for "this New Age, which is the **Age of Aquarius**—a new cosmic cycle." Creme calls the Aquarian Age a hard scientific/astronomical fact in which the sun comes into alignment with the magnetic energy of the constellation. Pisces, the age of individualism, is now being superseded by the time for the group—foreshadowed already in 1675 with the growing awareness in humanity of such a thing as society.

In Creme's formulation, the spiritual custodians are humans who have gone before us and do not need further incarnation. In other words, these are people who have become masters of themselves. These masters of wisdom and lords of compassion have, since the break-up of **Atlantis** some ninety-eight thousand years ago, lived in the remote parts of the world: in mountains and deserts. However, Blavatsky, like Jesus Christ and Leonardo de Vinci, is only a fourth degree initiate— the level just below the masters. It is the cosmic plan of evolution of which the masters are the custodians, and while they tend to appear to humanity as angels, Maitreya has promised that when the world is ready by its own free will to share and take the first steps into right human relationships, he will come with a tangible group of masters. He lays claim already to causing the end of the cold war as well as apartheid. At a London talk on 8 February 2001, Creme proclaimed that Lord Maitreya now says that he will appear even though humanity is not yet prepared. This will be the "Day of Declaration" in which Maitreya will present himself on television and radio to the entire world— speaking telepathically in everyone's own language. Creme's own organization, formerly the Tara Center in Los Angeles and the Tara Press in London, is known as the Share International Foundation. Like both the Aetherius Society and the **Raelian movement**, it promotes Maitreya's basic message: "Share and save the world. . . . Take your brother's need as the measure for your action and solve the problems of the world. There is no other course."

CYBERNETICS. A transdisciplinary "science of control and communication in the animal and the machine" named in 1947 by the mathematician Norbert Wiener and physician Arturo Rosenbleuth. The term, first used by André-Marie Ampère in the nineteenth century has been derived from the Greek $\kappa v \beta \eta \rho \eta \tau \epsilon \varsigma$ "steersman" to suggest that adaptive control is something that flourishes under a helmsman rather than a dictator. Cybernetics studies effective organization and the importance of feedback. Along with feedback loops, fluxes, emergent behaviors and unified but dynamic wholes, cybernetics has mutated in time into the related areas of chaos and complexity theory, robotics, artificial life, cognitive science, network dynamics and general systems theory. It is particularly concerned with spontaneous self-organization along with when and how something becomes more than simply the sum of its constituent components. Complexity theory in particular suggests the notion of "spiritual cybernetics" that can be possibly discerned behind religion in general as well as the specific personal and collective quest of New Age. *See also* BIOFEEDBACK.

-D-

DASS, RAM (Richard Alpert; 1933-). Key New Age spokesperson who first popularized the term "New Age," promoted the concept of New Age consciousness and is responsible for much of the subsequent influx of Eastern spiritual (chiefly **Hindu**) ideas into the West. Receiving his Ph.D. from Stanford University, Alpert conducted LSD-based research into human consciousness with the Department of Social Relations and the Graduate School of Education at Harvard University in collaboration with Timothy Leary, Aldous Huxley and Allen Ginsburg between 1958 and 1963. Because of the controversial nature of this project, Alpert and Leary were eventually dismissed from the Harvard faculty. In 1967 and 1968, Alpert traveled to India and there met and studied under Neem Karoli Baba, a disciple of Nityananda. His guru gave him the new name of Ram Dass ("servant of God"). He has since promoted a Hindu-**Sufi** spiritual practice based on **meditation** and has been strongly influenced by **Maharaja Ji**. In 1997, Dass suffered a massive cerebral stroke from which he has steadily recovered in the following years.

The books of Baba Ram Dass include *The Only Dance There Is* (1970, 1974), his bestseller *Be Here Now* (1971), *How Can I Help: Stories and Reflections on Service* (1985), *Compassion in Action: Setting Out on the Path of Service* (1995), *Soma: The Divine Hallucinogen* (1999) and *Still Here: Embracing Aging, Changing, and Dying* (2000).

Ram Dass created the Hanuman Foundation in 1974. Beside being the organizing vehicle for Dass' lectures and workshops, the foundation sponsors numerous projects—including the "Prison-Ashram Project" and the "Living Dying Project." Dass has also established the Seva Foundation as an international organization dedicated to service and the relief of suffering in the world. Among its projects are attempts to reduce blindness in Nepal and India, the restoration of agricultural life in Guatemala, providing primary health care for American Indians, and efforts to deal with homelessness and environmental degradation in the United States. Through these various undertakings, Ram Dass has emerged as a leading promoter of the social service and reform program component of the New Age movement. Along with **Marilyn Ferguson** and **David Spangler**, Dass directly links self-transformation with social action. He further sees meditation as providing the optimum of self-integrity and for infusing each moment with "space, peace, equanimity, joy and lightness." For Dass, meditation becomes a device by which one can live in the immediate moment and, at the same time, recognize the relativity of the single perspective. His "meditation-in-action" is a means for attuning the physical and mental to the spiritual. He stresses a **vegetarian** diet, the use of fasting, and regular meditation in a specially reserved space. Dass argues that the aims more usually associated with **human potential** (power enhancement, increase of pleasure, relief of psychological and/or physical pain) are egoistically limited and superseded by the spiritual liberation that he perceives to be the true goal and product of **meditation**.

DHARMAWARA MAHATHERA BELLONG, THE VENERABLE (1888-1999). Theravadin **Buddhist** monk from Cambodia, given the name Bhante by his followers. Originally a judge, Bhante knew from the time he spent the obligatory year as a monk in his youth that he wanted the monastic and celibate life on a permanent basis. After his daughter had grown and his family was provided for, he became a forest monk in his forties. Forest monks in the Theravada tradition do not stay in one place for longer than three days but continue to walk as a form of **meditation**. Bhante accordingly walked from Cambodia to India and down to Sri Lanka. Through color **healing**, Bhante cured one of the parents of Jawaharlal Nehru in the late 1940s. In gratitude, Nehru gave the monk a former Moghul pleasure garden (Merhauli) thirty kilometers south of Delhi. Beginning in 1950, he restored the run-down and overgrown location as his center, Ashoka Mission Vihara, from which he disseminated his teachings of **chromotherapy**. He eventually settled in Stockton, California, where he established a refugee center for Cambodian exiles. He lived in relative poverty with no institutional structure developed around him.

Bhante's approach to healing and **alternative medicine** was, like his life in general, one of basic simplicity. He began all treatment with the use of enemas. He considered that sickness mostly begins with morbid matter. He stressed healthy diet and, in the latter years of his long life, ate only fresh fruit and vegetable juices. Though he preferred **vegetarianism**, as a Buddhist monk he accepted the foods that were given to him. He considered the sun as the source of life and contended that the universe is composed, as are our bodies, of colors—both those we see and those we cannot see. All things emanate color, and everything (organ, thought, etc.) corresponds to a particular color. Illness results when a particular bodily organ loses its color intensity, while curing is effected through rebuilding balance in the body.

The colors Bhante advocated almost exclusively are green, yellow and blue. His students were taught to avoid the color red. This last is reserved only for particular cases of paralysis. In his understanding of chromotherapy, green as the middle color of the spectrum is a neutral, harmonizing and balancing color to be used for reenergizing, reharmonization and the treatment of depression, tiredness, exhaustion, shock and trauma. Yellow, as a warm color, is used to treat disease associated with chilling: digestive ailments such as constipation affecting stomach, liver, intestines; nervous disorders; allergies; bronchitis and colds if unaccompanied by fever. Blue, the cold color of ice, is considered a natural antibiotic and is used for cooling the body—treating fever, infection, burns, etc. Green and blue are employed also for the eyes, ears, bruises and cuts. Bhante essentially followed Edwin Dwight Babbit's method of "charging" spring water by putting it into a sterilized colored bottle and placing it for forty-eight hours in the summer sun. He also used oils as well as light (e.g., from a spotlight). He advocated the use of small quantities: small sips of green water before meals, yellow water after meals, and blue water away from meals.

DIVINE HIERARCHY, THE. The cosmos as described by **theosophy**. The Divine Hierarchy is centered at the top on the Cosmic Logos or God which is expressed as a Trinity (Creator, Preserver and Destroyer) and under which seven Planetary Logoi rule every star in the universe. Our own sun and solar system come under the jurisdiction of the Solar Logos who is humanity's God and who emanates a Trinity of Father, Son and Holy Ghost. Once again, there are seven *logoi* beneath the Trinity who, in turn, are associated with lesser angelic beings known as *devas*. Linking humanity and the divine bureaucracy are the mahatmas or masters, men and women of the **Great White Brotherhood** who have progressed beyond the need to incarnate but nevertheless do so to assist the rest of humanity.

According to the notion of the **seven bodies of the individual** as reflections of the seven stages of the universe, in humanity's evolutionary development, the first three stages of the earth and universe comprise steps toward materialization. The fourth stage is known as crystallization, while the final three are stages of spiritualization and the return of spirit. Theosophy holds that humanity at present is in the fourth stage, and theosophy's purpose is to become conscious of the higher levels of cosmic vibration and freedom from the levels of denser substance, i.e., to become free from matter. This historical evolution takes humanity through seven root races—each of which have seven subraces. The first three races—culminating with the Lemurian—are those that perfect the union of spirit and matter; the fourth race, the Atlantean, is the expression of the union and the paradisiacal origins of the human race; and the last three races are those of the spirit struggling to be free of the physical. Humanity is currently the fifth root race, the Aryan, in which its spiritual culmination is the Anglo-Saxon subrace and from which we will evolve into spiritual adepts.

The hierarchy of masters, intermediate between humanity and the Solar Rulers, parallels the organization of the Solar Hierarchy. At its top is the Lord of the World—the agent of the Solar Logos. Beneath him is the Trinity of Buddhas. The Lord of the World is often known as Sanat Kumara, and the three Buddhas as the Three Kumaras. Beneath these last are the three department heads of Will, Love Wisdom and Intelligence. Each head has a chief representative as well as assistants (the **Seven Rays**) who manifest the department heads to humanity. The first three of these are known as the Three Aspects or Major Rays; the remaining four, as the Four Attributes or Minor Rays. They employ the colors of the rainbow in aiding people to free themselves from rebirth and return their spark of divinity (manifest as a trinity of spirit, intuition and mentality) to its spiritual home. The Divine or Spiritual Hierarchy has been further elaborated by **Alice Bailey**. *See also* "I AM" RELIGIOUS ACTIVITY.

DIVINE LIGHT MISSION. *See* MAHARAJ JI, GURU.

DIVINE SCIENCE. Though not explicitly identifying as New Age, one of the leading components of the **New Thought** alliance. Like **Unity**'s stress on affirmation, the Divine Science Federation International rejects any notion of prayer as supplication. It centers instead on **meditation** in which it contemplates the limitless Being of God. In other words, Divine Science affirms the omnipresence of God over any mortal mind/immortal mind distinction. God is pure spirit. Creation is simply the emanation of life and substance from God. Creation is therefore explained as God in self-manifestation. Spirit and Substance are merely two aspects of the same reality; matter is divine energy manifest as form. In essence, the human is divine and one with the Creator. According to Divine Science, if the individual does not realize that each person is an individualized center of God's activity, confusion, turmoil, illness and poverty can manifest.

DOWLING, LEVI H. (1844-1911). Ohio-based pastor known for transcribing or **channeling** from The Book of God's Remembrance (the **Akashic Records**) *The Aquarian Gospel of Jesus the Christ* (1908) that describes Jesus' lost years. Emphasizing unconditional love, Dowling's work has formed much of the foundation of New Age Christology.

DREAM-WORK. A psychotherapeutic method used for the interpretation of dreams, behavioral patterns, disturbing events and synchronicities for insight, transformation and **healing**. Dream analysis has become a standard **therapeutic** tool since Sigmund Freud's understanding of the dream as an access to subconscious wishes and fears. Apart from employing dream-work for purposes of health and well-being, New Age also considers the dream as a vehicle for the transmission of **clairvoyant** and/or spiritual knowledge as well as contact with the powers of the spirit world. *See also* SHAMANISM.

DYER, WAYNE (1940-). Prolific writer, seminar facilitator and lecturer in the field of self-empowerment. Having received his doctorate in counseling psychology, Dyer became one of the original instigators of the self-development movement. His fans consider him the "father of motivation." His first book, *Your Erroneous Zones* (1976), focusing on guilt and worry, became a bestseller. Continuing to address motivational topics, Dyer adopts a holistic approach to physical, mental and spiritual concerns. Using a **New Thought** perspective, he stresses that one can manifest anything in life once he or she connects with the abundance of the universe. Something must be wished for, desired fully and sought after with complete will, intention and a passion that ignores the doubts of others.

As a modern personal growth and spiritual teacher, Dyer remains a leader in the self-help/transformational field of New Age spirituality. Some of his more than a dozen books include *Pulling Your Own Strings* (1978), *The Sky's the Limit* (1980), *You'll See It When You Believe It* (1989), *Real Magic* (1992), *Your Sacred Self* (1995), *Manifest Your Destiny: The Nine Spiritual Principles for Getting Everything You Want* (1992/1997), *Wisdom of the Ages: 60 Days to Enlightenment* (1998) and *There's a Spiritual Solution to Every Problem* (2001).

-E-

EARTH-BASED SPIRITUALITY. One of the stronger links between the New Age and **Neo-pagan** movements. Earth religions focus on a spiritual appreciation of nature as well as ecological restoration. They are part of the emerging concept of **Gaia** consciousness that tends to occur more in New Age circles rather than strictly pagan ones—despite the incongruence of nature spirituality with the underlying impetus of **New Thought** and transcendental **theosophical** foundations that informs New Age. From an earth-based spiritual perspective, experience is emphasized over doctrine, immanence over transcendence and the multiple over any single pathway to the divine. A spirituality that understands the tangible imbued with the divine or an inherent vitality is a form of animism. James Lovelock's hypothesis and theory from which much of the nature religion aspects of New Age derive does not understand this animistic dynamism of the earth as conscious or teleological.

EASTERN MYSTICISM. The more canonical expressions of **Hinduism** and **Buddhism** that, in the wake of **theosophy** itself, have come to inform and participate in the New Age Movement of the west. These are to be distinguished from the great body of eastern concepts and terminologies that have developed in the west through the theosophical focus on the Bodhisattvas, or Ascended Masters. Part of this trend was prefigured in the teachings of **Krishnamurti** who renounced his position as World Teacher (Lord **Maitreya**) and disbanded the Order of the Star of the East organization and embarked on a career of disseminating more traditionally eastern ideas. Consequently, on the one hand, there are people like the **Maharishi Mahesh Yogi** (transcendental meditation), **Swami Muktananda** (Siddha Yoga Dham of America), Yogi Bhajan (Sikh Dharma, i.e., Healthy, Happy, Holy Organization or 3HO), **Guru Maharaj Ji** (Divine Light Mission/Elan Vital), Bhagwan **Raj-nesh/Osho** (Osho International), Kirpal Singh (Ruhani Satsang), **Paramahansa Yogananda** (Self-Realization Society), Trungpa Rinpoche (**Naropa Institute** of **Tibetan Buddhism**), or even such westerners as **Baba Ram Das** (Hanuman Foundation), Ma Jaya Bhagavati (Kashi Ashram), Da (Bubba) Free John/Adidam (Johannine Daist Community/the Religion of Adidam/**Adi Da Samraj**) and John-Roger Hinkins (**MSIA**: Movement for Inner Spiritual Awareness) who promote various eastern meditative practices aiming toward an ultimate mystical or spiritual release, or, on the other hand, those people like Krishnamurti, **Rudolf Steiner, Sri Aurobindo** and now Guru Maharaj Ji, who teach or have taught a more secularized or western version of eastern spirituality and insight.

EDDY, MARY BAKER (1821-1910). Founder of Christian science. Eddy was another long-time sufferer who was cured by **Phineas Quimby** and became one of his pupils. Eventually, she founded her own movement, and the First Church of Christ, Scientist (the Mother Church) was formed in Boston in 1892. Eddy emphasized the notion of God as healer versus Quimby's idea of the mind as healer. The contrasts between Quimby/**New Thought** and Eddy/Christian science concern the existence of matter, the role of religion, and the pure idealism of Eddy in contrast to the mind-matter dualism of Quimby. Eddy affirmed the sufficiency of the Bible, God as supreme and infinite, salvation through Christ, and the crucifixion and resurrection of Jesus. For her, all is Infinite Mind in which Spirit is immortal Truth while matter is mortal error. Mankind, as the Image and likeness of God, is spiritual. While Christian science does not identify itself as New Age, Eddy's student **Emma Curtis Hopkins** developed the school of New Thought, itself one of the chief predecessors of New Age thought. *See also* HEALING.

ELAN VITAL. *See* MAHARAJ JI, GURU.

EMERSON, RALPH WALDO (1803-1882). A leading figure of the American transcendentalist movement, strongly influenced by the writings of **Emanuel Swedenborg**. Emerson had also been deeply affected by **Hinduism** through his reading of the *Bhagavad Gita*. A third influence came from European romanticism. As the chief exponent of New England transcendentalism, Emerson argued for a unitive world based on the priority of mind (God). Emerson developed a form of nature mysticism. Others included in the philosophic and literary group centered in Concord, Massachusetts, were Henry Thoreau, Amos Bronson Alcott and Margaret Fuller. Founded on a Kantian idealism that posited the primacy of the spiritual and super-individual against the material and empirical, the movement incorporated both Platonic and Eastern ideas as well as the Unitarian reaction against Calvinism. Its characteristic tenets were shaped by an advocacy on intuition and an extreme belief in the positive potential of human nature. As a leading component of the **American metaphysical tradition**, Emerson's transcendentalist movement prefigures much of what reappears in the New Age movements of the twentieth and twenty-first centuries.

END TIMES. The **apocalyptic** events leading to the **Christian** millennium and/or the New Age "**Age of Aquarius.**" Many sources of prophecy belief are to be found in the Bible, including the Old Testament books of Daniel and Ezekiel, and the Christian New Testament Gospel of Matthew. The primary source, however, remains the Book of Revelation. The word "revelation" is a translation of the Greek word "apokalypsis" referring to the unveiling of hidden information concerning future human events. Through revealing secret knowledge, the words "apocalypse," "revelation" and "prophecy" are closely related. By definition, prophets are apocalyptic.

A large "end times" subculture is to be found in the United States, even though it often remains opaque to outsiders and is misunderstood by many in a secular society. Media coverage of millennial expectation has opened a window on the various enterprises within this huge collection of diverse industries that yearly supply merchandise to tens of millions of Christian consumers. The central plank in this subculture is rapture, the Christian expectation of transportation to heaven. In the Christian context, those who believe they will be raptured seek to convert non-believers. A significant product of this effort are the "postrapture ministries" that comprise evangelical outreach materials for the benefit of those who will be left behind once the authors are raptured up to heaven.

With the approach of the year 2000, biblical prophecy bookshelves increasingly reflected the belief that the "end times" might have already begun and that the rapture could be close at hand. While this is largely a Protestant phenomenon and the Roman Catholic Church officially discourages "end times" speculation, a small but significant collection of apocalyptic Catholics also appeared to see the millennial year 2000 connected to apocalyptic prophecy. In addition, there are secular versions of apocalyptic **millennialism**. Relevant information is collected by the Center for Millennial Studies, which maintains a website that includes a useful glossary and bibliography.

For several of the leading New Age writers, especially those of an essential Christian persuasion (e.g., **Ruth Montgomery** and **Edgar**

Cayce), apocalyptic earth changes are expected to precede the transition into the new times. These changes include the possibilities of world war, devastating earthquakes and *tsunami*, volcanic eruption, pole shift as well as famine and plague. *See also* CHRISTIANITY; CHURCH UNIVERSAL AND TRIUMPHANT.

ENNEAGRAM. An ancient **Sufi** teaching introduced by **Gurdjieff** to his students around 1916. The enneagram is a nine-pointed diagram that allegedly maps the human psyche and provides a guide by which a person may achieve understanding of both self and interactions with others. The nine independent but interconnected systems of the human body and soul are represented by enneagons. **Oscar Ichazo** identified these enneagons as ego types. **Claudio Naranjo** and Helen Palmer evolved these into personality types as part of Western psychology. In 1992, the **Arica** Institute sued Palmer over copyright infringement following the publication of her book on the enneagram in 1988 but lost the case.

ENVIRONMENTALISM. Concern with restoring an ecological balance to planet earth. While much of the focus on planetary healing is more **Neo-pagan** than New Age, even within the latter there is a detectable ecological preoccupation with the well-being of the planet as a living entity. The interplay between the two movements on the environmental issue is ambiguous and often contentious, and in New Age there is a tendency to focus more on personal health than on global ecological concerns or a love of nature. Nevertheless, British pagan Mike Howard argues that the area of ecology based on an understanding of the sacredness of life and a reverence for Mother Earth may become the spiritual foundation for the **Aquarian Age**. Along with new science, new psychology and spiritual dynamics, **William Bloom** presents ecology as one of the four major fields of New Age. For him, New Age ecology is one that accepts responsibility for the total planetary state through interdependence and interpenetration. **José Argüelles** foresees the emergence of a locally operative planetary society that will rest in part on what he understands as the "shaman's environmental resilience." The notion of reaffirming humanity's stewardship of the earth and the green movement as a chief political expression for any New Age/pagan alliance are part of the social reform efforts that equally comprise New Age identity along with its interest in the occult and/or spiritual. *See also* EARTH-BASED SPIRITUALITY, GAIA HY-POTHESIS.

ERHARD TRAINING SEMINARS (*est*). An early and influential **human potential** program developed by Werner Erhard (Jack Rosenberg, 1935-). Combining Eastern mystical practices such as **yoga** and Zen **meditation** with elements of psychology, business management and **cybernetics** along with ideas taken from **Mind Dynamics**, **Scientology**, **Abraham Maslow**'s self-actualization, **Gestalt therapy** and **psychosynthesis**, Erhard taught what was at first an intense and controversial developmental psycho-technology. Originally, the program involved a sixty-hour training experience over two successive weekends in groups numbering approximately 250 people. "Verbal flagellation" was employed to "open" the trainee to objective self-observation. The purpose aimed to transform the level at which one experiences life toward a horizon of expanding satisfaction. Belief systems are condemned as myths developed from non-experiential knowledge and replaced by a process of increased observation. In the developmental awareness which results, God and the self are recognized as inseparable. Due to persistent accusations of fascism, minimalism, narcissism and brainwashing, *est* was modified in 1984 into the less harsh training known as The Forum. This program is sponsored by the Network—also known as The Centers Network or The Society for Contextual Studies and Educational Seminars. This broader association sponsors its foundation (through which financial grants are made for welfare and educational concerns) as well as such philanthropic projects as the Youth at Risk community program. The underlying maxim of *est*/The Forum is that "we are each the cause of our own experience and responsible for everything that happens in it."

ESALEN INSTITUTE. Birthplace of the **human potential movement** and "granddaddy" of New Age. Founded by Michael Murphy and Richard Price in 1962 on lands and a graveyard originally belonging to the Esselen Indians of Big Sur, California, Esalen became a seminar and conference center that also offered a series of residential work-study programs. Names associated with this metaphysical "Grand Central Station" include Jack Kerouac, Ken Kesey, **Abraham Maslow**, **Fritz Perls**, Alan Watts, Aldous Huxley, Joseph Campbell, George Leonard, **Buckminster Fuller**, **Moshe Feldenkrais**, Ralph Metzner,

Ida Rolf (*see* **Rolfing**), John Lilly and **Stanislov Grof** among many others. Stanford professor of comparative religion Fredrick Spiegelberg introduced Murphy and Price to Eastern philosophy, **yoga** and the teachings of Sri **Aurobindo**. They in turn established Esalen as a center for personal and social transformation with a focus on holistic and complimentary medicine. Research and study are conducted into blending Eastern and Western philosophies, psychology, comparative religious studies, education, sociology, somatics, the arts, ecology and human evolution. The Esalen center is also famous for its natural hot springs and for the development of Esalen **massage**.

est. *See* ERHARD TRAINING SEMINARS.

EVANS, WARREN FELT (1817-1887). A minister in the Swedenborgian Church of the New Jerusalem who had been formerly trained in Methodism. He later received healing from **Phineas Quimby** and proceeded thereafter to study under him. After Quimby's death, Evans returned essentially to a Swedenborgian framework in which he expanded Swedenborg's interpretation of healing and health. He also reemployed a mesmeric model in which he identified the Swedish scientist's notion of divine "influx" as healing power. Along with **Emanuel Swedenborg, Franz Anton Mesmer, Ralph Waldo Emerson** and Quimby, Evans was a major contributor to the common language concerning spiritual immanence as the source for healing.

-F-

FAITHIST. One of the first teachings to have been received through what is now referred to as **channeling**. Between 1881 and 1882, the spiritualist John Ballou Newbrough (1828-1891), as a light trance channel, produced by means of automatic writing the thousand-page *Oahspe: A New Age Bible*. *Oahspe* foretells the Kosmon Era as a time in which new people would emerge and transform the world into one of peace and happiness. Angelic forces are the guides of humanity through its seventy-eight thousand years of existence, beginning with human origins on the pacific continent of Pan (akin to Lemuria), and continuing under twelve religious prophets from Zarathushtra to Joshua (i.e., Jesus). This terrestrial transformation and the ascent of humanity take place within a typical **galactian** spiritual hierarchy multitude. Over the years, individual Faithist groups have both arisen and dissolved, but the membership network is maintained by the Universal Faithists of Kosmon that is headquartered in Salt Lake City.

FARM, THE. A countercultural commune established in rural Tennessee in 1970 by Stephen Gaskin and his followers. Following a series of Monday evening talks at San Francisco's Family Dog during the latter half of the 1960s, Gaskin led a fleet of buses across the United States before purchasing land and settling the commune. At its peak, residential membership approximated one thousand five hundred, but following a 1974 raid by state narcotic agents (Gaskin was imprisoned for a year for marijuana possession) and financial mismanagement, The Farm was reorganized in 1983 into a cooperative village. It continues to promote countercultural and now New Age values, has become financially self-sufficient (the manufacture of Geiger counters being one of its products) and undertakes various charity projects (e.g., hurricane relief work and aid in Central America).

FELDENKRAIS METHOD. A form of subtle touch **massage** developed by Moshe Feldenkrais and used for pain relief, the development of more comfortable posture and to deepen learning. Much of the method concentrates on bodily movement sequences that seek to transform habitual non-functional and tension-caused patterns. There is a Feldenkrais Guild of North America that accredits instruction and practice of the method.

FEMINIST SPIRITUALITY. The reinterpretation of religion, spirituality and theology that has developed from the political and reformist movement of feminism. The woman's liberation movement of the 1960s took formative root chiefly in the United States and France. It agitates for the political and legal rights of women and other minorities (e.g., people of color, those with nonconformist sexual preferences, the physically infirm, the economically disenfranchised, etc.). Names associated include those of Simone de Beauvoir, Betty Friedan, Kate Millet and Germaine Greer, among others. In the rewriting of cultural history from this emergent perspective, new interpretations of history (feminist history or "herstory") and theology ("thealogy") have been developed.

Feminist spirituality has both **Christian** and **pagan** dimensions. For the former, a key figure has been Catholic theologian Rosemary Radford Ruether. One effort here is the liberation of the churches from male domination (e.g., ordination of female priests). There is also an effort to understand God as other than "the Father." A significant book expressing these ideas is Ruether's *Sexism and God-Talk* (1983).

In general, the women's spirituality movement sacralizes women's experience and seeks empowerment for self-transformation and life change. It takes a holistic perspective to humanity, nature and the cosmos. Employing both psychological and ecological insights, much feminist spirituality is pagan and focuses on "The Goddess" rather than the Judeo-Christian father-god. Some key works that have helped to shape Goddess spirituality include Esther Harding's *Woman's Mysteries* (1971), Merlin Stone's *When God Was a Woman* (1976), Miriam Simos/Starhawk's *The Spiral Dance* (1979), *Dreaming in the Dark: Magic, Sex and Politics* (1983) and *Truth or Dare* (1990), Marija Gimbutas' *The Goddesses and Gods of Old Europe* (1982), Hallie Iglehart's *Womanspirit: A Guide to Women's Wisdom* (1983), Barbara Walker's *The Women's Encyclopedia of Myths and Secrets* (1983) and *The Women's Dictionary of Symbols and Sacred Objects* (1988), and Elinor Gadon's *The Once and Future Goddess* (1990). A prime example of feminist shamanism is the work of **Lynn Andrews** who endeavors to help women find their own means of self-empowerment.

Much of the language, outlook and practice of feminist and Goddess spirituality has been incorporated into the wider New Age movement. Through the high profile of women in **New Thought, theosophy** and the **American metaphysical movement** (e.g., **Mary Baker Eddy, Emma Curtis Hopkins, Helena Blavatksy,** Annie Besant, **Alice Bailey**)—movements from which New Age has developed, there is already the tendency within New Age spirituality to accord women a higher status than is the norm in most mainstream traditions. Consequently, there are numerous female leaders across the New Age spectrum—e.g., **Terry Cole-Whittaker, Marilyn Ferguson, Shakti Gawain, Louise Hay, Barbara Marx Hubbard, JZ Knight. Elizabeth Kübler-Ross, Denise Linn, Mother Meera, Ruth Montgomery, Caroline Myss, Pat Rodegast, Virginia Satir, Caroline Shaffer, Penny Torres** and **Marianne Williamson**. In **Wicca** and **Neo-paganism**, the role and leadership of women are even more prominent. A typical fusion of Christian, Neo-pagan and New Age elements that is expressive of the non-denominational nature of Goddess spirituality in itself is the veneration of Brigid/Brighid/Bridget/Bride as, variously, a Celtic goddess or Christian saint. Female icons, symbols and deities become tools for redressing the imbalance of patriarchy, and New Age no less than any other modern-day movement becomes a forum for feminist spiritual practice and gender-affirming self-expression. On the other hand, feminism becomes a standard against which contemporary spiritualities, including New Age, are currently assessed and judged. *See also* CHRISTIANITY.

FENG-SHUI. The Chinese system of geomancy that considers how to situate constructions in a landscape to maximize the harmonious influence of the energizing principle (*ch'i*) that connects the spiritual and terrestrial. For *ch'i* to flourish, it cannot stagnate or be blocked, but must be able to flow freely. The primary forces that affect *ch'i* are wind (*feng*) and water (*shui*). Feng-shui is, accordingly, the art of understanding the physical setting, its positive potential and possible detriments, and how to modify the subtle influence of the environment for an optimal effect on the psychic well-being of its human inhabitants. In applying the principles of the female **yin** and male **yang**, the most propitious point is considered to be where the two currents meet. Rocky hills and cliffs are yang; ground that is gently undulating is yin. The ideal proportion between the two is 2:3. The art of feng-shui recommends how to orient a building properly and how to rectify unfortunate influences through the use of rocks, plants, mirrors, other objects and avoidance of straight lines that allow *ch'i* to flow too quickly through a construction. In the West, much of the New Age employment of feng-shui techniques is concerned with the art of interior decoration, namely, designing and decorating one's dwelling space with a view of creating spiritual balance and the advantageous and unrestricted flow of energy. The number of books on feng-shui home design attest to the popularity of this approach for New Agers. *See also* SPACE CLEARING.

FERGUSON, MARILYN (1938-). New Age reformist visionary who sees the New Age as the eventual product of a peaceful network of dissolving and re-coalescing holistic, spiritual and ecologically minded components. Longtime editor of the Los Angeles-based *Brain/Mind Bulletin* and *Leading Edge Bulletin*, Ferguson published *The Brain Revolution* in 1973. But it is chiefly through her 1980 book, *The Aquarian Conspiracy: Personal and Social Transformation in the 1980s*, that Ferguson has fostered the image of New Age "global consciousness" as a humanitarian and environmental movement. Her spiritual "conspiracy" includes individuals, businesses and various organizations that have emerged to sponsor transformational and/or **healing** techniques or to market the various New Age products ranging from crystals, incense and **yoga** to health foods and **human potential therapy**. For Ferguson, New Age is less a spiritual movement than a social effort that seeks the conscious transformation of society itself. Her central concept is that of Thomas Kuhn's "paradigm shift" that suggests sudden and new ways of thinking about old problems.

For the individual, the deep inner change of personal consciousness is a form of shamanic transformation that is often deliberately sought through various "psychotechnologies." Cumulatively, such shifts of perspective allow for the breaking of the kind of "cultural trance" that allows parochial perceptions to become confused as universal truths. This sudden opening of understanding Ferguson sees as collective paradigm shift—a consensual transpersonal evolution that can occur "when a critical number of thinkers has accepted [a] new idea." Consequently, she welcomes conflict and struggle as positive goads that can unfold social transformation. For Ferguson, the transcendent and holistic forms of consciousness and their non-linear dynamics are best apprehended through paradox, **meditation** and mystical experience. Her **Aquarian Age** is a collective concern with both material well-being and psychological liberation.

Ferguson is a member of the Association of Humanistic Psychology as well as the Association of Transpersonal Psychology. She also serves on the board of directors for the Institute of Noetic Sciences. Her Aquarian perspective argues that after the dark and violent age of Pisces, we are now on the brink of a new millennium of love and light.

FINDHORN FOUNDATION. An international center of spiritual education and personal transformation located in Forres on the north coast of Scotland and comprising the "**Esalen**" of the United Kingdom. The Foundation is the legal charity that has grown out of the Findhorn

Community established by Peter and Eileen Caddy and Dorothy Maclean in 1962. Based on spiritual values and direct communication and cooperation with the "kingdoms of nature," the Caddys and Maclean developed a now-legendary vegetable garden on an inhospitable tract of land in a caravan park near the Findhorn Bay. In time, and attracting numerous spiritual seekers, the community dedicated to the evolutionary expansion of consciousness infused with spiritual values emerged. It now consists of approximately 450 residents in the local area, nearly 100 staff and an extensive international outreach. In developing the interrelationship between the **environment**, economics, social life and spiritual principles without dogma or creed, Findhorn offers adult holistic educational programs and courses. The American **David Spangler** became a co-director between 1970 and 1973. The Community recognizes **Alice Bailey** as a prophet of the New Age movement.

With an overriding focus on the "God within," the Findhorn Foundation has sponsored the Moray Steiner School, Earthshare—an organic community subscription agricultural scheme, Trees for Life—a Scottish reforestation plan, the Ecovillage—a self-sustainable community experiment to combine spiritual perception and cooperation with nature and the Findhorn Foundation College—an accredited holistic educational initiative that seeks to integrate and balance physical, mental, emotional, spiritual and relationship developments. In 1997, the Foundation was recognized as an official United Nations Non-Governmental Organization.

FIORE, JOACHIM DE (1145-1202). Thirteenth-century commentator on the Apocalypse. He described the three ages of mankind in terms of the Christian Trinity: God the Father corresponds to the ancient patriarchal ideal, God the Son conforms to the birth of Jesus the Nazarene and the time for the masses to be freed from oppression and God the Holy Spirit coincides with the third period, that of the Truth-Principle or Mother-Principle. **Emma Curtis Hopkins** maintained that the Age of the Spirit is the time for the rise of women (see **New Thought**). Fiore's third age is frequently also recognized as the New Age of Aquarius. *See also* AGE OF AQUARIUS, PRECESSION OF THE EQUINOXES.

FORD, ARTHUR (1879-1971). Spiritual medium known as "America's Sensitive of the Century." Ford became famous when he revealed Houdini's after life message as a verification that communication with the dead is possible. The Unification Church's Sun Myung Moon had sittings with Ford as did New Age figure **Ruth Montgomery**. His message concerns everlasting life and the survival of consciousness after death. He co-founded the Spiritual Frontiers Fellowship that stresses that "Prayer is talking to God. **Meditation** is listening to God." According to Ford and the Fellowship, the purpose of life is "to be one with God again." Ford published *Unknown But Known: My Adventure into the Meditative Dimension* in 1968 and *The Life Beyond Death* in 1971. To continue his work and teachings, Patricia Hayes founded the Arthur Ford International Academy in 1974. It awards "Certifications of Mediumship."

FORUM, THE. *See* ERHARD TRAINING SEMINARS.

FOX, MATTHEW TIMOTHY (1940-). Originally, a Roman Catholic Dominican priest (ordained in 1967) who became a "self-appointed" emissary to the New Age movement. Strongly influenced by the ideas of Meister Eckhart (thirteenth/fourteenth century German mystic), Fox founded the Institute in Culture and Creation Spirituality in Chicago in 1977. This was moved in 1983 to the Holy Names College in Oakland, California. Fox was silenced by the Vatican for a year from 15 December 1988. He has since left the Catholic Church to become an Episcopal priest (in 1994) and now serves as president of the University of Creation Spirituality. He also serves as the co-chair of the **Naropa** University Oakland Campus and is the founder of its Master's Program. Fox has engineered the "reinvention of worship" through his **Techno Cosmic Mass**.

The Friends of Creation Spirituality, Inc. was established in 1984 to educate the general public in creation-centered spirituality. In his 1983 *Original Blessing: A Primer in Creation Spirituality* (revised edition in 2000), Fox shifted Christian emphasis from original sin to original blessing. His creation spirituality blends Christian mysticism, feminism and **environmentalism**. Fox's message may be summed up as mystical, ecological and social justice. Creation Spirituality elucidates four spiritual pathways: the Via Positiva of awe, wonder, joy and gratitude; the Via Negativa of darkness, silence, grief, pain and release; the Via Creativa of creation, renewal and rebirth; and the Via Transformativa of compassionate activity, manifestation of justice and the celebratory act.

As a postmodern theologian, Fox is a prolific writer. Some of his nearly two dozen works include *On Becoming a Musical, Mystical Bear: Spirituality American Style* (1972), *A Spirituality Named Com-*

passion (1979), *Passion for Creation: The Earth-Honoring Spirituality of Meister Eckhart* (1980), *Meditations with Meister Eckhart* (1983), his edited *Western Spirituality: Historical Roots, Ecumenical Routes* (1981), *The Coming of the Cosmic Christ* (1988), *Creation Spirituality: Liberating Gifts for the People of the Earth* (1991), *Wrestling with the Prophets* (1995), *The Reinvention of Work* (1995), *Natural Grace—* with **Rupert Sheldrake** (1996), *The Physics of Angels: Exploring the Realm Where Science and Spirit Meet—*with Rupert Sheldrake (1996), *Sins of the Spirit, Blessings of the Flesh* (1999) and *One River, Many Wells: Wisdom Springing from Global Faiths* (2000). Through his books and worldwide talks, Fox has emerged as an articulate spokesperson for a grounded New Age perspective that combines the ecological and the mystical in a manner that bridges the traditional and innovative. His autobiography is titled *Confessions: The Making of a Post-Denominational Priest* (1997).

FREEMASONRY. Along with **Rosicrucianism**, one of the first western developments leading to the ancient wisdom tradition of **theosophy**, namely, the notion of hidden wisdom that can be traced to a remote past. The Freemasons originated in the Middle Ages as various guilds of bricklayers and stone artisans. Over time, the professional secrets of the different orders became occult secrets, and the guilds emerged as occult orders. The interaction between Freemasonry and Rosicrucianism has been a persistent feature.

FULLER, RICHARD BUCKMINSTER (1895-1983). Scientist, philosopher, designer-prophet and discoverer of synergetics: the geometrical coordinate system that bases structure on the triangle. In 1949, Fuller conceived the geodesic ("earth-dividing") dome as a network of triangles forming a spherical surface. As an organic structure that combines the "energetic-synergetic geometry" of nature's coordinate system, the geodesic dome is able to enclose much more space using far less material than conventional buildings. Fuller desired to improve human housing as efficiently as possible in keeping with his motto of "doing more with less." The geodesic dome is the lightest, strongest and most cost-effective structure ever devised.

    Fuller's concern was "Comprehensive Anticipatory Design Science" or the attempt to anticipate and solve humanity's major problems with more life support for everyone utilizing fewer resources. His technological visions form much of the optimism behind **Marilyn Ferguson**'s Aquarian conspiracy and that branch of New Age and reformist thought that works toward a populist technology in harmony with the organic rhythms of nature. Fuller promoted the notion of "Spaceship Earth" (first coined by Barbara Ward) to encourage thinking of the planet as a single system with a common interest in successful survival. He authored twenty-eight books among which are *Operating Manual for Spaceship Earth* (1963) and, with Adjuvant Kiyoshi Kuromiya, *Critical Path* (1981). To continue Fuller's ideas, the Buckminster Fuller Institute has been established in Santa Barbara, California.

-G-

GAIA HYPOTHESIS. Conjecture made by British chemist James Lovelock (1919-) in his 1979 book, *Gaia: A New Look at Life on Earth*, that the Earth and its inhabitants is a single living organism. This idea that the planet is a complete, self-sustaining and self-regulating system has been translated into the idea of New Age holism. It is further linked to current chaos, catastrophe or complexity theory that pictures the quantum development of consciousness as part of natural evolution. Lovelock and New Age thinkers such as **William Bloom** understand the evolution of technology—particularly telecommunications, electronic networks and information processing—as part of this same process. There is a parallel here in the sequential process described by **Teilhard de Chardin** in terms of the geosphere to biosphere to noosphere. While Lovelock's hypothesis is now accorded the status of a theory, it was not originally intended to suggest teleology or self-conscious purpose. Nevertheless, the holistic ontology of Gaia theory has appealed to environmentalists and ecological activists as well as the spiritual reformist movements collectively known as New Age. Lovelock has been joined in his work by American scientist Lynn Margulis, and together they have further refined the notion of the Earth as a closed-loop self-regulating system that produces emergent properties in which the whole becomes more than the sum of its parts. The Gaia hypothesis and now theory have provided much of the impetus behind **earth-based spirituality**, Earth religions, the green movement and New Age concepts of Gaia consciousness. Lovelock has further expanded his ideas in *The Ages of Gaia: A Biography of Our Living Earth* (1988) and *Gaia: The Practical Guide to Planetary Medicine* (1991).

GALACTIANISM. A branch of New Age thought that focuses on a galaxy-oriented terminology—including the phenomena of UFOs or flying saucers, pyramid power, **Atlantis**, Lemuria, genetic engineering, extraterrestrials or space brethren and the Pleiades as a command center of higher forms of consciousness. The general theosophical inspiration behind New Age has frequently led to belief in a meta-galactic interpenetration of endlessly multiple dimensions. If, however, the transcendental is eliminated from this view of the cosmos, reality is seen more in terms of an underlying and immanent monism. In contrast to New Age's essential gnostic derivation, much of its galactian formulation understands deity not as supernaturally transcendent but as extraterrestrial or interdimensional being. In other words, the supernatural or miraculous is replaced by the supertechnological. This last is accepted as the accomplishment of superior or "more advanced" races: essentially sensuous humanoids as opposed to strictly spiritual beings from beyond space and time. Consequently, we have two general branches of New Age galactianism: one gnostic and holding ultimately to the unreality of nature or its final worthlessness or both; the other cosmic and seeing nature as the only reality—albeit a nature of enormous size if not also of multiple dimensions.

Much of the Galactian inspiration of New Age clearly derives from **theosophy** and especially its understandings of the **Great White Brotherhood**. But while Guy and Edna Ballard's **"I AM" Religious Activity** or Mark and Elizabeth Clare Prophet's Summit Lighthouse/**Church Universal and Triumphant** (CUT) stress the principle of cosmic law, there is not the same kind of emphasis on galactic engineering codes, electro-magnetism, wave-form harmonization or what **José Argüelles** refers to as "faulty genetic circuits" that are found in the Galactian branches of New Age. At the same time, while spiritual seeking through Galactian frameworks often intersects with ufology, not all flying saucer cults are necessarily Galactian or can even be considered as New Age. More typical of the Galactian cosmology of absolute and material immanence in which life is not the result of a process of natural evolution, but one of extraterrestrial biotechnological fabrication, is Claude Vorilhon's **Raëlian movement**, Urantia, James Jacob Hurtak's *Keys of Enoch*, Ron Hubbard's Church of **Scientology**, and Marshall Applewhite's Heaven's Gate. Closer to the gnostic galactianism position that considers supersensuous possibilities that transcend the natural might be George King's **Aetherius Society** and Ernest and Ruth Norman's Unarius. But like New Age's lack of clearly articulated differentiation between its gnostic and **pagan** elements, the same fluid confusion exists between galactianism's gnostic and cosmic formulations. Elements of both appear throughout the various UFO or flying saucer groups as well as in Argüelles' *Surfers of the Zuvuya* or **Benjamin Creme**'s teachings on **Maitreya**.

From the galactian position, especially its more cosmic perspective, the idea of *samadhi* or final release is dismissed as a state of illusion in which one comes to believe that further spiritual evolution is no longer necessary. In Galactian mysticism, spiritual purpose, instead, is found in eternal evolution rather than *nirvana* or oblivion. Typical of its thinking is the concern with "interdimensional reality." The Galactian spiritual hierarchy often exists on multiple levels or dimensions of cosmic reality. In the Urantian understanding of the cosmos, however, the *Urantia Book*'s elaborate polytheism is presented as not outside our space-time but one in which its higher beings live on various spheres to be found within our universe. This more corporeal notion of the heavenly hosts may reflect Mormon theology as well as that of the more contemporary Unification Church. More usually, however, Galactian theology comprehends its enormous hierarchical bureaucracy of spiritual beings (angels, deities, evolved souls and ascended masters) in a plenitude of realms that extend not only throughout our own three-dimensional world but beyond it as well.

Invariably, there is one ultimate God at the Galactian center. In other words, the Galactian world-view extends the gnostic and medieval chain of being into an infinite plenum of multiple dimensions. The divine source of all being is usually understood in masculine terms—e.g., Urantia's Fatherhood of God and Brotherhood of Man. Although the heavenly bureaucracy is also portrayed as male, Urantia does speak of a Mother Spirit. But it is rather with the Universal **Faithists** of Kosmon (headquartered in Salt Lake City) that a Galactian understanding is encountered in which half the heavenly hosts are female. For the Faithists, the godhead is both masculine and feminine.

The central rupture in Galactian spiritual history is the Luciferian rebellion. This was the free will breaking on higher dimensions with the even higher law of cosmic harmonics and its plan for intergalactic evolution. As a segment of the heavenly hosts broke away under the leadership of Lucifer, on earth this constituted the events in the story of the Watcher Angels (the "sons of God" in Genesis 6:2) as recorded in the apocryphic Book of Enoch. In violation of their assigned role, the Watcher Angels along with their leader came to earth and had intercourse with female humans. Their giant offspring have given rise to "genetic aberrations" within the human race that account for the corruption that is now found on earth. In CUT's understanding, the descendants of the Watcher Angels head the world's governments, financial institutions, multinational corporations and the underworld drug cartels.

Eventually, the rebels are to be defeated by the archangel Michael, imprisoned and finally secluded in permanent torment. While CUT's theological position is essentially theosophical, that of Hurtak is chiefly Enochic, Cabalistic and Christian with Egyptian, Tibetan and Mormon overtones. That of Argüelles is a **Zen** compilation on a Mayan base. All, however, entertain the notion of damnation—one that is eternal according to CUT, *The Keys of Enoch* and the *Urantia Book*. It is chiefly in the Faithists' *Oahspe* and for the Aetherius Society that there is no ultimate annihilation, that finally all souls are believed to become cleansed and that there will be no hell of everlasting punishment. Basically in Galactian mystic theology, the purpose of existence is the continual progression of the human soul toward perfection.

Consequently, Galactian mysticism and theology are to be seen as a loose mix of related but highly varied scientist and cosmological concepts that constitute a particularly popular current of thought within the New Age movements. Galactianism is gnostic inasmuch as it desires release from physical confines, but it occupies a middle ground between **Neo-pagan** affirmation of the tangible and the non-dual gnostic emptiness of a thinker like **Ken Wilber**. The non-supernatural and non-gnostic forms of galactianism are best understood as **astral** religions.

GASKIN, STEPHEN. *See* THE FARM.

GAWAIN, SHAKTI (Lili Fournier). A leading author of the self-help, growth and consciousness movements. Gawain offers assistance to people who wish to access their own intuition and inspiration. Individuals are encouraged to find and develop their inner guide for ongoing intuitive guidance. Questioning any traditional New Age transcendental spiritual path, Gawain teaches people to work with and augment all four levels of human existence: the physical, emotional, mental and spiritual—not just the spiritual alone. She also advocates working with our disowned energies or inner shadow self. But at the same time, Gawain stresses that true prosperity is not monetary gain but something that operates within the heart and soul. Through books, tapes and workshops on guided **meditations**, she teaches the use of contemplative reflection and exercise for **healing** purposes. Students are taught to master creative **visualization** through daily affirmations. In Gawain's vision of the future world, ancient wisdom is combined with modern technology for a naturally balanced life. Among her several publications, there are *Creative Visualization* (1978, 1985), *Living in the Light* (1986, 1998), *The Path of Transformation: How Healing Ourselves Can Change the World* (1993) and *Creating True Prosperity* (1997).

GESTALT. *See* PERLS, FRITZ.

GNOSTICISM. Various pre-Christian **pagan**, Jewish and early **Christian** sects that stressed the value of revealed divine knowledge (*gnosis*) as the vehicle for attainment of spiritual redemption. Among Greek philosophy and Hellenic mystery cults, the Orphic cults are the exemplary instances of gnostic perception. The belief system itself probably derives from Babylonian and Egyptian mytho-religion. Christian gnostics became particularly active in the second century C.E., and much of the doctrines of **Christianity** were formulated in reaction against the understandings of the gnostics. Revivals of gnosticism have occurred since the time of the Alexandrian conquests of the fourth century B.C.E. into the twelfth and thirteenth centuries C.E. with the ascent of the Albigenses, or Cathars, in Languedoc. One of gnosticism's fullest expressions was established by the Persian prophet Mani who lived in the third century C.E. Similar to Manichaeanism is the Islamic gnostic sect of the Mandeans, who originated in Jordan and still exist in Iran and Iraq.

Gnosticism is a dualistic orientation that identifies the spiritual as the good and contrasts it with matter as evil. It embraces the *soma sema* concept of the body being a tomb. Accordingly, the cosmos has become a vast prison that is subject to the rule of the Demiurge and his seven archons. These have enslaved the human spirit and prevent the divine spark of the human soul from returning to God despite the body's death. Because true knowledge of God is obscure or hidden, salvation is possible only through mystical revelation or *gnosis*. This last may be brought to humanity through the efforts of a savior or special prophet, but it may also be obtained by an individual through **meditation**, the practice of various austerities or other techniques.

In spite of being denounced virtually from the inception of the Christian Church with adherents being persecuted and executed as heretics well into the Middle Ages, influences of gnosticism are to be seen in **Freemasonry** and **Rosicrucianism** (from whence it influenced **Rudolph Steiner**) and in the alchemical efforts of C. G. Jung. As a generic adjective, "gnostic" refers to the transcendental religions that view life as a "fall" and matter as ultimately either illusory or valueless. In contrast to **pagan** religiosity that views life and evolution as an open-ended cyclic process that originates in the matrix of the physical, the gnostic orientation seeks to "escape" the tangible and "return" to some original source or preexistent state. In paganism, consciousness is an emergent; in gnosticism, it is an *a priori* reality. From this perspective, and despite the ecclesiastical condemnations, much of the official dogmas of Christianity and the other Abrahamic faiths as well as of

Buddhism and Vedantic **Hinduism** are gnostic. Vernacular practice, on the other hand, even in the world's major religions, is often pagan, this-worldly rather than otherworldly, and focusing on welfare, health, success and practical concerns rather than spiritual salvation. *See also* ASTRAL.

GOLDEN DAWN. Properly, the Hermetic Order of the Golden Dawn, a pseudo-Masonic and quasi-**Rosicrucian** secret society founded in 1887/1888 by William Wynn Westcott (1848-1925) and Samuel Liddell MacGregor Mathers (1854-1918). The group was popular during the 1890s and attracted such luminaries as W. B. Yeats, Bram Stoker, A. E. Waite, Florence Farr, Arthur Machen, Algernon Blackwood and, in 1898, Aleister Crowley (1875-1947). It was the first to gather together a complete magical system which it formulated as a sort of Western **yoga** aiming to develop human consciousness and obtain mystical experience. As an occult society, the Golden Dawn competed with the Esoteric Section of the **Theosophical Society** from whom it adopted **Blavatsky**'s **Great White Brotherhood**—renaming her guiding Hidden Masters as the Secret Chiefs. While both Blavatsky and Mathers allowed that these wisdom entities incarnated on the physical plane, it was the former Golden Dawn initiate, Dion Fortune, who, after the decline of the Hermetic Order and the founding of her own organization, the Society of the Inner Light, claimed that the Inner Plane Adepti or Hidden Masters had their natural locus in the **astral** plane. Consequently, while branches of the Golden Dawn exist today in the United States and New Zealand, it has disappeared as a formal organization in Great Britain, the land of its birth. Nevertheless, it played an important historic role not only in the dissemination of esoteric teachings concerning psychic development and astral projection but also in the development of the characteristic New Age phenomenon of **channeling**. It was Fortune, however, who shifted from **spiritualist** trance mediumship to what is now the more prevalent form of psychic mediation. The Golden Dawn based its own rituals and initiatory stages on the Tree of Life of the Jewish **Kabala** along with an overlay of Christian, Egyptian and some Eastern elements. *See also* FREEMASONRY.

GRAY, SPAULDING. American writer, actor, performer and monologist. Spaulding has created eighteen different monologues that include *Monster in a Box* and *Swimming to Cambodia,* for which he won an Obie Award. He performs in the United States, Europe and Australia and, because of his challenging ideas, was cited by **Marilyn Ferguson**

as an Aquarian conspirator. In 1977, he founded the Wooster Group, an experimental media and theater ensemble that is based in New York. Beside writing and performing his autobiographical trilogy, *Three Places in Rhode Island*, Gray has published a novel, *Impossible Vacation* (1993), and *Gray's Anatomy* (1994).

GREAT INVOCATION, THE. One of **Alice Bailey**'s chief contributions to the New Age movement:

> From the point of Light within the Mind of God
> Let light stream forth into the minds of men.
> Let Light descend on Earth.
>
> From the point of Love within the heart of God
> Let love stream forth into the hearts of men.
> May Christ return to Earth.
>
> From the centre where the Will of God is known
> Let purpose guide the little wills of men –
> The purpose which the Masters know and serve.
>
> From the centre which we call the race of men
> Let the Plan of Love and Light work out.
> And may it seal the door where evil dwells.
> Let Light and Love and Power restore the Plan on Earth.

This prayer is not only used by Bailey's Arcane School but often appears in many other New Age venues—particularly theosophical but others as well. Through use of the Great Invocation, the individual intends to visualize the power of the cosmic hierarchy as it funnels down to earth. *See also* DIVINE HIERARCHY.

GREAT WHITE BROTHERHOOD, THE. Not a racial designation but a **theosophical** reference to the "brightness of enlightenment or wisdom." The Ascended Masters are those who have learned the lessons of earthly life and have no need for further incarnation. But rather than securing a final cosmic extinction or nivanic oblivion, such masters chose instead to pass their wisdom on to those still caught in the cycles of transmigration. Their concern is to assist and help those yet living on earth. In this sense, the Ascended Masters are a version of the

Bodhisattvas who have denied the possibility of Buddhahood until everyone on earth has achieved enlightenment and release as well.

The present bearers of the Ancient Wisdom lineage hail from remote regions of Tibet, Egypt or Arabia. Sometimes they have returned to civilization in order to help humanity and assist in spiritual development. In the understanding of the Great White Brotherhood, these beings may be thought of as living on the earth (frequently in the Himalayas) or as non-corporeal beings who on special occasions appear in human bodies. These masters are believed to speak in cognitive language that masks hidden (occult) knowledge. It is the higher self alone that is able to apprehend the master's wisdom. *See also* **Seven Rays**. For the fullest elaboration of the Ascended Masters of the Great White Brotherhood, see the CHURCH UNIVERSAL AND TRIUMPHANT. More is to be found under BENJAMIN CREME. *See also* REINCARNATION.

GROF, STANISLAV (1931-). A founder and chief theoretician of **transpersonal psychology**. Czech-born, Grof received his M.D. from Charles University, Prague, in 1956 and his Ph.D. in medicine from the Czechoslovakian Academy of Sciences in 1965. He emigrated to the United States in 1967 and became active in the origin of the **Esalen Institute** from 1973. Between 1978 and 1982, he served as president of the International Transpersonal Association.

Grof conducts research on the therapeutic and heuristic aspects of non-ordinary consciousness as well as in the use of psychedelics and non-drug techniques in experiential psychotherapy. A lecturer and facilitator of workshops, Grof is now best known for his work in **holotropic breathwork**. Among the numerous books he has written, co-authored or edited, there are *Realms of the Human Consciousness* (1976), *The Human Encounter with Death* (1977), *LSD Psychotherapy* (1980), *Ancient Wisdom and Modern Science* (1984), *Beyond the Brain: Birth, Death, and Transcendence in Psychotherapy* (1985), *The Adventure of Self-Discovery* (1987), *Human Survival and Conscious Evolution* (1988), *The Holotropic Mind* (1992), *Books of the Dead: Manuals for Living and Dying* (1994), *The Cosmic Game* (1997) and *Psychology of the Future* (2000).

GURDJIEFF, GEORGE IVANOVITCH. (*c.* 1870-1949). Greek-Armenian mystic teacher who has been influential on several New Age movements. Espousing a radical form of **gnosticism**, Gurdjieff was the first to promote the western esoteric notion that "consciousness" is the object of spiritual endeavor. He considered that the normal conscious state is essentially a hypnotic trance from which the enlightened person needs to awaken, and he identified this condition of hypnosis as the result of the **kundalini** of imagination. In the Gurdjieffian perspective, the human being is basically a machine, and the purpose of life is to awake to our non-mechanical essence or soul. This last, however, is an *opus contra naturam* and a process in which the soul is not a given but something that is "made" by the individual. Students of Gurdjieff refer to the awakening undertaking or mindfulness that leads to enlightenment as the Work or Fourth Way—one which begins through rigorously recording personal thoughts, emotions and behavior objectively and continues with the practice of various spiritual exercises.

According to Gurdjieff's student Pyotr Demainovitch Ouspensky, "man is a plurality" of constantly changing thinking, emotional, perceiving, desiring egos. No one "I" is any more authentic than the next. The sense of being a unified being is instead a fictional delusion. Nevertheless, through the awakening process of the Work, a person can free himself/herself from automatic and socially dictated behavior and come to direct the machine that he or she is. The general thrust of Gurdjieff's teachings have strongly influenced the **human potential movement, Esalen,** and such movements as *est* and L. Ron Hubbard's **Scientology**. The emphasis of spiritual development is to be able to take full responsibility for our individual and personal actions. There is also a decided stress placed on developing awareness of the presence of the body—in keeping with the **Sufi** goal of making a person whole.

Gurdjieff's principal research center was the Institute for the Harmonious Development of Man at Fontainebleau, outside Paris, that operated between 1922 and 1934. A central activity of the Gurdjieffian institutes was the study and practice of the master's choreographed dances—originally designated "Sacred Gymnastics" and now known as "Movements." Following in the Sufi tradition, Gurdjieff stressed throughout his teachings that the process of students' dispassionate self-observation required strict supervision by an already awakened master. The permanent disciple-teacher relationship is integral to the Work, and the overall practice remains an oral tradition despite the publication of writings by both Gurdjieff (*Beelzebub's Tales to His Grandson* and *Meetings with Remarkable Men*) and Ouspensky (*In Search of the Miraculous* and *Tertium Organum*). Nevertheless, rather than contemplative withdrawal, practitioners are instructed to remain pragmatically engaged with ordinary life and to live as fully as possible in the present moment. The only things of importance are ideas, music and sacred gymnastic movement for the development of inner faculties. Gurdjieff's teachings concerning the **enneagram** as a universal symbol dating to 1916/1917 have become incorporated into several New Age movments—especially through the work of **Oscar Ichazo** and **Claudio Naranjo**.

GURU. Popular New Age term for "spiritual teacher"—imported from **Hinduism**. If a composite of Sanskrit *gu* "darkness" and *ru* "light," the designation parallels the western *educator* as "one who leads out [from ignorance or darkness]." The guru is a significant leader across the New Age spectrum and indicates the formative Hindu influences on the movement as a whole. Sometimes the guru operates through the **magic** of *siddha* (*see* **tantra**; *see also* **Swami Muktananda, Sai Baba**), but more often through providing an exemplary model for disciples to emulate. Because of the often mesmeric powers or hypnotic charisma of the guru, and perceived or actual abuses engendered through authoritarian control over acolytes, the term "guru" has acquired negative connotations for many in the West. The *bhakti* tradition that stresses total devotion and even veneration of one's guru has on occasions exacerbated this acquisition.

Nevertheless, in the context of Hindu origins, the guru is an inspirational teacher who works with the student on a one-to-one basis and almost invariably seeks to aid and encourage the disciple in renouncing worldly tendencies to obtain a **gnostic** state of transcendental awareness. In **Hinduism**, Sikhism and **Buddhism**, the guru is accepted by a master in an established lineage tradition. In the wider New Age market, however, gurus are frequently self-appointed. The most noteworthy of these is probably **Osho/Rajneesh**. New Age also uses the term for such world-teachers as the Buddha, Jesus Christ and Mohammed, among others.

-H-

HARNER, MICHAEL. Former teacher at **Esalen** (Big Sur) and the California Institute of Integral Studies (San Francisco) and, along with **Carlos Castaneda**, one who has done much to promote New Age or Neo-**shamanism** as a popular western spiritual pursuit. He directs the Foundation for Shamanic Studies. While Harner originally did some solid anthropological ethnographic work in South America, his subsequent construct of the concept of "core shamanism" is a creative and imaginative work. What occurs in a Harner workshop, in which he replaces shamanic journeying with guided imagery, will not be found in any single indigenous tribe. Moreover, **dream-work** itself is largely absent in Harner's development of core-shamanism that follows in the wake of Mircea Eliade's "construction" of shamanism and Castaneda's incorporation of a great deal of fantasy in his works. Among the salient features of Neo-shamanism is its orientation toward personal and spiritual empowerment for its practitioners. As a Neo-colonial intrusion, it is seen to be a "fake" practice from the Native American perspective, but with its emphasis on the "imaginal" (as opposed both to the imaginary and to Carl Jung's archetypal), the power and process of imagining becomes a way to develop intuitive and spiritual insight without appropriating from indigenous cultures. Harner's seminal work is his 1980 *The Way of the Shaman.*

HAY, LOUISE (1930-). Successful and influential New Age writer on illness. She contends that "all disease comes from a state of unforgiveness" and that the person most difficult to forgive is oneself. Following in the tradition of *A Course in Miracles*, Hay believes that we create the bodily illnesses from which we suffer. Since we create our own truths, when we create negative truths, we are in effect creating an imbalance in the physical/emotional body. But through the process of positive affirmation, we can reprogram the mind and thereby heal ourselves. The controversy over Hay's method lies in its extreme simplicity and unreal expectations. Her method is in fact judgmental in allowing disease to occur in abnormal and unnatural contexts from which the individual must extricate himself/herself. Despite the successful influence that imagery and **visualization** can have on the body and its immune system, it may not always be so easy to take control of one's own mind. Among Hay's more popular works is her 1988 *You Can Heal Your Life*. *See also* HEALING.

HEALING. A central preoccupation for much of the New Age in its search for holistic approaches that combine body, mind and spirit. The extraordinary medical advances in the first half of the twentieth century (antibiotics, vaccines, miracle drugs, anesthetics and complex surgical procedures) produced the expectation that health and well-being are the norm, but with the subsequent diminishment in medicine's dramatic successes and the various side effects and other unpleasant aspects of conventional treatment becoming apparent, the west's **New Thought** heritage was reactivated and rebolstered with the influx of eastern ideas that began in the 1960s. While New Age often insists that "we are a spirit having a physical experience," there is an apparent contradiction in its extreme concern with illness and fear of death. Through its **human potential** origins, New Age appears obsessed with pain and suffering.

A common theme found in such popular New Age writers or healers as **Louise Hay, Caroline Myss, Deepak Chopra, Bernie Siegel** and **Stephen Levine** is the power of the mind. Illness is no longer understood as purely physical or accidental but the result of imbalance in the individual's complex system of energy expression. Healing is believed to begin through holistic perception and a basic "change of mind." New Age's central teaching is for the individual to take responsibility for his or her condition.

While acknowledging that the mind can indeed affect the physical condition, a major criticism leveled against New Age is its tendency to convert complex ideas into simple programs. Overgeneralizations are often couched in pseudo-scientific language. New Age believers are expected to develop an omnipotent ability to control their universe. Much of this paradigm of thought and expectation derives from the immensely popular *A Course in Miracles*, which claims that illness is essentially a mistaken way of being. The *Course* advocates a shift from fear, the source of all illness, to love. This shift depends on forgiveness, and this in turn requires development of the realization that all sin is an illusion. In general, the *Course* and other forms of New Age healing affirm an underlying principle of self-empowerment. *See also* ACUPUNCTURE, ALEXANDER TECHNIQUE, ALTERNATIVE MEDICINE, LYNN ANDREWS, ARICA, AROMATHERAPY, AURA-

SOMA, WILLIAM BLOOM, EDGAR CAYCE, TERRY COLE-
WHITTAKER, WAYNE DYER, MARY BAKER EDDY, WARREN
FELT EVANS, FELDENKRAIS, SHAKTI GAWAIN, GESTALT
THERAPY, STANISLAV GROF, HOLOTROPIC BREATHWORK,
HOMEOPATHY, EMMA CURTIS HOPKINS, BARBARA MARKS
HUBBARD, IRIDOLOGY, GERALD JAMPOLSKY, KINESIOL-
OGY, KIRLIAN PHOTOGRAPHY, ELIZABETH KÜBLER-ROSS,
DENISE LINN, ABRAHAM MASLOW, MASSAGE THERAPY,
MEDICINE WHEEL, FRANZ ANTON MESMER, MIND DYNAM-
ICS, NATUROPATHY, LEONARD ORR, FRITZ PERLS, PSYCHO-
SYNTHESIS,   QIGONG,   REBIRTHING,   REFLEXOLOGY,
WILHELM REICH, REIKI, JOHN ROBBINS, ROLFING, VIRGINIA
SATIR, SHAMANISM, SHIATSU, BERNARD SIEGEL, SILVA
MIND CONTROL, SUBUD, THERAPY, VISUALIZATION, AN-
DREW WEIL, MARIANNE WILLIAMSON.

HERMETIC ORDER OF THE GOLDEN DAWN. *See* GOLDEN
DAWN.

HINDUISM. A label applied by western academics to the indigenous,
Dharmic practices of the Indian subcontinent. The term expresses a
theological body of thought that has grown from the originally pagan
spirituality of the Vedic peoples, possibly incorporating pre-Aryan religious notions and deities, and taking codified form through the specula-
tions of the late portions of the *Rigveda*, the *Atharvaveda*, the *Brahma-
nas* and *Upanishads*, and the *Mahabharata* (including the *Bhagavad
Gita*) and the *Ramayana*. The more popular forms of Hinduism are
rooted in the *Puranas* or "Ancient Tales"—largely sectarian texts that
are devoted to a particular deity.

Hinduism possesses countless gods and goddesses—many of
whom are known only regionally or locally. The more ubiquitous figures are the preserver Vishnu with his various incarnations—Rama and
Krishna being the most revered, the destroyer Shiva, the feminine
power Devi in numerous manifestations (principally Shiva's wife
Durga, Parvati, Kali, Vishnu's consort Lakshmi and the spouse of
Brahma, Sarasvati), Shiva's elephant-headed son Ganesha and the
monkey-god Hanuman. Devotees of the sun-god, Surya, though few in
relative numbers, represent another long-established sectarian expression that appears across India.

Along with the creator Brahma, Vishnu and Shiva form a trinity (*trimurti*) of supreme figures. Brahma receives little or no devotion. The gods (*devas, devatas*), however, though often worshipped for this-worldly favors and as vehicles for the expression of devotion (*bhakti*), are, along with the apparent world itself, illusions (*maya*), and the Hindu's transcendental goal is to achieve liberation (*moksha, samadhi*) through union with the Ultimate Reality (*Brahman*) or identification of the true self (*Atman*) with the Absolute. To this end, the various techniques of **meditation** and **yoga** are employed toward realizing enlightenment, fulfillment and release. Hinduism, despite its sectarian divisions, is in general a tolerant and all-encompassing spirituality. Nevertheless, its ultimately world-denying philosophy—expressed best perhaps in its underlying Advaita Vedanta monistic theology—represents an eastern form of **gnosticism**.

Through both its numbers of adherents and the Indian diaspora, Hinduism is one of the world's major religions. With the rescinding of the Asian exclusion laws in the United States in 1965 and henceforth the putting of eastern immigration quotas on par with that of other nations, the increased availability of Hindu (as well as other spiritual) teachers became a seminal factor in the emergence of religious seeker-ship options that has largely coalesced as the New Age movement. Hinduism has become a major influence in the development of New Age belief and practice. Through such figures as the **Maharishi Mahesh Yogi, Guru Maharaj Ji, Osho/Rajneesh, Paramahansa Yogananda, Ramana Maharshi, Sai Baba** and, eventually, people like **Baba Ram Das, Deepak Chopra, Mother Meera,** and **Adi Da Samraj,** among others, Hindu teachings reformulated chiefly for a western audience have built upon the earlier transcendentalism of **Ralph Waldo Emerson** and **theosophy** of **Helena Blavatsky** and **Alice Bailey.** *See also* EASTERN MYSTICISM.

HINKINS, JOHN-ROGER. *See* MSIA.

HOLOTROPIC BREATHWORK. A program developed by transpersonal trainer **Stanislav Grof** for experiencing breathwork and the transpersonal perspective. Holotropic ("moving toward wholeness") breathwork researches consciousness through depth and transpersonal psychology as well as anthropology, Eastern spiritual practices and the mystical traditions of the world. The process on which the program is centered involves accelerated breathing along to evocative music in a special set and setting. Its purpose is to enter a non-ordinary state of consciousness and to activate the natural inner **healing** process. It is usually conducted in groups in which people work as pairs alternating between the roles of experiencer and "sitter."

HOLY ORDER OF MANS (HOOM). Incorporated in California in 1968 as a "New Age School of Christian Initiation" by Earl W. Blighton (1904-1974). Drawing from his interests in **Freemasonry, Spiritualism, Roscrucianism** and the Subramuniya **Yoga** Order, Blighton combined traditional **Christian** monasticism with **New Thought**, esotericism, **millennialism** and **tantric** ideas and practices into his "Science of Man." He argued that humanity was entering a New Age of spiritual enlightenment that required initiation rites. The priests of the Order were trained to provide these. With its headquarters in San Francisco, men and women took traditional monastic vows similar to those of Roman Catholic orders: pledges of poverty, obedience, purity, humility and service. They observed regular periods of prayer and fasting, wore clerical clothing and engaged in collective ownership. Mission stations and training centers were established in over 60 cities by the early 1970s—with membership peaking in 1977 at approximately 3,000. Along with its New Age belief in the universality of the spiritual path and the incorporation of eclectic practices, it also stressed the ordination of women priests. Lay people who wished to remain financially separate were encouraged from the early 1970s to become part of the Order's coeducational membership and organize local "Christian Communities" that the order priests headed. Celibate suborders were also established. At this stage, personal experience of the sacred was the foundation of authority, and the group was non-dogmatic. Emphasis was on the spiritually ecstatic and charismatic, individual exegesis and innovation. Following Blighton's death as well as the 1978 mass suicide of the People's Temple in Jonestown, Guyana, Blighton's successor, Andrew Rossi, began to shift the group's focus from missionary work to that of localized Christian spiritual communities that emphasized traditional values. The Holy Order of MANS (HOOM) is interesting because of its eventual transformation from a New Age community into an Eastern Orthodox Christian institution. HOOM was disbanded in 1986.

HOMEOPATHY. A holistic method of **healing** based on low potency use of "mother tincture" remedies and first developed by German physician Samuel Hahnemann (1755-1843). In contrast to allopathic medicine, homeopathy approaches body organs and systems as interacting parts of a whole and thereby treats the complete organism rather than simply the infected part. Remedies are developed through succussion of minute doses of an original substance based on "the law of similars." In Great Britain, the Cooper School of Robert Thomas Cooper (1844-1903) has been instrumental in the wider acceptance of homeopathic treatment.

HOPKINS, EMMA CURTIS (1853-1925). Original student of **Mary Baker Eddy**, who subsequently broke with her in 1885. Hopkins then began her own organized movement based on Christian science. She attracted and ordained mostly women. In fact, Hopkins emphasized what she referred to as the key position of women in God's activity in history. She employed the historization of the Trinity first proposed by **Joachim de Fiore** (1145-1202), in which God the Father corresponds to the ancient patriarchal ideal, God the Son conforms to the birth of Jesus the Nazarene and the time for the masses to be freed from oppression, and God the Holy Spirit coincides with the third period, that of the Truth-Principle or Mother-Principle. Hopkins maintained that the Age of the Spirit is the time for the rise of women. Through her students, the **New Thought** Alliance eventually developed.

HOROSCOPE. *See* ASTROLOGY.

HORWITZ, JONATHAN. Neo-shaman practitioner involved with ritual and psychotherapeutic recovery of soul-loss. Studying and working with **shamanism** since 1972, Horwitz was a staff member of the United States-based Foundation for Shamanic Studies. With an M.A. in anthropology, he co-founded the Scandinavian Center for Shamanic Studies in 1986. The Center's activities include the practice, teaching and research into shamanism as well as grassroots shamanic networking. Unlike traditional forms of shamanism that attempt to combat and conquer disease spirits, Horwitz advocates treating the negative with respect and love. In this, he shares a "New Age" shamanism theodicy that denies intrinsic reality to evil. He also rejects the indigenous notion of the shaman as a singular and specialized calling and sees instead that shamanic work is something available to everyone—providing the possibility to contact the powers of the universe directly. Through Horwitz's shamanism with its similarities to the teachings of both **Carlos Castaneda** and **Michael Harner**, anyone can receive universal power and wisdom without the need of a middleman. But Horwitz also stresses the necessity to employ the power of the universe as something "on loan" and for the betterment of the planet. For him, the challenge for the new generation of shamans is to "network nature" and reestablish contact between human beings and other inhabitants of the earth. In particular, the contemporary shaman's priority is to stop the slaughter of the environment, to rectify the damage already done, and to trust that the planet will nourish us both physically and spiritually.

HUBBARD, BARBARA MARX (1931-). Educator, futurist, 1984 U.S. vice presidential nominee and New Age prophetess. Influenced by **Abraham Maslow**, **Teilhard de Chardin** and **Buckminster Fuller**, Hubbard stresses human responsibility for the evolutionary process on planet earth. She understands evolution as an organic process of evolving consciously and argues that emotional maturity is dependent on the fusion of feminine and masculine consciousness. In 1994, she proclaimed that "**New Thought** is now or will become in the next thirty or fifty years the most important single movement on earth." Hubbard speaks of the coming birth of humankind as one body, recognizes "cultural creators" as people who are changing their values toward a more planetary and global culture, and sees the new type of human that she calls the *Homo universalis* or *Homo noetica*, as prefigured in the great saints, seers and mystics of human history.

In 1982, Hubbard published *The Evolutionary Journey: A Personal Guide to a Positive Future*. This was followed in 1989 by *The Hunger of Eve: One Woman's Odyssey Toward the Future*. Some of her other books include *The Revelation: Our Crisis Is a Birth (The Book of Co-Creation)* (1993), *The Revelation: A Message of Hope for the New Millennium* (1995), *Conscious Evolution* (1998) and *Emergence: The Shift from Ego to Essence* (2001). Hubbard is the founder of both the World Future Society and the Society for the Universal Human. She now serves as the president for the Foundation for Conscious Evolution in Santa Barbara.

HUMAN POTENTIAL MOVEMENT. A loose congeries of "technical" approaches to empirical-experiential immediacy found in individual practices as well as various religio-therapeutic movements (e.g., **gestalt**, encounter, **Scientology**/dianetics, *est*, **Zen**, aikido, transactional analysis, **reiki**, transcendental meditation). While drawing on the ideas of William James, Aldous Huxley and Alan Watts, human potential coalesced around the works of **Abraham Maslow**, Roberto Assagioli and **Fritz Perls** in the 1960s. Its central venue became the **Esalen Institute** at Big Sur, California. Human potential embraces the concerns of self-growth, self-help, self-focus and self-development—recognizing the spark of divinity within each individual and, hence, the potential for unlimited personal improvement. The chief criticisms leveled against Human Potential are those of narcissism (deification of the isolated self), self-indulgence, anti-rationalism and pseudo-mysticism. The movement retorts with the claim that experience of self encourages service to others. Human Potential groups are essentially developments or extensions of various meditative techniques ranging from concentration, mantra recitation, contemplation, devotion, **visualization**, body movement, mindfulness, **meditation** in action, and meditation without form. These techniques are recognized as legitimate means toward legitimate ends. They become helpful tools toward business success, economic management, political achievement, military effectiveness and increased satisfaction in general. In many respects, the contemporary New Age movement is to be seen as the spiritualization of the earlier human potential movement.

-I-

"I AM" RELIGIOUS ACTIVITY. A movement founded by Guy
(1878-1939) and Edna (1886-1971) Ballard following in the theosophical tradition of discarnate spirits, spirit guides, devas and angels.
Though the "I AM" Religious Activity does not explicitly identify itself
with or as New Age, it continues the **theosophical** essentials which
have been hallmarks of much of the movement. In short, the Ballards
fully endorse the iconographic symbolism of theosophy.

In 1929/1930, Guy Ballard visited Mt. Shasta in California—
reputedly the home of mystical adepts from **Atlantis** who lived inside
the mountain. While there, Ballard claims to have encountered the
eighteenth-century occultist, Comte de Saint Germain, who had since
become an Ascended Master, the Lord of the Seventh Ray (*see* **Seven
Rays**). Saint Germain designated Ballard, his wife Edna and their son
Donald as the only Accredited Messengers of the Ascended Masters,
and he bequeathed to them the Instruction of the Great Law of Life.
Their task became that of initiating on Earth the Seventh Golden Age—
the permanent "I AM" Age of Eternal Perfection. In 1932, the Ballards
formed the Saint Germain Foundation as the corporate expression of
the "I AM" Ascended Master Religious Activity.

According to "I AM" Activity, the purpose of individual life is to
develop contact with the Ascended Masters of the **Great White Brotherhood** and cooperate with their work. Endeavors release the "I AM"
power within each of us so that it can be used toward the elimination of
evil in the world and the promotion of freedom and justice to replace all
evil. The One God, omnipresent, omniscient and omnipotent, rules all
creation and constitutes the Life of the Universe. The dominant form of
divine reality is that of light. The source of God's power and authority
is the Great Central Sun that emanates as the "Mighty I AM Presence."
Each individual begins as a spark from this divine flame. In other
words, through the individualized "I AM Presence," God becomes the
Presence and Master within each person, namely, the Christ Self. God
is likewise individualized within each member of the Ascended Masters
of love, light and perfection. By attuning themselves to the "I AM Presence," the Masters have overcome the need for further physical incarnation and ascended into light. Master Jesus is one of these who, through
his ministry and ascension, released the Christ Light, the "Mighty I AM
Presence," for the earth's movement into the Light of Divine Love.

Consequently, along with a portrait of Saint Germain, every "I AM" sanctuary is adorned with a picture of Jesus.

The Ascended Masters are conceived of as each radiating the light of a particular color. In "I AM" teachings, the individual human is understood as surrounded by a column of purple flame. "I AM's" iconography depicts the enveloping purple light as connected via a shaft of white light to the "I AM" Presence. This last is shown as a person clothed in golden light and surrounded by a circular rainbow of light indicating the accumulated good of previous lives. This fusion of theosophical ideas with color symbolism has become integrated into the New Age worldview with its emphasis on light and color. In the "I AM" context, the colors of black (symbolizing hate, death and destruction) and red (indicating anger, irritation and impurity) are avoided.

For the followers of the Ballards' teachings, the "I AM Presence" is invoked by a series of affirmations (declarations affirming the individual's attunement to God and the consequent blessings therefrom) and commands called decrees (fiats spoken on behalf of the higher self). The repetitive use of decrees becomes a central activity and is the tool for calling upon the "I AM Presence" and activating the violet flame around each person as the means to purify from undesirable personal conditions. Negative decrees are also employed toward annihilation of discord and imperfection, but these may not be directed against individuals. Along with the use of decrees and affirmations, "I AM" members also resort to quiet contemplation.

One of the criticisms of the Ballards' teachings is that the combination of the "I AM" with the use of decrees had been earlier taught by Annie Rix Militz, a popular metaphysician of Los Angles. Other commentators have remarked on the similarity of the Ballards' understanding of the Ascended Masters and the separate teachings of Will Garver and Baird Spaulding. What is clear at least is that there has been much fluidity and exchange between **theosophy**, "I AM" and such groups as the Summit Lighthouse/**Church Universal and Triumphant** as well as the broader range of New Age movements. And while the I AM Religious Activity does not overtly identify as New Age, many of its teachings and practices have been incorporated into the wider movement.

ICHAZO, OSCAR (1931-). Bolivian-born student of **Zen, sufism, yoga, Buddhism**, Confucianism, **I Ching** and the **Kabala** who developed **Arica**—a nine-level hierarchy of training programs that seeks the human individual's total development. Ichazo became involved in the early 1950s with a Buenos Aires "mystery school." In 1970, he conducted a nine-month training course in Arica, Chile. The Arica Institute was incorporated in New York the following year. In 1992, Arica lost a copyright infringement case against Helen Palmer.

Using the **enneagram**, Ichazo's practice focuses on imbalances or "fixations" that he describes as personality shaping accumulations of life experiences that have formed during childhood. He developed a set of twenty-three breathing and movement exercises called psychocalisthenics or kinerhythm that are designed to awaken the vital energy during **meditation**. The School of T'ai Chi Chuan was founded in 1976 by Patrick Watson (1935-1992), a student of both Ichazo and Grand Master Cheng Man-Ch'ing (1901-1975).

I CHING. The Chinese "Book of Changes" dating to 2498-1150 B.C.E. and consisting of perhaps the world's oldest surviving fortune-telling system, that of the Tortoise-Shell Oracle. The *I Ching* consists of sixty-four hexagrams with brief statements explicating their meaning along with additional commentary including annotations made later by Confucius. The hexagrams are composed of broken (*yin*) and unbroken (*yang*) lines forming trigrams and supposedly representing stylized forms of the cracks which would appear in a tortoise shell as it was heated. It was these cracks as well as the subsequent lines determined by the casting of lots or coins that were interpreted in response to specific questions. As an ancient system of divination, the *I Ching* has become popular within Western metaphysical and New Age circles. While purporting to divine answers concerning personal, family, business and social problems, the *I Ching* nevertheless is itself a profoundly philosophical collection of thought.

IRIDOLOGY or iris diagnosis. A system of analysis developed by Hungarian physician Ignatz von Peczely in the nineteenth century that diagnoses disease and a person's state of health by interpreting the color, texture and location of various pigment flecks of the eye. The eyes are considered "windows of the soul." Iridology was revived in twentieth century America by Bernard Jensen (1908-2001). Particularly popular in France and Belgium, the iris is charted into various zones that are believed to correspond to all areas of the body. The art and/or science divides people into personality types (jewel, flower, stream and shaker) as well as inner- or outer-directed and left-brain or right-brain developed. When subjected to scientific testing, iridology has tended not to fare convincingly. Perhaps for this reason, there is also a shift toward psychotherapeutic application and rapid eye technology. The Rayid Model employs a flickering strand of light coming from a central point (for example, the flickering movement of a hand-held white wand by the iridologist or rapid eye technician) in order to reveal deeper levels of mind using patterns through the eyes in response to a series of questions. This methodology aims to reveal the essential core of one's personality and the balance between the person's mental, emotional, physical and spiritual components.

Books on iridology include Jensen's *Science and Practice of Iridology* (1952) and *Iridology Simplified* (1980), Jim Jenks' *Basic Iridology* (1988), Ladean Griffin's *The Essentials of Iridology* (1988), *Visions of Health: Understanding Iridology* (1992) by Bernard Jensen with Donald V. Bodeen and Donald R. Bamer's *Practical Iridology and Sclerology* (1996).

-J-

JAMPOLSKY, GERALD G. (1925-). Popular psychologist and child and adult psychiatrist working within a Christian New Age framework. A Stanford Medical School graduate, Jampolsky advocates the use of love and forgiveness on psychological, social and spiritual levels as a **healing** medicine. For him, people must learn to let go of fear and guilt both to find inner peace and to live in the moment. He calls love our natural state of being. Jampolsky lectures and consults on transformation in government, issues of health, education and business, the areas of psychology and psychiatry, and life transitions. His thinking may be described essentially as **New Thought**, and he has been strongly influenced by *A Course in Miracles*.

Jampolsky's original bestseller is *Love Is Letting Go of Fear* (1979). Among his fifteen books, there are also *Teach Only Love: The Seven Principles of Attitudinal Healing* (1983)—revised as *Teach Only Love: The Twelve Principles of Attitudinal Healing* (2000), *Good-Bye to Guilt* (1985), *Love Is the Answer: Creating Positive Relationships* (1990), *Change Your Mind, Change Your Life* (1994)—with his psychotherapist wife Diane Circincione, *Forgiveness: The Greatest Healer of All* (1999), and *Shortcuts to God: Finding Peace Quickly Through Practical Spirituality* (2000). Jampolsky is the founder of the Center for Attitudinal Healing in Tiburon, California. The Center, now with over 150 affiliates in twenty-eight countries, offers peace of mind and transformation training for children and adults facing life-threatening diseases. In 1982, he founded Children as Teachers of Peace and, in 1987 with his wife Dr. Cirincione, the AIDS Hotline for Kids.

-K-

KABALA (also Kabbala, Cabbala, Cabala, Qabala, etc.) The mystical strand of classical Judaism having roots in the Torah and believed to have been received by revelation to either Abraham or Moses, though Rabbinical tradition holds that the Kabala was first taught to Adam by the Archangel Gabriel. Being transmitted from father to son or from tutor to pupil, the Kabala was at first an oral tradition, but in the twelfth century Abraham ben Huya incorporated the cabalistic doctrine into the *Sefer Bahir*. The most famous codification of the Kabala appeared as the *Zohar* in the thirteenth century—probably the work of Moses of León. Cabalistic mysticism also appears heavily indebted to both **gnosticism** and Neo-platonism. The historical source of the Kabala itself is considered to be the *Sefer Yatsira*, a third to fifth century book that discusses cosmology and cosmogony and claims that the world was created through thirty-two secret "paths of wisdom"—the ten *sefirot* "ciphers, spheres" plus the twenty-two letters of the Hebrew alphabet. The visual glyph, model or representation of the *sefirot* and the paths between them is known as the Tree of Life. As the archetype by which creation is ordered, the cabalistic tree depicts the balancing pillar of Will, the dispensing pillar of Mercy, and the containing pillar of Severity. Each *sefira* is understood as an attribute of God. As the descending *sefirot* emanate from the crown *sefira* of Kether, British occultist Steve Wilson describes the Tree of Life as an upside-down growing tree.

The cabalistic tradition has taken different forms in different countries and at different times. Nevertheless, its basic approach for spiritual growth has remained consistent. The Kabalist attempts to reach the highest planes and ultimate union with the divine through contemplation on successive features of the Tree in conjunction with **visualization**, correspondence and use of subtle body energy. In many respects, there is a similarity here with the consciousness-raising techniques used in **Hindu yoga** or **Buddhist meditation** involving the body's **chakras** or energy centers. Cabalistic practice has played a significant role in **Christian** mysticism and especially within the western high or ceremonial **magical** tradition. Its identification of the *sefirot* with angelic forces who are invoked by the aspirant as **astral** teachers in seeking "re-union with godhead" betrays an underlying gnostic worldview and the concomitant recognition of a higher transcendental self that bridges the conscious and unconscious minds. The use of pathworking and creative visualization, the understanding of the divine spark within each individual, and the belief in spiritual evolution that are all characteristic of cabalistic thought have equally become hallmarks of New Age spirituality.

KARMA ("work," "action"). The consequences of one's actions within one existence that influence the character of the individual's succeeding existence. Karma refers to the spiritual law of cause and effect. From an eastern perspective, primal karma (*adi karma* or the pre-karmic state) consists of the action of creative force alone. This force allegedly brings souls to the material plane so that they may begin to acquire experience under their own initiative. In this way, an individual establishes the law of his/her own life. It comes to enjoy, suffer, reap rewards and pay penalties. The series of earth-lives are considered to become the occasions by which the individual soul stores up karma.

In **Hinduism**, karma signifies the law of nature that requires that every doer receive the exact result or reward of its actions. The equivalent of spiritual karma in physics is the law of compensation or the balance of equilibrium; in jurisprudence, it becomes the law of justice. In ethics, as in civil and criminal law, the basis of rewards and punishment is the decisive principle of right and wrong conduct. Correct or good actions create good karma; bad or wrong actions create bad or negative karma. The underlying principle holds that every act performed by anybody must be followed by its natural and legitimate result. Accordingly, Hinduism elaborates three kinds of karma: *Pralabdh* or "fate" karma, referring to that which has been earned through previous lives and upon which the present life is based; *Sinchit* or "reserve" karma which, unlike fate karma that must be paid off in the present life, is that which cannot be drawn upon through the will of the individual but is subject to the will of the "lord of karma"; and *Kriyaman* or "daily" karma whose payment of suffering or reward may occur at once or at least some other time in the present life or might be stored as *sinchit* karma to be drawn upon at some future lifetime according to the will of the "lord of karma."

In Galatians 6.7-10, St. Paul says, "Whatever a man soweth, that shall he reap. Make no mistake about this: God is not to be fooled; a man reaps what he sows." In Eastern thought and Eastern-influenced Western belief, the notion of karma is translated into the doctrine of **reincarnation**. In **gnosticism**, gnostic **Christianity**, **theosophy** and

New Age, karma is understood as what creates the circumstances of one's next incarnation. Above and beyond being a system of reward and punishment, karma is believed in eastern and New Age circles to be what "rounds out" one's experience. In the fulfillment of karma, the soul advances to "higher levels" of existence or even attains final release (*moksa, nirvana*) from the *dharma* of rebirth. From the spiritual perspective, karma does not equate with fate but with evolution. It is involved not only with actions and events but also with attitudes, thoughts, desires and ingrained habits. It operates on personal, group, racial, collective and cosmic levels.

KHAN, PIR VILAYAT INAYAT (1916-). **Sufi** exemplifier of the global consciousness of the emerging holistic age. Born in London, Khan graduated from the Sorbonne in 1940 with a degree in psychology. He studied with Sufi masters in India and became an acknowledged Pir in the lineage of the Chishti Sufi Order of India. Khan was also trained in Hindu, Buddhist, Judeo-Christian and Islamic traditions. He was named by his father (Hazrat Inayat Khan) in 1926 as his successor in the **Sufi Order** and the Confraternity of the Message.

Khan has directed the Sufi Order toward "awakening to the divinity within." He employs **meditation** techniques from various traditions and seeks to combine science, religion and holistic medicine. Khan endeavors to have people give up resentments and prejudices that individually hinder "our unfoldment toward becoming our highest ideal" and collectively cause wars. Some of Khan's published works are *Toward the One* (1974), *The Message in Our Time* (1978), *The Call of the Dervish* (1981), *Introducing Spirituality into Counseling and Therapy* (1982), *That Which Transpires Behind That Which Happens* (1994) and *Awakening: A Sufi Experience* (1999).

KINESIOLOGY. The "study of body movement" using gentle muscle testing. Kinesiology developed out of the Academy of Physical Education organized in Maine by Luther Halsey Gulick in 1904/1905 and, subsequently, with the founding in 1926 of the American Academy of Kinesiology and Physical Education in New York City. In essence, kinesiology derives from medicine, chiropractic, osteopathy, **acupuncture** and biochemistry. It is based on chiropractic procedures of manual manipulation of spine, extremities and cranial bones. As a non-invasive energetic **healing** science, it has become a popular **human potential**

technique that seeks to bypass the conscious mind in the determination of subconscious, bodily and etheric causes of energy blockages. The argument behind kinesiological therapies is that by deleting inappropriate reactions based on past experiences, the individual is allowed the freedom to create his/her own choices for positive change and balance. Being closely linked to acupuncture, the fundamental assumption of kinesiology is that the body possesses innate healing energy. This can be employed for purposes of reestablishing health, well-being and vitality.

Kinesiology is part of the natural health field comprising a method for identifying bodily stresses and structural, chemical and/or emotional imbalances in order to enable their correction through manual as well as non-manual therapy. It focuses on energy flows in the muscles, tissues and organs. Corrective measures include stimulation of the spinal-reflex, neuro-emotional, neuro-lymphatic and neuro-vascular systems as well as acu-points, meridian energy flow, emotional stress release, nutritional support, exercise and lifestyle improvements.

There are over fifty methods of muscle testing **biofeedback**—including applied, clinical, bio-, wellness, manual, transformational, **cybernetic** and health kinesiologies. Applied kinesiology is a 1960s body-work development of Detroit-based George Goodheart that combines Western and Eastern techniques—in particular, elements of Chinese medicine. It sees that disease is manifested structurally in identifiable muscle weakness patterns. Rather than endeavoring to relax a tight muscle, Goodheart's method is to strengthen the muscle's spinal or extremity opposite. Applied kinesiology attempts to stimulate muscles through massage of the acu-points as a means of restoring energy balance.

KIRLIAN PHOTOGRAPHY. A process developed in Russia by Semyon Davidovitch Kirlian (1898-1980) to record a person's **aura** as well as energy field images of natural substances. Kirlian discovered in 1937 a means of photographing an electric corona discharge using a metal plate and a generator or oscillator capable of producing a high voltage field of variable pulse and frequency. This has in turn become a standard New Age means for "reading" an individual's "life energy," "bio-energy" or "astral body." Heavily debunked by skeptics and scientists, the Kirlian diagnostic method persists in the world of alternative therapy. Much of the popularity of Kirlian photography as a medical tool is due to University of California, Los Angeles parapsychologist Thelma Moss (1919-1997). Among her works, there are *The Body Electric* (1979) and *The Probability of the Impossible* (1983). Another important work promoting this field is *The Kirlian Aura* (1974) edited by Stanley Kripner and Daniel Rubin.

KNIGHT, JZ (1946-). Née Judith Darlene Hampton, icon of American New Age spirituality. Knight remains one of the most charismatic and controversial spiritual leaders of the New Age movement. Reputedly, Ascended Master Ramtha, a 35,000-year-old Cro-Magnon Lemurian warrior from **Atlantis**, first appeared to Knight in 1977. In his own lifetime, he commenced a war against all tyrants and has survived in legend as the Hindu warrior-god Rama. He chose Knight as his vehicle as she is the **reincarnation** of his own daughter but also not to reinforce the outdated exclusive association of spiritual truth with the masculine. Ramtha/Knight are responsible for the popularity of the term "**channeling**." Much of Knight's story has been chronicled in **Shirley MacLaine**'s book *Out On a Limb*.

In 1988, Knight founded Ramtha's School of Enlightenment: The American Gnostic School—now known as Ramtha's School of Enlightenment: The School of Ancient Wisdom, located on Knight's ranch in Yelm, Washington. Knight is also the president of JZK, Inc. and chairman of the JZ Knight Humanities Foundation. She conducts nationwide forums called "Dialogues." In 1992/3, the divorce case between JZ and her ex-husband Jeffrey Knight was reopened. The landmark significance of these proceedings was that all references to "cult activity," "brainwashing" and "mind control" were banned. Additionally, 1995 and 1997 Austrian court rulings against Julie Ravell decreed that Knight is the only person allowed to channel Ramtha. Among the numerous books and videos released by JZK, Inc. are the joint works of Knight/Ramtha, namely, *Ramtha: The White Book* (1987, reissued 2001), *UFOs and the Nature of Reality: Understanding Alien Consciousness and Interdimensional Mind* (1991), *A Beginner's Guide to Creating Reality: An Introduction to Ramtha and His Teachings* (1997), and *The Two Paths* (1999). Works listed under Ramtha's name alone include *I Am Ramtha* (1987) as well as *The Mystery of Birth and Death* and *The Spinner of Tales*. Knight's own story is found in *A State of Mind, My Story: The Adventure Begins* (1987).

Knight's teachings constitute a form of **gnosticism** holding that the world is an increasingly dense and less spiritual emanation from a transcendental and ineffable divine source. The human individual represents a spark of divinity that has fallen into and is now trapped by matter. The essential Ramtha/Knight message is that preoccupation with the ordinary and mundane prevents new thought and engagement with the extraordinary. The School of Enlightenment endeavors to introduce the dynamics of breath technique, consciousness and energy and, at the same time, form a synthesis between science and spirituality. It adheres to a **New Thought** perspective and proclaims: "As a spiritual being, when we have created the image in the brain, we have created reality."

KRISHNAMURTI, JIDDHU (1895-1986). A fifteen-year-old youth brought from India to England to be groomed for his future role as the next World Teacher. Krishnamurti was formally recognized in 1925 by the **Theosophical Society**'s Annie Besant (1847-1933) and Charles Leadbeater (1854-1934) as **Maitreya**. The Order of the Star of the East had been created to be his vehicle, and he was placed at its head—a move that precipitated the rupture between **Rudolf Steiner** and the Theosophical Society. However, in 1929, Krishnamurti himself repudiated the Society's contentions regarding his preordained position and dissolved the Order. He chose to remain unaffiliated to any institutionalized religion in order to be an independent spiritual teacher. He stressed personal spiritual responsibility for the individual and denied all restrictive mental and religious dogmas.

On land purchased on his behalf by Besant in Ojai, California, in 1922, Krishnamurti's own transformation began there with an experience of deep spiritual insight that he termed "the process." He rejected the alleged religious authority of the **guru** or spiritual master and pursued thenceforth essentially the Advaita Vedanta understanding of **Hinduism**. Self-observation and concerted effort are what lead to enlightenment and freedom. His independence and use of Hindu vocabulary suggest a close influence upon and conformity with New Age thought. His first published work had been *At the Feet of the Master* in 1911, but following his break with theosophy, he taught principally through lectures as well as further publications: e.g., *Freedom from the Known* (1963), *Think on These Things* (1964), *The Awakening of Intelligence* (1973) and *The Future Is Now: Last Talks in India* (1989). The popularity of his teachings led to the establishment of the Krishnamurti Foundation in Ojai in 1969.

KÜBLER-ROSS, ELIZABETH (1926-). The first to bring to the attention of the medical professions as well as the general public the **near-death experience** frequently reported by patients. After visiting concentration camp survivors in 1945, Kübler-Ross was directed toward her life's concern with the process of dying. She earned her medical degree from the University of Zurich in 1957 and a degree in psychiatry from the University of Colorado in 1963. In 1969, she published her first book, *On Death and Dying*, in which she sought to break through the professional denial that prohibited the dying from expressing their fears and worries. This was followed by a long series of works—including *Questions and Answers on Death and Dying* (1974), *Death: The Final Stage of Growth* (1975), *To Live Until We Say Goodbye* (1978), *Remember the Secret* (1982), *On Children and Death* (1983), *AIDS: The Ultimate Challenge* (1987), *On Life After Death* (1991), her autobiography *The Wheel of Life: A Memoir of Living and Dying* (1987), and *Life Lessons* (2000) which deals with life and living. In 1977, Kübler-Ross founded and then directed Shanti Nilaya in Escondido, California. Later this became the Elizabeth Kübler-Ross Center and was moved to rural Virginia. Following a series of strokes, she retired in 1995 and no longer teaches, lectures or leads workshops. Her spiritual message is best summed in her statement: "There are no mistakes, no coincidences. All events are blessings given to us to learn from."

KUNDALINI (Sanskrit "coiled"). The psycho-spiritual energy that is alleged to lie dormant at the base of the spine. In various yogic, esoteric and Vedantic systems, the "awakening of the kundalini" is considered an essential part of spiritual deveopment. The kundalini is likened to a coiled serpent sleeping at the base **chakra**. Through breathing and concentration exercises, the kundalini is "aroused" to stimulate the other chakras as if the serpent has uncoiled and stands upright. Focus on the kundalini has come to preoccupy a segment of New Age meditators. *See also* GURDJIEFF, GEORGE IVANOVITCH.

-L-

LABYRINTH. A maze constructed with intricate passageways and blind alleys that, in the New Age context, is employed as a religious symbol and locus for **meditation**. Jean Houston used the labyrinth in her Mystery School from which Lauren Artress, a San Francisco Grace Cathedral Episcopal priestess, developed in the mid-1990s the idea to install labyrinths in churches, schools, hospitals and other public places. Proponents argue that this practice can be traced to medieval **Christianity**. Critics consider labyrinth installation part of New Age narcissism.

LEVINE, STEPHEN. Director, along with his wife Ondrea, of the Hanuman Foundation Dying Project. In his work with the grieving, terminally ill and dying, Levine has had close relationships with **Elizabeth Kübler-Ross**, **Baba Ram Dass** and **Gerald Jampolsky**. His main issue is that it is mind alone that creates suffering, that is, the cognitive capacity that has become diminished by a deeply conditioned sense of self is what keeps us apart, creates the world, creates suffering in the world, and blocks the heart. Nevertheless, the mind is only part of the equation. In order to overcome the confusion and frustration of the mind, the mercifulness of the heart must be integrated in order to achieve balance and **healing**. Following in the tradition of Ram Dass, Levine acknowledges the many different healing techniques currently available but argues that **meditation** is the most valueable and productive.

In Levine's understanding, true healing results when we meet our suffering or illness and, instead of attempting to drive it away through fear, loathing, hate, anger or distrust, encounter it with "lovingkindness, awareness, mercy and balance." Healing the body without including the mind and allowing the process to enter the heart achieves at best only removal of the symptoms or surface discomforts. The core problem of suffering and grief remains untouched. Levine's metaphysics understands the body as "solidified mind." Only when the mind softens the areas we have abandoned through fear can mercy and compassion flow into them so that healing may begin. Striking a consistent New Age chord, Levine finds love as the answer. Illness becomes an opportunity to explore the depths of our being beneath superficial relief to find its very essence: "life itself, pure awareness, pure love." Two of Levine's books are *Guided Meditations, Explorations and Healings* (1993) and *Embracing the Beloved: Relationship as a Path of Awakening* (1996).

LILLY, JOHN CUNNINGHAM (1915-2001). Neuroscientist, brain researcher and inventor of the isolation tank in the 1950s. An associate of Aldous Huxley, **Buckminster Fuller**, Alan Watts, **Fritz Perls, Oscar Ichazo** and **Baba Ram Dass**, Lilly developed the theory of internal realities and the hardware/software model of the human brain/mind. He also initiated efforts for interspecies communication through his work with dolphins. He wrote a dozen books: *Simulations of God: The Science of Belief* (1956), *Man and Dolphin* (1961), *The Dolphin in History* (1963), *The Mind of the Dolphin* (1967), *The Scientist* (1967), *Programming and Metaprogramming in the Human Biocomputer* (1967), *The Center of the Cyclone* (1972), *Lilly on Dolphins* (1975), *The Dyadic Cyclone*, with Toni Lilly (1976), *The Deep Self* (1977), *Communication between Man and Dolphin* (1978), *John Lilly, so far . . .* , by Francis Jeffrey with Lilly (1990) and *Tanks for the Memories* (1995).

LINN, DENISE (1951-). New Age healer and teacher offering seminars and workshops in guided **meditation** to enable people to sense and balance energy fields. Linn, now based in central California, connected with her Native American heritage after a **near death experience** at the age of seventeen. She developed an awareness of energy flows and a closeness to the earth and came to believe that each person possesses an inner ability to find within the answers to life questions. Linn is particularly known for her teachings concerning "**space clearing**" that employs **feng-shui** techniques for purification and blessing purposes. Her specific method is called "synchro-alignment" and is concerned with learning how to sense and harmonize the energy field of oneself, one's clients and home environments. Students are taught to align their inner life with their outer environment. Using a Native American spiritual orientation, Linn employs personal allies and animal totems from the spirit world as well as such Amerindian paraphernalia as sage, drums, rattles, **medicine wheels**, blessing altars, etc.

Linn is known for a series of best-selling inspirational books: *Sacred Space: Clearing and Enhancing the Energy of Your Home* (1995), *The Secret Language of Signs: How to Interpret the Coincidences and Symbols in Your Life* (1996), *Past Lives, Present Dreams: How to Use Reincarnation for Personal Growth* (1997), *Sacred Legacies: Healing Your Past and Creating a Positive Future* (1999), *Altars: Bringing Sacred Shrines into Your Everyday Life* (1999), *Quest: A Guide to Creating Your Own Vision Quest* (1999), *Space Clearing: How to Purify and Create Harmony in Your Home* (2000) and *Secrets and Mysteries: The Glory and Pleasure of Being a Woman* (2002).

LOVELOCK, JAMES. *See* GAIA HYPOTHESIS.

LUCIS TRUST. *See* BAILEY, ALICE.

-M-

MACLAINE, SHIRLEY (1934-). Hollywood actress who has emerged as a leading promoter of New Age thought. She continues to publish books detailing her inner spiritual odyssey: *Out On a Limb* (1983), *Dancing in the Light* (1985), *It's All in the Playing* (1987), *Dance While You Can* (1991) and *The Camino: A Journey of the Spirit* (2002). MacLaine pursues the various notions that have emerged as the New Age *lingua franca*: the God within, Christ-consciousness, self-responsibility, **karma**, **reincarnation**, spirit guides, higher self, **meditation**, **out-of-body experience**, spiritual evolution, cosmic union, **astrology**, sacred immanence, earth energies, holy spots, talismans, **magic** as unlimited possibility, **yin and yang**, the Divine Universal Energy Source, the Goddess aspect of the God-force, **channeling**, extraterrestrials, etc. For her, the Old Age represented the domination of masculine energy that is now becoming obsolete and superseded by a more equitable spiritual gender balance. Like **Ruth Montgomery**, MacLaine is comfortable with a New Age biblical hermeneutic and understands the apocalyptic transition into the new era as a global karmic clean-up. Nevertheless, she sees evil as relative and not an intrinsic or extrinsic absolute. Her position is **gnostic** in that she understands two planes of existence: the illusory earth-plane physical level of pain, difficulty and joy, and the spiritual level of infinite wisdom and true reality. Echoing a common New Age sentiment, for MacLaine, religion itself need not have anything to do with spirituality. Dogma and ritual are more often than not mechanisms to augment and exploit power.

MAGIC. Primarily, any attempt to transcend or bypass the empirical laws of nature. There are many different understandings of magic including the art of deception, the art and science of causing change through will, the medieval grimoire-based art of conjury, and an operation of the supernatural. In general, magic is associated more with contemporary Western **paganism** than with New Age, though the New Age expectation of radical change and/or a quantum leap of collective consciousness is a magical one when it is expected as a supernatural *deus ex machina* operation. For the individual, the contemporary understanding of magic in much of both contemporary Western paganism and New Age is a psychological discipline that works with archetypal constructs, self-growth developing and **human potential**.

MAHARAJ JI, GURU (Prem Pal Singh Rawat) (1957-). Successor of his father Sri Hans Ji Maharaj in 1966 to the Divine Light Mission that had been founded six years earlier. Conforming to the Sant Mat understanding that stresses lineage and the teacher-disciple relationship, Maharaj Ji was recognized as the latest *sataguru* following in the tradition of Krishna, Buddha, Christ, Mohammed, etc. Divine Light Sant Mat emphasizes transmitting "Knowledge" from one master to another via the techniques of **meditation** (*satsang*). As part of this tradition, the goal of the Maharaj's teaching is spiritual realization. His followers were known as "premies." They lived often in ashrams, as families or in small groups of devotees, renounced drugs, alcohol and meat, and were originally strictly and hierarchically controlled.

Completing his schooling in 1971, Maharaj Ji began a world tour as leader of the Divine Light Mission to help people find inner peace and God realization. In the United States, because of his youth as well as a reputed fondness for Rolls Royce automobiles and other secular pleasures, he became a controversial figure in the media despite his popularity among the counterculture. When, as a teenager of sixteen, he married his twenty-four-year-old secretary, his mother in India deposed him as leader of the Mission and installed another son in his place. A year earlier (1973) he had attempted to launch the spiritual millennium or New Age at the Houston Astrodome, but poor attendance resulted in financial disaster. As a result, Maharaj Ji changed the name of his remnant movement in the early 1980s to Elan Vital, progressively eliminated the Indian and **Hindu** elements, dismantled the structure of communal homes, and has distanced himself from his former status as divine **guru**. He has acquired an essentially **human potential** emphasis and lecture/workshop format in disseminating knowledge, and the other teachers of his movement are no longer known as mahatmas but now simply as instructors.

Maharaj Ji's teachings are focused on experiencing the immediate present with little interest in either postmortem existence or the Hindu doctrine of **reincarnation**. They emphasize that what is sought is already within and that the route to this understanding is gained through the cultivation of inner stillness. Today, Maharaj Ji lives as a private citizen in the United States with his wife and four children and earns an income through teaching tours. He considers himself an educator rather than an Eastern guru. While there are about a quarter million followers of the Divine Light Mission in India itself, those practicing Elan Vital's "techniques of Knowledge" in Britain, the United States, Europe, Australia and Africa number approximately 75,000.

MAHARISHI MAHESH YOGI (*c*.1918-). Hindu guru teaching a form of **meditation** known as transcendental meditation, or TM. The Maharishi became known to the west when the Beatles visited him in Rishikesh, India. He also taught the Beach Boys around the same time. After establishing the Spiritual Regeneration movement in Madras, he traveled to California, New York and Europe to disseminate the TM technique as it reached a peak of popularity. The adept is given his or her own personal and secret mantra consisting of one, two or three syllables upon which the individual concentrates and eliminates all other thoughts while silently repeating the mantra. Practitioners argue that TM became the origin of the **human potential movement** that emerged in the 1960s and 1970s as well as the fitness, holistic and New Age movements of the 1980s. Surveys of New Age seekers indicate familiarity with TM among the highest elements shared in common. The Maharishi now supplements TM teaching with instruction in ayurvedic medicine. He claims to foster an educational rather than a religious movement and sponsors the meditative concept of "critical mass" (*see* **Cayce, Edgar**) by which a disproportionate number of people (the square root of one percent of the world's population) meditating collectively can reduce or eliminate violence, hostility, war and many of the planet's other ills.

MAITREYA. The name of the future Buddha. Until his appearance, Maitreya resides as a bodhisattva, a person who out of compassion for the enlightenment of all humanity, refrains from entering *nirvana*. In the **theosophical** teachings of **Helena Petrovna Blavatsky**, Maitreya is identified with Jesus Christ as a central figure in the **Great White Brotherhood** of Ascended Masters, the spiritual hierarchy that mediates between the human and divine worlds. Blavatsky became convinced that a fifteen-year-old Indian boy, Jiddhu Krishnamurti (1894-1985), was the incarnation of the World Teacher, but in 1929, Krishnamurti renounced this role. In 1948, a former disciple of Blavatsky, **Alice Bailey**, published *The Reappearance of the Christ* which reaffirmed the coming of Buddha/Christ as the instigator of the **Age of Aquarius**. Following in this tradition, British painter **Benjamin Creme** began to receive telepathic messages in 1959 from the Ascended Masters foretelling the arrival of Maitreya as the head of the Great White Brotherhood. Creme announced in 1972 that the arrival of Maitreya/Christ was to occur shortly.

MANDALA "circle." A reference to a Buddhist sacred area such as the place beneath the bodhi tree where Sakyamuni Buddha first obtained enlightenment. The mandala also refers to the schematic diagram in circular form representing the cosmos and used for **meditative** concentration and **visualization**. The symbol may also represent the iconography and soteriology of an individual Buddha. The mandala is particularly associated with **Tibetan Buddhism** in which elaborate symbolic circles are constructed laboriously by monks, often for months, using particles of colored sand only to be swept away at the conclusion of the accompanying ritual.

MASLOW, ABRAHAM (1908-1970). The "father of American humanism" in psychology. Introduced to self-actualization at Brandeis College by Kurt Goldstein in the 1950s, Maslow began a crusade for humanistic psychology and developed a hierarchy of needs ranging from the physiological to safety and security requirements to the needs for love and belonging, then those for esteem and finally the need to actualize the self, that is, growth motivation and being needs. Studying such people as Benedict Spinoza, Thomas Jefferson, Abraham Lincoln, William James, Mahatma Gandhi, Albert Einstein and Eleanor Roosevelt as illustrative examples, he concluded that the self-actualized person is one who is reality-centered, focused on life problems rather than personal difficulties, concerned with means more than ends or with means as ends in themselves, who has a need for privacy, is basically independent of culture and environment, is affirmative of democratic values, is compassionate and usually enjoys intimate personal relations. Such people also have a non-hostile sense of humor, an acceptance of both self and others, spontaneity and non-pretentiousness, a freshness of appreciation, a creative nature and more peak experiences than the average person. Maslow understood the peak experience as those mystical experiences that transcend the self and give one the feeling of being part of the eternal and infinite whole. Along with **Fritz Perls** and **Roberto Assagioli**, Maslow was instrumental in coalescing the **human potential movement** in the 1960s. He was also influential in the development of **transpersonal psychology**. His most important books are *Toward a Psychology of Being* (1968), *Motivation and Personality* (1954, 1970) and *The Further Reaches of Human Nature* (1971).

MASSAGE THERAPY. "Structured touching," or touching with a purpose, that has emerged as a popular foundation to the self-help/**human potential**/body-work concerns of the New Age movement. Massage **therapy** involves the non-invasive application of manual techniques and possibly adjunctive therapies with the intention of improving the health and well-being of the client. It seeks to relieve muscle pain or stress, increase body awareness and/or bring equilibrium in a crisis. Tangible outcomes are sought through active stimulation of the skin, lymph and blood as well as relaxation of the muscles and nervous system, the elimination of metabolic waste and the stretching of connective tissues. Effort is also made to tranquilize the entire organism through the parasympathetic nervous system.

There are numerous forms of massage that range from soft tissue, deep tissue or sports massage, Swedish or relaxing massage, **shiatsu** or pressure point massage, **Esalen** massage and **tantric** or sexual massage. With soft tissue manipulation there is an emphasis on holding, causing movement and/or applying pressure to the body. Sports massage is employed primarily for athletes. Swedish massage is understood as a form of gymnastics that concerns precise work with muscles and the circulatory system. As a part of Gestalt psychotherapy, Esalen massage is a cross between classical Swedish massage and the deeply personal sensing work developed originally by Charlotte Selver in Germany. Tantric massage involves erotic stimulation within a framework that endeavors to conserve sexual energies and desires and transmute them for spiritual purposes. *See also* FELDENKRAIS METHOD.

MEDICINE. *See* ALTERNATIVE MEDICINE

MEDICINE WHEEL. A geophysical ritual device depicting cosmic harmony. Its prototype is the "medicine wheel" in the Bighorn Mountains of northern Wyoming—possibly several thousand years old and preceding the Crow, Shoshone, Arapaho and other northern Plains tribes who subsequently used that area. The medicine wheel device became popular with Hyemeyohsts Storm's 1972 publication of *Seven Arrows*. **Sun Bear** and his Bear Tribe encouraged use of Medicine Wheel ceremonies to provide meeting points between Amerindian practices and New Age beliefs. Occurring in North America and Europe, medicine wheel ceremonies to heal the earth are held at various intervals and usually within specially designed stone circles representing the universe and sacred natural balance. The wheel is to function as an interpretive tool for guidance, growth and the acquisition of wisdom for the health of Mother Earth. Ohky Simine Forest, a Mohawk elder, has combined Mayan and Mongolian **shamanism** elements to create a Native medicine wheel ceremony for **healing** between the four races: White, Native American, Asian and African. Each race is associated with a particular direction as well as gift, power animal, fear and obstacle to be overcome. For example, white is linked to north, mind, wolf, fear of self and the wall of conditionings. Red connects to south, heart, deer, fear of death and the wall of shame. Nevertheless, promotion of the medicine wheel by such people as Jamake Highwater, Loren Cruden, Sun Bear and Sun Bear's wife, Wabun Wind, has been attacked by Native American critics as an inauthentic New Age application.

MEDITATION. Psychologically, techniques that produce a fourth state of consciousness beside the ordinary waking state, sleep and hypnotic trance. The state of enlightenment or ecstasy toward which disciplined mind techniques aim is a hypometabolic condition of mental alertness. In the New Age context, meditation becomes a means for introspection and discovery of the inner self, soul or spirit. It is also used in conjunction with creative **visualization**. In the meditative effort to produce a different state of consciousness, the meditator may concentrate undividedly on various simple images or ideas such as a mantra, **mandala**, deity, saint, holy person or visual object in order to suspend the active calculating momentum of mental life and obtain a superconscious state of observation and attentiveness. In this type of meditation, one seeks a form of heightened concentration, total absorption, transcendence of external stimuli and ultimately the experience of ecstasy. This kind of consciousness-altering technique is typical of **yoga** as well as various forms of Christian and **Sufi** mysticism.

Another basic form of meditation is that which involves the detached examination of the individual stream of consciousness. The meditative person endeavors to become unattached to the ephemeral quality of all phenomena and passively arrive at a state of superawareness. The mind becomes an "empty vessel." This form of meditation is more typical of **Buddhism**.

There are a multitude of techniques of contemplation and concentration encompassed by the umbrella term of "meditation." These are variously incorporated into such traditions as **Zen Buddhism**, yoga, transcendental meditation, Sufi twirling, Whirling Dervishism, Christian mystical union, as well as the state of "relaxed alertness" for the reception of **clairvoyant** impressions in the New Age art of **channeling**.

MEDIUM CONSULTATION. Use of a medium in the sense of agent, vehicle or instrument to communicate with or receive messages/information from the etheric world of the departed, spirit entities or ascended masters. A development of the **spiritualist** movement, in the New Age context, the medium has become a **channel**. As an intermediary or go-between, the medium or channel mediates on behalf of his or her clients with the unseen psychic dimension. Sometimes known as a psychic, **clairvoyant**, automatist or sensitive, the medium's function is to transmit knowledge relating to **healing**, protection, success, self-improvement, spiritual growth and/or material manipulation. He/she often, though not invariably, experiences trance in which either the vehicle becomes possessed by a spirit entity or, more akin to the **shaman**, the mediator enters the spirit world itself. On the other hand, "waking" mediums or channels may simply speak with discarnates without undergoing either possession or flight-of-the-soul. These latter tend to remain in control of their normal mental faculties and awareness. Despite the wide range of differing forms, medium consultation is a popular recourse in spiritualist and New Age circles—whether in the form of the more traditional séance or in the more contemporary channeling session.

MEERA/MOTHER MEERA (1960-). A popular New Age Hindu "avatar"—especially well-known in Germany where she lives in Dornburg-Thalheim between Cologne and Frankfurt with her constant companion, Adilakshmi. Born as Kamala Reddy in Chandepalle, Andhra Pradesh, India, she first attained *samadhi* at the age of six. She was introduced to **Sri Aurobindo** and Sweet Mother in Pondicherry and began giving *darshan* or audiences around 1980. Mother Meera is known as a silent avatar of the Divine Mother for our turbulent times. Operating without an ashram, interviews, tapes, chanting, mantras, music, incense, international organization or even words, her service is personal and silent. Her unique gift to the world is to make available the radical transformative Light of Paramatman, the Supreme Being. She offers a path of joy and transformation and claims that all divine incarnations are equal. Mother Meera does not encourage **meditation** since it can increase spiritual pride. She also does not require celibacy but prefers **vegetarianism**. Her only publication is *Answers*, an account of the working of the Divine Mother in the world. The book is based on questions her devotees have asked about her identity, work and path. Mother Meera refers to the Overmind, the Supramental, and four even higher planes of consciousness. She advocates surrender to the god force in all that one does.

MEHER BABA "Loving Father" (1894-1969). Merwan Sheriar Irani, of Parsi descent from Puna, India. He was recognized by several female **Sufi** leaders: Hazrat Babajan (who predicted his spiritual leadership), Upasui Maharaj (who imparted Divine Knowledge to him), and Rabia Khan (a successor to Hazrat Inayat Khan, founder of the Sufi movement—who declared Irani as the Qutb or central being of the universe). Rabia Khan transferred property to what became Sufism Reoriented, an important group within the Meher Baba organization. Irani received the name Meher Baba from his disciples. His initial ashram was near Bombay/Mumbai, and later he established his center in the region of Ahmednagar. Meher Baba's organization has no formal creeds but teaches that God alone is real and identical with the self, that through love one can become one with God, that God is to be known within everyone, that one should renounce selfish desires and submit to God's will in tranquility. **Vegetarianism** is not enforced, but use of recreational drugs and premarital sexual congress are not allowed.

In 1925, Meher Baba permanently entered "the Silence" and suspended further oral teachings—communicating instead through writing.
He also made several trips to Europe, the United States and Australia
starting in 1931. From 1956, he began conveying his ideas through
hand gestures alone. He maintained his silence until his death forty-four
years later. Meher Baba claimed himself to be the seventh and last avatar for the present era—completing the cycle begun by Zoroaster and
including Krishna, Rama, the Buddha, Jesus and Mohammed. In exchange for the intense veneration received as an exemplary charismatic
figure of advanced consciousness, Meher Baba bestows on his followers an "avataric push" in their own spiritual evolution. Friends of Meher Baba hold that this can still occur even after the master's physical
passing. "Baba lovers" are generally understood as part of the New Age
spiritual movement. One of Meher Baba's disciples was Paul Brunton
(1898-1981) who, in his own teachings, combined Indian concepts with
western esotericism. **Alice Bailey** wrote a forward to Brunton's book,
The Secret Path: A Technique of Self-Discovery. See also SUFISM

MESMER, FRANZ ANTON (1734-1815). A Swiss-Austrian physician who came to work in France. He reputedly effected cures by strok-
ing diseased areas of the body with magnets. He argued that a subtle
fluid existed that was uniformly diffused through nature—one that
linked the microcosm of the human body with the macrocosm of the
universe. This he referred to as a magnetic force. Disciples of mesmerism first appeared in America in the 1830s. Eventually, the mesmeric
sleep that they advocated was separated from the notion of animal
magnetic fluids. While Mesmer's fluid has been transformed into electromagnetic energy, the magnetic state itself survives as the hypnotic
state, that is, an altered state of consciousness brought about primarily
by suggestion. Mesmer became a formative influence on the **American
metaphysical movement** and through it on the subsequent developments of **New Thought** and New Age.

MILLENNIALISM. Belief in an ideal society characterized by peace,
freedom, material prosperity and rule of righteousness. Its Christian
version derives from Revelation 20:1-20, describing the binding of the
devil and his imprisonment in a bottomless pit for a millennium or
"thousand" years. With the removal of satanic influence, the resurrected

Christian martyrs will reign with Christ for this period of time. Unlike the predominant Christian focus on the prospects for the individual in this world and the next (death, immortality, rewards of the just, punishment of the damned), millennialism is concerned with the future and chronology of coming events for the human community on earth. End of the world scenarios are generally derived from the books of Daniel and Revelation.

The Christian attitudes toward the millennium are traditionally labeled premillennialist, postmillennialist and amillennialist. The first holds that Christ's return will be preceded by catastrophic signs (war, famine, earthquake, apostasy, the appearance of the Antichrist and the great tribulation). These events will be followed by the second coming and the period of peace and righteousness under Christ and his saints. Postmillennialism, by contrast, considers that the millennium of a godly, peaceful and prosperous world will precede the second coming, the resurrection of the dead and the last judgment. The gradual elimination of evil in the world results from Christian teaching and the solving of economic, social and educational problems. This millennium then culminates with the return of Christ. Finally, the amillennialist position sees a continuous development of good and evil in the world until the second coming when the dead shall be raised and the judgment conducted. Amillennialists believe that the kingdom of God is already present in the world with the victorious Christ ruling his church through the Word and Spirit. From this perspective, the future kingdom is thought to refer to the new earth and life in heaven. Revelation 20 becomes therefore a description of the souls of the dead believers reigning in paradise with Christ.

In New Age, the millennium is frequently interpreted as a literal or metaphorical understanding of the **Age of Aquarius** as a collective quantum change in consciousness. While the New Age millennium is similarly described as a peaceful, harmonious era of freedom and prosperity, it often follows one Christian trajectory or the other in how it is achieved. While **Marilyn Ferguson**'s "Aquarian Conspiracy" can be classified as postmillennialist in that the world's paradisiacal transformation will be accomplished peacefully through education and eco-social reform, a spectrum of New Age thought expects the new era to be preceded by violent and catastrophic earth-changes. Forecasts of apocalyptic **end-times** including a final battle between satanic and anti-satanic forces are predicted by **Nostradamus, Edgar Cayce, Levi Dowling**, Elizabeth Clare Prophet and **Ruth Montgomery**. These last comprise a "premillenialist" cohort within the Christian wing of New Age. *See also* CHRISTIANITY.

MIND DYNAMICS. A four-day training program established by Alexander Everett (1921-) along with his experiential **human potential** training organization in 1968. Everett moved the headquarters of Mind Dynamics Incorporated from Fort Worth, Texas, to San Francisco, California, in 1970. The organization was closed down four years later, but its influence continues in related developments and spin-offs: William Penn Patrick's Leadership Dynamics; Bob White, Randy Revell, Charlene Afremow and John Hanley's 1974 Lifespring; Werner Erhard's 1971 *est*/The Forum (**Erhard Training Seminars**); Stewart Emery's Actualizations; Bob White's Life Dynamics; Randy Revell's Context Trainings; Howard Nease's Personal Dynamics; Jim Quinn's Lifestream; Thomas Willhite's PSI World Seminars and the present-day development of Everett's training program now known as Large Group Awareness Trainings.

Like **Silva Mind Control**, Everett's Mind Dynamics is a non-confrontational methodology in self-hypnosis. Everett considers the seminal influences on his program to be the ideas of **Edgar Cayce, theosophy**, Rosicrucianism, egyptology, Silva Mind Control, **Unity**, the **Esalen Institute** and **Gestalt therapy**. While related, it differs from such "hard hitting group encounters" as Leadership Dynamics or the original *est*. Following encounters with Eastern spirituality, Everett has developed a two-day seminar called Inward Bound and focused on "complete centering."

MONTGOMERY, RUTH SHICK (1913-2001). Former White House correspondent who, through automatic writing and numerous books, became known as "The First Lady of the Psychic World." Her fifteen publications include her 1966 bestseller *A Search for the Truth, Here and Hereafter* (1968), *A World Beyond: A Startling Message from the Eminent Psychic Arthur Ford from Beyond the Grave* (1971), *Born to Heal* (1973), *Companions Along the Way* (1974), *The World Before* (1976), *Strangers Among Us* (1979), *Threshold to Tomorrow* (1982), *Aliens Among Us* (1985), *Ruth Montgomery: Herald of the New Age*

(1986)—with Joanne Garland, and *World To Come: The Guides' Long-Awaited Predictions for the Dawning Age* (1999). The "spirit message" that she conveys is an insistence on oneness with God, the unlimited inner capacity of the human being, and the good one does on earth as the fuel for soul advance.

In all fundamentals, this is a **gnostic** position in which each created entity or person, despite the obstacles, immediately seeks reunion with its "Maker." Montgomery interprets her psychic worldview through a Christian and biblical framework. Opposing the limitations of both "scientific materialism and philosophical rationalism," she argues that in **Christianity** the universal psychic experience has been given "an ethical coloration" for the first time. In the quest for eternal truth and "Oneness with God," the material has no importance and physical incarnation represents only a minor segment in the soul's millennia-long ascent. The great obstacle of earthly existence, however, is temptation—the very thing Christ was able to reject and, consequently, is now able to return repeatedly to earth "without any of its hampering limitations of time and space and body." Montgomery, however, has also expressed a New Age sentiment that is frequently criticized by others, namely, that physical hardship and deformity are "chosen" by those who suffer from them in order to progress their souls more rapidly.

Influenced by **Arthur Ford**, **Edgar Cayce** and Cayce's son Hugh Lynn Cayce as well as **Nostradamus** and **Levi Dowling**, Montgomery denies the reality of death and places a strong emphasis on the efficaciousness of prayer—a psychic experience she considers similar to **meditation** and dreams. She also accepts the notion of **reincarnation** or a succession of terrestrial lifetimes all designed and chosen with the intention of encouraging "spiritual progress." Other ideas presented and explored through her spirit guides include the compatibility of Christianity and Judaism with Eastern philosophy, the therapeutic value of understanding past lives, postmortem existence in the **astral** plane, cocreation, earth changes and the coming planetary axis shift, magnetic healing, Lemuria/Mu and **Atlantis**, extraterrestrial space visitors, the intergalactic universe-federation, the **walk-in**, and the **millennialist** conformity of the New Age transition with the apocalypse of the Book of Revelations. Montgomery foresees a final battle between Satan/the Antichrist and a coalition of humanity, walk-ins and extraterrestrials preceding the establishment of the New Age as a paradise on earth.

MOVEMENT OF SPIRITUAL INNER AWARENESS. *See* MSIA.

MSIA (pronounced "messiah"). The Church of the Movement of Spiritual Awareness, founded by John-Roger Hinkins (1934-) in the late 1960s. A former student of ECKANKAR that is centered on John Paul Twitchell's understanding of ECK (Spirit or the Cosmic Current) as the "divine essence of God within each of us," Hinkins has established in Los Angeles the PRANA (Purple Rose Ashram of the New Age) Theological Seminary and College of Philosophy. Twitchell (1908/1912?- 1971) had himself been an associate of **Scientology** and Sant Mat master Kirpal Singh, founder of Ruhani Satsang. He developed a form of surat shabda **yoga**—a series of physical exercises and spiritual practices that aim to allow the soul to travel beyond physical limitations to the impersonal and infinite source of all life. In Hinkins' movement, the focus is the consciousness of the founder himself. He is believed to be able to "read" the **karma** of each person and assist the individual in developing complete awareness of God. The goal of the Insight Transformational Seminars, short-term intensive growth experiences for individuals, that Hinkins founded in 1978 is to facilitate "soul travel" or soul transcendence to the original home beyond the **astral**, causal, mental and etheric dimensions. MSIA techniques include **aura** balancing, light studies and becoming aware of one's programmed responses. Insight claims to help individuals develop greater self-confidence, self-esteem, communication skills, motivation, enthusiasm, productivity and improved relationships. Hinkins has also established in Santa Monica, California, both the Baraka Holistic Center for Therapy and Research and the KOH-E-NOR University. MSIA also promotes **healing** and holistic health.

MUKTANANDA, SWAMI (1908-1982). Teacher of a form of **yoga** known as kundalini. Muktananda was initiated into Kashmir Shaivism by his **guru** Bhagwan Sri Nityananda in the late 1940s and achieved enlightenment (*samadhi*) in 1956. The kundalini represents the spiritual energy thought in **Hinduism** to reside within the first **chakra** at the base of the spine. This energy is believed to be fundamental to both sexual desire and higher consciousness. It is considered metaphorically a serpent that can be awakened and made to rise through the remaining chakras of the central nervous system, culminating in the seventh at the

124 The Dictionary

crown of the head where it induces the blissful state of *samadhi*. (*See also* **Sikh Dharma**). Muktananda's innovation for the West is that the kundalini can be aroused directly through the grace of the guru rather than strictly through the individual's own effort. This transmission is known as *shaktipat* initiation. It can be bestowed through touch (Muktananda often used peacock feathers) or simply by thought.

Nityananda founded the Ganeshapuri Ashram northeast of Bombay/Mumbai in 1949 as the meditation center of the Siddha Yoga tradition. Following an invitation by Werner Erhard in 1974 to come to the United States, Muktananda established a headquarters in the Catskill Mountains near South Fallsburg, New York. This had followed an early world tour in 1970 that included Europe, America and Australia and during which Muktananda was accompanied for much of the time by **Baba Ram Dass**. A third visit was undertaken in 1978. The result of these travels has been the worldwide establishment of hundreds of meditation centers. The Siddha Yoga Dham Associates Foundation was created in 1975. Muktananda's spiritual autobiography, *Play of Consciousness*, was published in 1978. He promoted the notion of *darshan* or the seeing of one's guru as more important than advance through **meditation** itself. With Siddha Yoga, a typical practice consists of chanting the guru's name. Other foci include service to others as part of one's devotion to the guru.

Muktananda designated a brother and sister as his successors. However, Swami Nityananda (1963-) renounced his sannyasin vows and position in 1985—leaving his sister **Chidvilasananda** (1956-), known as Gurumayi, in control of the movement and headquartered in Ganeshpuri. Pursuing at first a career as a private meditation teacher, Nityananda established the Shanti Mandir (Peace Temple) in 1987, but in 1989 he recommitted to his former sannyasin status and reclaimed his position as co-leader of the Siddha Dham movement. His sister has not recognized his claims and maintains herself as sole successor of Muktananda. In 1995, Nityananda was inducted by an important group of leaders in the broader lineage of Kaula Tantric Kashmir Shaivism. *See also* TANTRA.

MYSS, CAROLINE. Best-selling author in the field of **alternative medicine** who focuses on self-**healing** based on spiritual ideals. Her leading books are *Anatomy of the Spirit* (1997) and *Why People Don't*

Heal and How They Can (1998). Myss has been much influenced by Dr. C. Norman Shealy, M.D., a research and clinical professor of psychology, founder of the Shealy Institute for Comprehensive Health Care, and author of several books of his own and others in collaboration with Myss. In his *Sacred Healing: The Curing Power of Energy and Spirituality* (1999), Shealy maintains that "illness stems from an imbalance or sickness in the spirit of the individual patient." In her turn, Myss has been proclaimed by Shealy to be the equal of the past "talented intuitives and mystics who have sensed the power centers of the human body." As a, if not the "medical intuitive" of today, Myss employs an intuitional ability to perceive a person's energetic body and thereby understand the emotional, psychological and spiritual foundations of illness. According to Shealy, Myss' techniques constitute the basis of medicine for the twenty-first century.

Myss' message is that power lies at the root of all health and disease. She argues that the purpose of our lives is to assume responsibility for this power and to redirect spirit away from negative investment to the positive. Since our spirits are "ultimately our true power," life is to be lived from a spiritual nucleus. Her central point is that the individual biography becomes one's biology. Our biological health constitutes a living and breathing biological statement that conveys our strengths, weaknesses, hopes and fears. Since how we think, feel and behave is recorded within ourselves—producing a self-accountable result, we must learn to read our individual energy systems. In order to penetrate the obscuring miasma of emotions, patient or healer must develop an intuition that he/she can trust.

Along with the principle that biography becomes biology, Myss also stresses that illness and powerlessness are interconnected, and in understanding personal power issues, healing involves our individual ability to listen intuitively to bodily messages and know what augments or decreases energy. A third central plank to her philosophy is that the individual must take full responsibility for the creation of his or her health. Since energy medicine reveals that we are responsible for our health, we participate in the creation of whatever illnesses from which we suffer. For Myss, this translates into the need to focus on emotional, psychological, physical and spiritual factors in the healing process rather than on the illness itself. In this, she is distinguishing between curing (a passive process that involves relinquishing self-power to an external authority) and healing (an active and internal process of self-investigation leading to self-empowerment). Cures seek simply to make the symptoms disappear, whereas healing is positivistic and involves the whole person.

According to Myss, illness results from either a dominating negative attitude or a dependence on external authorities. She feels that although we create our own diseases through behavioral patterns and attitudes, this is rarely a matter of conscious choice. Unlike **Louise Hay**, Myss does not accept that we can avoid all problems through positive affirmation and absence of negative thought. It would be unrealistic to believe that it is possible to have a whole life free of discomfort or challenge, and no spiritual tradition can guarantee pain-free living. Nevertheless, she does insist that, through the transmission of positive messages to the biological system, healing can be generated. She also points out that not everyone desires to be healed since some people use their suffering as a means for gaining attention from or power over others. Moreover, not all illness is a result of negativity. Disease, for Myss, can also spring from the need for major change or spiritual development. Like **Deepak Chopra**, she believes in "deep healing" in which the patient accepts the responsibility for how biography affects biology and feels truth as something both "visceral and cellular."

MYTHOLOGY. A usually ancient, cultural register of myths or narrative stimuli that were intended to activate psychic, mental and emotional behavior in the achievement of real ends. Together, myths, legends and fairy tales constitute metaphors to express non-empirical and/or non-directly accessible truth. Myths are distinguishable by their "sacred" content and are organized into religious mythologies. These last tend to symbolize a people's early beliefs, values, worldviews, understanding of deities and spirits and their relationships to them. They functioned as supplements to automatic reflex and, to the degree that they continue to express atavistic patterns embedded in the human psyche, they represent **archetypes** as well as archetypal stories or histories. The study of myth by New Agers is an attempt to detect the deeper meaning beneath the narrative surface. Mythic study is undertaken as a **therapeutic** aid toward self and collective transformation. If the importance of myth was originally its effectiveness, from a New Age perspective its significance lies more in the ability to unlock potential energies, creativeness and spiritual/integrated development. *See also* TRANSPERSONAL PSYCHOLOGY.

-N-

NARANJO, CLAUDIO B. Pioneer of the **human potential movement.** Naranjo studied medicine, music and philosophy in his native Chile and, in 1967, conducted experiments with ibogaine and iboga-extracts. After coming to the United States, he joined the staff of the **Esalen Institute** in its early days and eventually became one of three successors to **Fritz Perls.** Later influences on the development of his thought include **Swami Muktananda, Idries Shah, Oscar Ichazo** and **Tarthang Tulku Rinpoche.** Naranjo is an important figure in the **enneagram** movement, and if Ichazo is the "father" of the enneagram of character types, Naranjo is recognized as its "mother." He is also known for having introduced "Fourth Way" ideas to psychotherapy. With Kathy Speeth, he co-founded Seekers After Truth (SAT) in Berkeley, California. At present, Naranjo concentrates on integrative and **transpersonal psychotherapeutic** education in Europe and South America.

Naranjo's publications include *The One Quest* (1972), *The Psychology of Meditation* (1972), *The Healing Journey* (1974), *Consciousness and Creativity* (1978), *Ennea-type Structures* (1991), *Gestalt Therapy: The Attitude and Practice of an Atheoretical Experientialism* (1993), *Gestalt after Fritz* (1993), *The End of Patriarchy and the Dawning of a Tri-une Society* (1994), *Ennea-types in Psychotherapy* (1994), *Character and Neurosis: An Integrative View* (1994), *Transformation through Insight: Enneatypes in Life, Literature and Clinical Practice* (1997) and *The Healing Journey: New Approaches to Consciousness* (2001).

NAROPA INSTITUTE. Created by Chinese/Tibetan Chögyam Trungpa, Rinpoche (1940-1987) in Boulder, Colorado, as a center for disseminating the teachings of **Tibetan Buddhism.** With a lineage in both the Kagyu and Nyingma traditions of Tibet and recognized as a *tulku* or incarnation of a bodhisattva, Trungpa fled his homeland in 1959, went to Great Britain in 1963 and, following an auto accident in 1969, renounced his status as a monk and became a layman. He arrived in the United States in 1970 and first founded the Karme Choling center in Vermont—three years later incorporating it and the other centers he had founded subsequently into the Vajradhatu Foundation with its headquarters in Halifax, Nova Scotia. With more than one hundred local centers and possibly 5,500 members internationally, Vajradhatu is today among the largest Buddhist organizations in the West. In 1974, Trungpa established the Naropa Institute as the educational arm of Vajradhatu. Now known as Naropa University, it was modeled on the legendary Nalanda Monastic University, whose ruins can be seen in the Indian state of Bihar. As the first accredited Buddhist university in the United States, its goal is to unite Buddhist contemplative practice with Western academic subjects.

With his blatant fondness for sexual relations and alcohol, Trungpa was a controversial figure. His teachings combined "rough and humorous forms of **Buddhism**." He employed a confrontational and unpredictable teaching style that was intended to disrupt one's deepest sense of complacency. For instance, in 1975, he instructed his students to drag the poet W. S. Merwin and the poet's girlfriend before a large gathering and strip them naked. Negative repercussions ensued for the Institute following this incident for a number of years. In his 1973 book *Cutting Through Spiritual Materialism*, Trungpa introduced the new phrase of "spiritual materialism" into New Age vocabulary to describe the acquisitive impulse toward "collecting" spiritual experiences and initiations. Highly influenced by the western vocabulary of humanistic and growth-centered psychology, he emphasized Buddhism as a practice to awaken the mind and to subdue rather than pursue egotistical practice.

As part of the Naropa Institute, Allen Ginsburg and Anne Waldman established the Jack Kerouac School of Disembodied Poetics in 1974. The Naropa University's Allen Ginsburg Library was dedicated in 1994. The current student enrollment is approximately 1,000. Naropa's mission, which seeks to join intellect and intuition while avoiding intellectual pollution, is to cultivate awareness of the present moment, to foster a learning community, to cultivate openness and communication, to exemplify the Buddhist educational heritage, to integrate the world's wisdom traditions with modern culture and to be non-sectarian and open to all. In 2001, the president of the Naropa University was John Whitehorse Cobb. Vajradhatu International was subsequently headed by Osel Tendzin (Thomas Rich).

NATIVE AMERICAN SPIRITUALITY. The religious understandings and practices of the Amerindian peoples—particularly those of North America. For the New Age movement, American Indian ceremonies (e.g., the sweat lodge, vision quest, **tribal dancing and drumming**) and paraphernalia (e.g., the dream-catcher, **medicine wheel**) have become direct and reputedly accessible native sources of a presumed holistic but indigenous spirituality and inspiration. Native American sensitivities underlie much of the **dream-work, pathworking** and **visualization** employed throughout New Age gatherings. **Totemism** and use of power animals are further derivatives that have been incorporated into the mishmash of New Age eclecticism. But above all, it is under the broad umbrella of **shamanism** or Neo-shamanism that indigenous influence is probably the strongest. Shamanic orientations have emerged as the practice most associated with American Indians that has now become a New Age staple in the development of its worldview and transformational technique. *See* CARLOS CASTANEDA, MICHAEL HARNER and LEO RUTHERFORD.

The relationship between Native Americans and Euro-American New Age spiritual practice is riddled with **controversy**. In this case, the concern and bitterness engendered have to do with perceptions of appropriation of Amerindian institutions by descendants of the very people who are known to have "stolen the land" from its native inhabitants. Now, New Agers are seen as cultural imperialists who are also stealing the religion and culture of the aboriginal peoples of North America. Particularly irksome is the romanticizing and commercialization of spirituality that often comprises the most salient aspects of the New Age identity. While much of the hostility is spearheaded by the Lakota peoples, the American Indian community is itself contentiously divided over the issue. Many leaders contend that their traditional practices will not survive unless they are taught and exported to Euro-Americans. Foremost among these was **Sun Bear**. Others that are more open to sharing native spirituality with outsiders include **Lynn Andrews, Denise Linn, Jamie Sams** and **Tony Shearer**. For New Age itself, with its argument of collective ownership of all spirituality, the question comes down to attitudes of respect and sensitivity—attitudes that are frequently not readily apparent if and when they are present at all.

NATUROPATHY. A system of **alternative medicine** that employs natural agencies in the treatment of disease. It avoids allopathic medicines and chemical drugs and turns instead to herbs, roots and other plant derivatives along with fresh air, sunshine, exercise, **massage**, fasting, and a diet of unprocessed whole food. Naturopathy's principal emphasis is to encourage the body to become strong and resist illness rather than to attempt eradication of the disease itself. As a holistic discipline, it affirms "the healing power of nature" and living in attunement with it.

The origins of naturopathy are to be found in the second half of the eighteenth century as a reaction to the emergence of medicinal practice based on empirical and methodological controls. The seminal figures to its development include Samuel Thompson (1769-1843)—use of **Native American** herbal knowledge; Per Henrik Ling (1776-1839)—Swedish **massage**; Vincent Preissnitz (1791-1851)—use of cold water and massage; Sylvester Graham (1794-1851)—advocate of **vegetarianism**; and Father Sebastian Kneip (1821-1897)—developer of hydrotherapy. Naturopathy has become a major part of New Age concern with **healing**. In the nineteenth century, it became the umbrella term for the alternative methods of curing that coalesced around hydrotherapy, the popular water cure of the day. Consequently, like **theosophy** and **New Thought**, naturopathy was a well-established tradition by the time the New Age began its development in the late 1960s. Through New Age, it has augmented its focus to include such related disciplines as chiropractic, **iridology**, **aromatherapy**, **yoga**, **acupuncture**, **Alexander Technique** and other **therapeutic** practices. All these various disciplines are integrated together by the naturopathic understanding that disease results essentially from the accumulation of bodily toxins, stress, structural imbalance and unhealthy habits. It differs from New Thought in accepting disease as real but something that can be eliminated through a change in lifestyle rather than a cultivation of a radically new mental perspective that denies physical reality. In naturopathy, the emphasis is placed firmly upon the body's own natural power to heal. *See also* HOMEOPATHY.

NEAR-DEATH EXPERIENCES (NDEs). A **transpersonal** experience alleged to occur when one is close to death. In general and as the consciousness of the individual appears to detach from his/her body as that body faces imminent demise, the NDE feeling is reported to be pleasant and free of fear. Along with heightened awareness and greatly accelerated mental activity, there is a profound feeling of peace and acceptance as well as a rapid review of one's life along with visual and auditory experiences. Raymond Moody (*Life After Death*, 1975) discovered fifteen separate elements described by those who had shared an

NDE. Moody elaborated another four elements two years later which were less common: a vision of universal insight, a luminous city, a realm of bewildered spirits who are unable to detach from the physical world and supernatural rescue from physical death by a spiritual agent. Others (e.g., **Blackmore**) claim that NDEs are triggered by the brain as it begins to die. This is known as cerebral anoxia or the result of a lack of oxygen in the brain. But many within the New Age orientation see NDEs as spiritually real and transformative experiences. *See* OBE.

NEO-PAGANISM. A broad outgrowth of chiefly **Wicca** and **feminist spirituality**. Neo-paganism is not to be confused with contemporary Western **paganism** in general, which includes reconstructions of ancient paganisms as well as importations of various present-day indigenous and folk-oriented practices. From within the broader contemporary pagan scene, it is increasingly emerging as a distinct spirituality to be recognized by its conformity to a bi-theistic focus on "The God and The Goddess," employment of Wicca's eight sabbats as its annual sequence of festivals, and its specific identification of the four cardinal directions of east, south, west and north with, respectively, air, fire, water and earth. While both male and female aspects of the godhead are acknowledged, there is an overriding emphasis on the Goddess *per se*.

Where Neo-paganism is similar if not identical or at least frequently confused with New Age is with its predilection of focus upon the self and personal development. Much Neo-pagan practice is also New Age in its often eclectic appropriation of other traditions and its reliance on total self exegesis. This manifests as Neo-pagan/New Age insistence on the freedom to use and interpret without consideration or sometimes even recognition of other proprieties and/or authorities.

NEO-SHAMANISM. *See* SHAMANISM.

NEURO-LINGUISTIC PROGRAMMING (NLP). A psychodynamic method of utilizing the individual's inherent abilities to learn, process, and utilize information and knowledge through awareness of one's mind and body. Developed by Richard Bandler and John Grinder, NLP has been used in overcoming fears, addictions, and destructive behaviors, and in enhancing health, creativity, and athletic performance. Its techniques have been clinically tested for at least three decades. NLP is particularly popular among executive managers, politicians and advertisers. It may be seen as a recasting of Norman Vincent Peale's "power of positive thinking" as well as an articulation of the essential dynamic behind **New Thought**.

NEW AGE CONTROVERSIES. *See* CONTROVERSIES, NEW AGE.

NEW THOUGHT. A chief predecessor of New Age, developed primarily through the teachings of **Emma Curtis Hopkins**. Hopkins' students established their own centers, adopted different names for them and began to differentiate themselves from **Mary Baker Eddy**'s Christian Science. Many of these groups tend today to identify or associate as New Age. These include **Unity**—founded by Myrtle and Charles Fillmore in Kansas City, **Divine Science**—founded by Melinda Cramer in San Francisco, and the Institute (later, the Church) of **Religious Science**—founded by Ernest Holmes in Chicago and now centered in San Diego. Each of these derives their authority for ministry from Hopkins and Eddy. The designation of "New Thought" was first suggested in the 1890s and by the beginning of World War I was generally accepted as the unifying designation for these related denominations.

While Christian Science, after Eddy's death, continues to be led by lay people, New Thought groups tend to have ordained ministries. Nevertheless, the movement as a whole remains decentralized as one that celebrates diversity of opinion. But without losing the healing emphasis of Christian Science, New Thought has developed an equal emphasis on **prosperity**. It reasons that poverty is as unreal as disease. Consequently, its students are taught to live out of the abundance of God. In general, New Thought advocates the more universal position that acknowledges the value of all religious traditions. In the early part of the twentieth century, a retired judge and New Thought lecturer, Thomas Troward, introduced new psychological concepts— specifically, the differentiation of the mind into objective (waking consciousness) and subjective (unconscious) aspects. In this manner, he opened the New Thought movement to the concept of the dynamic subconscious that was missing in both Eddy and Hopkins.

In 1914, the International New Thought Alliance was formed from the various groups founded by Hopkins' students. It produced a Declaration of Principles that was revised in 1957 but remains similar to the idealistic thought of Christian Science. Its differences include having no specifically Christian affirmations while it affirms belief in God as Universal Wisdom, Love, Life, Truth, Peace, Beauty and Joy. In other words, God is generally understood in non-anthropomorphic terms. The Declaration affirms the universe as the body of God, the human as an invisible spiritual dweller inhabiting a body, and that humans continue to grow and change after death. While remaining affirmative of Christian Science's common idealism, New Thought nevertheless assigns a more positive role to the body and the material world. Matter is not regarded as mortal error, but though it is considered a manifestation of spiritual reality, it is still something that is secondary in importance and veracity.

While Christian Science rejects **Phineas Quimby**'s adherence to magnetic **healing** as well as New Thought's abandonment of Eddy's essential Christian orientation, both movements look to a manifestation of the Truth they teach in the individual's life. This is usually referred to as a "demonstration." To move from sickness to health is to demonstrate healing. To move from poverty to wealth is to demonstrate abundance. While Christian Science rejects New Thought's emphasis on prosperity, it also rejects the latter's openness to various psychic and occult practices. Nevertheless, both movements advocate the role of a practitioner to aid in demonstration, that is, of a professional who has been trained in the arts of healing prayer. While all are different and use slightly different techniques, all the New Thought churches with the exception of the Unity School of **Christianity** provide their memberships with the assistance of healing prayer specialists. Some New Thought practitioners specialize in the manifestation of abundance. Unity, the major exception, has no practitioners but does have licensed Unity teachers who nevertheless function in a similar fashion.

Among the portfolio of New Thought groups, those which are chiefly significant for New Age include Unity, Divine Science, Religious Science, the Adventures in Enlightenment Foundation (*see* **Terry Cole-Whittaker**) and Miracle Experiences, Inc. (*see* *A Course in Miracles*). While most New Thought is to be found in America, New Thought groups exist throughout the world. Much of the New Thought-New Age international impetus is now led by the formation of *A Course in Miracles* study groups. In Japan, a significant New Thought presence is found in the movement of Seicho-No-Ie. Among New Thought North American denominations, Unity is the largest followed by Religious Science and then Divine Science. Approximately 350 institutions belong to the New Thought Alliance.

NHAT HANH, THICH (1926-). Vietnamese **Zen Buddhist** monk. Nhat Hanh founded in Vietnam the School of Youth for Social Services, the Van Hanh Buddhist University and the Tiep Hien Order (Order of Interbeing). He is chiefly known for his development and promulgation of the Buddhist perspective on non-duality. Exiled from Vietnam in 1966, he persuaded Martin Luther King, Jr. publicly to oppose the Vietnam War. He has taught at Columbia University and the Sorbonne and now lives in the monastic community of Plum Village in southwestern France. Nhat Hanh conducts worldwide retreats on the art of mindful living. He is a prolific author, and among his several books written on his own or in collaboration with others, there are *Being Peace* (1987), *Old Path, White Clouds: Walking in the Footsteps of the Buddha* (1991), *Peace in Every Step* (1991), *Touching Peace: Practice and Art of Mindful Living* (1992), *The Long Road Turns to Joy: A Guide to Walking Meditation*—with Robert Aitken (1996), *Breathe! You Are Alive: Sutra on the Full Awareness of Breathing* (1996), *Living Buddha, Living Christ*—with David Steindl-Rast (1997), *Moment by Moment: The Art and Practice of Mindfulness*—with Jerry Braga (1997), *The Heart of the Buddha's Teaching: Transforming Suffering Into Peace, Joy and Liberation* (1997), *For a Future to Be Possible: Commentaries on the Five Mindfulness Trainings* (1998), *Teachings on Love* (1998), *Going Home: Jesus and Buddha as Brothers* (2000) and *Anger: Wisdom for Cooling the Flames* (2001).

NITYANANDA. *See* MUKTANANDA, SWAMI.

NOSTRADAMUS (1503-1566). Latinized name of Michel de Nostredame, European prophet born in the French city of St. Remy de Provence. Eldest of five sons in a well-educated Jewish family, Nostradamus was exposed to the occult wisdom of the **Kabala** and, after his parents' conversion to Roman Catholicism, to biblical prophecy as well. The visions he experienced as a child were accepted as gifts from God. He enrolled in Montpellier University in 1552 where he obtained his degree and medical license. His treatment of plague victims was unorthodox: he made his own medicines and refused to "bleed" patients—the common practice of the day until the end of the nineteenth century. Despite professional opposition, he became famous for achieving many cures and for possessing an extraordinary gift of **healing**. However, he lost his wife and two children to the plague and, because of the aroused interest of the inquisition in his methods and friendships, was forced to leave his home base of Agen and lived a nomadic life throughout Europe for six or more years. During this time, his prophetic abilities began to manifest.

Eventually, Nostradamus resettled in Provence where he married a wealthy widow and fathered six more children. As his fame grew, he won the favor of Catherine de Medici who consulted him as an **astrologer**. He also became the physician of Charles IX. Nostradamus first began to record his prophecies in 1550. He scried alone every night in a secret study—beginning first with an inauguratory ritual and concentrating on a tripod brazier until it would appear to burst into flame. In the vaporous mists above the bowl, a spirit would appear and, in a frightening voice, dictate past history as well as present descriptions and future prophecies. Nostradamus recorded what he heard and saw even though the meaning was not always clear to him. Because of fears of the inquisition, he transcribed the prophecies into quatrains and anagrams using French, Provençal, Latin and Greek. They were not kept in chronological order and were first published in 1555 as "Les Prophecies de M. Michel Nostradamus." An expanded version appeared in 1558 containing 1,000 prophecies. By this time, he had won the protection of aristocratic circles as a respected prophet. Upon his death, Nostradamus was buried upright in a church wall in Salon de Provence. Superstitious soldiers opened his grave the following century, and his bones were subsequently reinterred in another church in the same town.

The prophecies of Nostradamus have become a major reference for New Age thought. While the enigmatic quatrains are open to conflicting interpretations, some scholars have argued that more than half his predictions have come true. The controversy is furthered by the fact that, despite the abstruse language, word meanings themselves have frequently shifted over time, but translations have not always taken this into account. Nostradamus is credited with forecasting the rise of Napoleon and the Napoleonic Wars; the civil wars in both England and America as well as other historical events in these countries; the assassinations of Abraham Lincoln and both Kennedies. He foresaw the developments of air, space and submarine travel as well as the atomic bomb. On the other hand, Nostradamus predicted the beginning of a third World War between 1994 and 1999 with the destruction of New York City by a Middle Eastern despot—a war which was to last twenty-seven years and then be followed by one thousand years of peace. For many, 1999 was accepted as the beginning of the New Age. Nostradamus' prophecies conclude with the year 3797 when the world is to end, but there is a lacuna of one century before that time.

NUMEROLOGY. The study and art of using numbers qualitatively rather than quantitatively. Numerology is a method of divination that seeks to discern information of the past, present and future through psychic rather than empirical means. As a form of esoteric hermeneutics, it is similar to **astrology**, dream interpretation, casting of lots, *I Ching*, **tarot** reading, and **channeling**. As such, it becomes a standard part of the New Age portfolio of mantic arts.

Numerology itself derives in part from the idealistic philosophies of Pythagoras, Plato and **Plotinus**. One of its more prevalent manifestations applies to determining the "inner essence" of a person's name by adding together the numerical values associated with each letter until one has a single digit number. In "occult addition," $22 = 2 + 2 = 4$; $19 = 1 + 9 = 10 = 1 + 0 = 1$, and so forth. The primary nine integers each have associated various qualities and portents. While numerology possesses many different interpretive systems, one that is particularly popular in New Age is gematria, in which the letters have values in accord with the Hebrew alphabet. Gematria forms a part of the esoteric study of the **kabala** and the determination of correspondences between unrelated phenomena through the derivative number produced in the spelling of their names. Despite the many variations of numerological systems, numerology is an essential component of New Age esoterica. For many, it constitutes the Philosopher's Stone of **alchemy**.

-O-

OMEGA POINT. The central apex of the cosmos in terms of space and time. For **Teilhard de Chardin**, the omega of science and the Christ of **Christianity** will converge through an ultimate unity and cohesion—culminating in a "divine, personal Omega." This represents the fulfillment of human evolution, a time when the light of consciousness will blaze across the planet. For Teilhard, the Omega Point is millions of years in the future, though he commented on the cosmic implications of an ever-increasing pace of development—especially the technological impact of radio and television—on the integration of humanity. Had he lived to see the emergence of computer networking and the World Wide Web, he might have seen the Omega Point as sooner rather than later.

For New Age writer Peter Russell, the Omega Point might signify the end of our ever-accelerating evolution. This is thought not to represent the end of the world but the end of human dysfunctionalism. Time will continue, and so will our bodies and the species, but, according to Russell, we might find ourselves in a totally different reality—perhaps even beyond the realm of space and time. Following the implications of Einstein's theory of relativity, Russell wonders whether light is more fundamental than either space or time and whether, once the light of pure consciousness radiates through humanity, deeper truths that transcend space and time as absolutes might then become manifest.

ORR, LEONARD (c. 1938-). Developer of **rebirthing**. Orr is a graduate of Los Angeles Pacific College who, in his teens, became a born-again Christian. He has also been influenced by **Phineas Quimby** and **New Thought** ideas. Orr claims to have experienced hundreds of spontaneous rebirthings between 1962 and 1974. In 1974, he "perfected" the method of rebirthing. He developed the first training center for rebirthers in his hometown of Walton, New York, in 1975 and, with Sondra Ray, published the "bible" of the technique in 1977: *Rebirthing in the New Age*. His stated goal is to help people achieve spiritual enlightenment and self-sufficiency. In 1997, during a trip to India, he claims to have met Babaji, the biblical Angel of the Lord, in a 9,058-year-old body. Among his over twenty books, there are *Physical Immortality for Christians* (1980), *Babaji: The Angel of the Lord* (1984), *Bhartriji* (1984), *Breath Awareness* (1986), *The Common Sense of*

Physical Immortality (1988), *The Story of Rebirthing* (1990), *Turning Senility Misery into Victory* (1990), *How to Make Democracy Work* (1990), *Government without Taxes* (1991), *The Healing Power of Birth and Rebirth* (1994), *About Your Femininity* (1994), *Secrets of Youth* (1994), *Personal Energy Management* (1996), *Fire* (1997) and *Breaking the Death Habit: The Science of Everlasting Life* (1998).

OSHO—formerly, Bhagwan Shree Rajneesh (1931-1990). Controversial but popular **guru** who relished jolting people out of their attachments to ethnic or religious beliefs. He contended that national, religious, gender and racial divisions are destructive. Osho was a New Age type of leader who promoted a spiritual practice along with a propensity to shock those more established in conventional mores and understandings.

Born in India as Rajneesh Chandra Mohan, his parents were Jains, but Osho himself claimed to have never subscribed to any particular religious faith. He also claimed to have received *samadhi* at the age of twenty-one. With a master's degree from the University of Sagar, he taught philosophy for nine years at the University of Jabalpur. He combined his academic life with work as a religious teacher. His early followers came from Europe and India. These he termed *sanyassins*— again flouting the established meaning of the designation which refers to spiritual celibates. Moving from Bombay to Poona, he founded an ashram in 1974. Estimates range to as high as fifty thousand westerners who came to him in their search for enlightenment.

Allegedly because of health problems, Rajneesh, as he was then known, left India in 1981 for the United States to receive medical treatment. With a group of followers, he settled on a 65,000 acre ranch in the state of Oregon which was renamed Rajneeshpuram. Difficulties with locals ensued, but eventually several *sanyassins* were elected to the city council, and the town of Antelope was renamed City of Rajneesh. As local tensions and scandals escalated, Rajneesh fled to Charlotte, North Carolina, where he was arrested by immigration authorities and was incarcerated. The conditions of a suspended sentence were that he leave the United States, and he returned to Poona in 1987. After a brief four-day period in which he accepted **Zen** Master Katzue Ishira's prophecy that he was a **reincarnation** of Sakyamuni, the Buddha, he then claimed that he was "Buddha in my own right"—rather than a reincarnation. In this self-proclaimed capacity, he adopted the name of

"Osho" which is reputedly derived from William James' expression "oceanic experience" but is usually simply translated as "master."

At its peak, Osho's organization had about 200,000 members and 600 centers around the world. The "official" religion of Rajneeshism was disbanded in 1985. Nevertheless, the external designation often remains as the "Rajneesh Movement." For insiders, the movement is simply "sannyas." The best-known of Rajneesh/Osho's practices is dynamic meditation that begins with strenuous physical activity and concludes with silence and celebration. This was designed to lead the individual to overcome repression, lower personal inhibition, develop a state of emptiness, and attain enlightenment. According to Osho, the person would then have "no past, no future, no attachment, no mind, no ego, no self." Osho's teachings comprise a form of monism that stresses that God is in everything and everyone. It denies any division between "God" and "not-God." People, even at their worst, are considered to be divine. Osho also recognized Jesus as having attained enlightenment, and he believed that Christ had survived the crucifixion and lived subsequently in India until the age of 112.

Before his death, Osho appointed twenty-one followers ("the Inner Circle") to look after the functioning of the ashram at Poona and handle the administrative affairs relating to his work. There are currently about twenty **meditation** centers based on his teachings worldwide. His main influence now operates through his writings and video recordings. His books remain popular among many New Agers.

OUT-OF-BODY EXPERIENCE (OBE). A state of consciousness separate and apart from the physical body. It is a waking form of ecstasy related to sleep, altered states of consciousness and sensory deprivation in which a person perceives the physical environment from a vantage incommensurate with the tangible location of his or her body. The OBE dream-like state of consciousness may be produced through hypnosis, nitrous oxide, drug-induction, the body's chemical imbalance or oxygen-deprivation that causes variation in the mid-brain stem's reticular activating system (RAS). It is similar to LSD experience but is accompanied by a form of muscular paralysis. It is popularly associated with the **near-death** experience as well as **shamanic** trance. Works on the OBE and its induction include Robert Monroe's *Journeys out of the Body* (1971), *Far Journeys* (1985) and *Ultimate Journey* (1994) and

Susan Blackmore's *Parapsychology and Out-of-the-Body Experiences* (1978) and *Beyond the Body* (1982).

-P-

PAGANISM. A religious option that reveres physical spirituality either as the exclusive parameter of the divine or as the initial source of evolutionary progress. Paganism holds that there is nothing beyond nature: nature is all that is. There are many variations to this religiosity that includes animism, polytheism, pantheism, humanism and **shamanism**. It is traditionally associated with the pre-Christian peoples of Europe (classical Greece and Rome, Druids and Celts, Germanic and Nordic peoples, etc.); tribal peoples of Africa, Oceania, Asia and the Americas; the Afro-Latin-Atlantic diasporas; Japanese Shinto and the classical Confucian and Taoist religions of China. In the contemporary West, many lost traditions are being reclaimed and reconstructed. Others are being invented.

As a present-day religious movement, paganism in the West is largely a rival or competitor to the New Age movements. New Age itself has no central authority that determines what is and what is not New Age and, as part of the diffuse spiritual consumer market, it does on many occasions include pagan elements (celebrations, sacred places, ritual circles, etc.) But in general, the bias of New Age is **gnostic** and transcendental rather than pagan. *See also* NEO-PAGANISM.

PATHWORKING. A technique employed in New Age gatherings as a form of collective **meditation**. Pathworking is also a mode of group **visualization**, and it is most likely a derivative of **shamanism** with its techniques for vision quest, **healing** and psychopompic guidance of souls of the dead to the afterworld. The pathworker initially will coach his or her audience into a relaxed state receptive to suggestion. People are encouraged to close their eyes and sit in a comfortable position. The guide for the pathworking will then describe the ensuing "journey" in visual and imaginative terms. Those traveling the "inner path" are ultimately encouraged to look deep within themselves to find their own personal truth, meaning or symbolic aid (power animal, color, etc.) to assist them in their future search for enlightenment. In spiritual terms, pathworking is a form of mediation between the individual, his or her community and the world of spirits—whether these last are animal spirits, those of the forces of nature, the Ascended Masters of **The Great White Brotherhood**, or one's "Higher Self." In essence, a successful pathworking is a form of hypnosis—one that may also be undertaken individually or privately as a type of auto-hypnosis.

PERLS, FRITZ (1893-1970). Jewish-German expatriate and pioneer at the **Esalen Institute** in California in the 1960s and later at his own center near Victoria in Canadian British Columbia. He developed the *Gestalt* methodology of verbal analysis and direct confrontation with the false roles the self creates for itself. Perls, along with such seminal thinkers as **Wilhelm Reich**, Otto Rank, Kurt Lewin, Carl Rogers, Roberto Assagioli and **Abraham Maslow**, has been significantly instrumental in launching the field of humanistic psychology from which the growth and the **human potential** and subsequent New Age movements took their birth. Perls' Group Gestalt Therapy places stress on the value of immediate, authentic experience within a framework that takes the mind/body as a holistic organism rather than a Cartesian dichotomy. His most significant works are *Ego, Hunger and Aggression* (1942/1947), *Gestalt Therapy* (1951) and *Gestalt Theory* (1969).

PLOTINUS (*c.*205-*c.*270). Egyptian-born, Roman Neo-Platonist, who developed the last great system of Greek speculative philosophy. Although Plotinus condemned **gnosticism**, he promulgated a type of gnostic thought that remains implicitly at the heart of most New Age theological speculation. He distinguished four kinds of knowledge: sense knowledge as an obscure representation of truth, reason cognition that provides knowledge of the essence of things, intellectual cognition that allows self-knowledge, and ecstasy that consists of the supernatural intuition of God and the cessation of natural knowledge in the divine unconsciousness. Plotinus' metaphysics delineate both a downward progression of divine emanations from God to the world and a moral upward movement from the world to God. The ladder of being suggests the One (or God) above all understanding from which the universe proceeds not by creation but by emanation—first the Nous as the intelligence of unchanging thought, second the World Soul, and finally the visible world of material nature. In its contemplative activity, the World Soul has the Nous as its object beyond both matter and time. On the other hand, in its plastic activity, the World Soul forms the various things of the universe on the basis of the ideas that it contemplates in the Nous. Consequently, particular souls originate in the Nous but come through the World Soul into the world: first, the souls that animate the sky; second, those of the stars; third, those of the demons; and last, the human souls that fell down into the world through sin. Having once been in a state of preexistence in the Nous, human souls are now imprisoned in the body. Matter is the final step of emanation and, according to Plotinus, it is darkness and evil.

Paralleling the two activities of the World Soul, the individual soul also engages in contemplative and plastic activities. In the human, the rational tends toward the formation of ideas. The informative, by contrast, informs the body. In his attempt to solve the question "What is man and what must he do to reach happiness?" Plotinus found the Stoics and Epicureans to be unsatisfactory and turned to a monistic resolution to overcome dualism. God is seen as the supreme inconceivable reality and also the source of all other realities: the invisible and visible worlds, including humanity. For the human, God is true happiness, but being unable to obtain complete knowledge of God through reason, the individual cannot possess full happiness. In order to reach God and possess him, the human being needs the superior help that comes from God alone. Beyond all the forces of reason, God's manifesting to the individual to make her/him happy is what Plotinus refers to as "ecstasy"—the state in which one loses his or her personality and becomes united with God. Plotinus had reputedly attained this state twice in his lifetime. After his death, his works were assembled under the title of *The Enneads*. The devaluing of the material world and nature that is found in both Plotinus' Neo-Platonism and the various schools of gnosticism remains an often unarticulated but discernible perspective of the "nature is ultimately illusion" position of New Age that exalts the spiritual over the tangible.

PRECESSION OF THE EQUINOXES. The earlier occurrences of the equinoxes in each successive sidereal year. The earth functions as a tilting gyroscope and, like the slow movement of the axis of any inclined spinning body around another axis, the resultant western or retrograde motion of the equinoctial points along the ecliptic changes the direction in which the axis points. In the case of the earth, the planet's polar axis gradually shifts relative to the fixed stars. The precession of the axis causes the zodiacal constellations to appear to rotate around the earth relative to any specific point (e.g., the spring equinoctial point). The zodiac shifts fifty seconds annually, approximately one degree every seventy-two years, one complete sign every 2,160 years, and a complete zodiacal revolution (one Platonic or great year) roughly every 26,000 years. Claudius Ptolemy defined the first thirty degrees of the sky as the sign Aries, and his tropical system of astronomy/**astrology** codified in the second century C.E. began at the spring equinoctial point or 0 degrees Aries. However, due to the retrograde motion caused by equinoctial precession, the sun is now in the sign of Pisces at the time of the vernal equinox around March 21. As long as it continues to be so, we are said to be in the Age of Pisces. However, when the zodiac precesses enough to cause the vernal equinoctial point to slip back into the sign that precedes Pisces, it is asserted by astrologers that we will then have entered into the **Age of Aquarius** which, in turn, is identified by many as the New Age. *See also* JOACHIM DE FIORE.

PRECOGNITION. The predictive ability to perceive events before they occur. Precognition includes prophecy and other forms of seeing into the future. Examples of biblical precognition are found in Matthew 2:1-2 and Acts 1:15-26, 11:28, 21:1-13.

PROSPERITY CONSCIOUSNESS. The **New Thought** "science" or "art" of manifesting abundance in all areas of one's life, including finance, health, relationships, etc. Also known as abundance consciousness and wealth consciousness, prosperity consciousness teaches the use of the "Universal Law of Thought Energy Manifestation" to create abundance. Since nothing "just happens" or is "by chance," we create everything in our lives—even what seems to come through outside forces—with our thought energy. If, however, we focus our thought energy on something (people, events, circumstances and/or objects), we draw it/them into our lives from all directions. People already do this unconsciously by simply allowing their unconscious mind to create what it wants. However, using thought energy consciously is to be aware of the thought energy manifestation process and in control of that energy by actively focusing on things desired. But there is also a third type of thought energy application known as super-conscious manifestation in which one aligns oneself with the Universal Spirit. This last, working through the individual, automatically manifests everything needed for fulfilling a "higher purpose." Highly advanced spiritual beings are cited as examples—people who wander the planet without possessions in order to help and teach others. But by letting God manifest all their needs for them, those who follow their "higher purpose" find food, water, shelter and other required things automatically provided.

Prosperity consciousness holds that poverty, like disease, is an illusion. It teaches that our "Higher Selves" already possess everything that exists in the universe and have the ability to do absolutely anything. We simply have to call forth whatever is desired. Those wishing to create prosperity in their lives are encouraged to think about it constantly, affirm that they already have it, write out their affirmations, thank the Universal Spirit for bringing it to them, and **visualize** how it feels to have what they desire. The assumption is that what is desired already exists on a different vibrational frequency but needs to be brought into the physical realm. The student is encouraged to affirm, visualize, **meditate**, act and speak as if he/she already has that which is desired. (*See further* **neuro-linguistic programming**.) However, along with this positive position of affirmation, the concomitant fact that we allegedly create and/or allow our own misfortune remains one of the more **controversial** aspects of New Age, according to its critics.

PSYCHIC DREAM EXPERIENCE. Working with and integrating information obtained through extrasensory means rather than the empirical input of the five bodily senses. Unlike standard dreams that concern personal growth processes, psychic dreams—whether spontaneous or intentionally induced—involve premonitions, **astral travel**, past lives and/or intuitive insights. The broad range of psychic dreams includes **precognition** dreams—especially those that serve as warnings and motivations for preventing or changing a possible future event, **telepathic** dreams in which communication from one energy source to another occurs without mechanical assistance, apparition dreams in which personal messages are conveyed from the deceased and **clairvoyant** dreams in which the event dreamed about occurs simultaneously. **Clairaudient** dreams involve the "hearing" of information; clairsentient dreams, the "feeling" of information. **Dream-work** or the working with dream material is a typical undertaking for many within a New Age orientation. Psychic dream experience refers not only to the dreaming activity itself but also to the conscious reflection and interpretation of one's dream experience to gain a more complete understanding of one's waking reality. The process often involves recording one's dream, highlighting the elements that seem significant and looking for symbolic associations. *See also* CHANNELING, SHAMANISM and SPIRITUALISM.

PSYCHOKINESIS. The ability to move objects through mental will and without the aid of physical tools. Essentially, psychokinesis refers to the exercise of mind-over-matter and extends into spiritual **healing**. For examples of psychokinetic healing, see I Kings 5:1-27, Acts 3:3-11. *See also* NEW THOUGHT; SPIRITUALISM.

PSYCHOSYNTHESIS. A method of psychological development and self-realization developed by Roberto Assagioli (1888-1974). Intimately related to the emergence of the **human potential movement**, psychosynthesis endeavors to allow people to become the masters of their own lives without passive submission to either inner phantasms or external influences. It is a form of **transpersonal psychology** and has been described as "a psychology with a soul." The basic assumption is that by employing a collection of techniques and exercises designed to expand consciousness, the client is moved away from negating habits and life blocks toward an opening of creative potential. Besides being a practical and working method for personal growth, psychosynthesis aims for harmonious personal relationships with others as well as with self. The values of intuition, inspiration and creative insight are stressed along with the mystical and esoteric. One of its techniques involves the development of guided imagery in which images and natural objects are invoked for purposes of **meditative** discourse.

Psychosynthesis endeavors to heal feelings of separation and foster realization of one's responsibility to both self and the world as a whole. It honors the human family itself and its coverage of the whole planet and suggests that within these parameters, we need to understand ourselves on both the individual and group participatory levels. The idea is to view oneself alongside others rather than above or below anyone else. In the obtaining of our wishes, this should not occur at the expense of others.

Assagioli claimed that psychoanalysis has to do primarily with the "basement of the psyche." The transpersonal or spiritual is missing in the strictly analytical mode. Psychosynthesis, by contrast, goes further by putting back together what analysis takes apart. By synthesizing the mental, emotional, physical and spiritual, a more harmonious whole is effectively created. In other words, psychosynthesis is more complete.

By discovering one's true spiritual nature, one is able thereby to transform everyday life. The two main crises from which people suffer are the "crisis of meaning" and the "crisis of duality." Psychosynthesis aims to heal these crises by bringing the divided parts into harmony—in other words, through synthesis. Assagioli stressed that psychosynthesis is not a doctrine or school of psychology, it has no orthodoxy, and there is no exclusive representative or leader—including Assagioli himself.

The discipline employs a map that it calls the "egg of being" and which purportedly represents our total psyche. Its three horizontal divisions depict in ascending order one's lower unconscious, middle unconscious and higher unconscious or superconscious. They also represent our past, present and future, and the egg itself is surrounded by the collective unconscious. At its apex sits the higher self, while the field of consciousness and the conscious self or "I" are to be found within the zone of the middle unconscious. The egg of being is a schematic metaphor that relates primarily to one's "inner journey." Its divisions represent the different aspects of ourselves as individual beings as well as our connections with other beings.

PURSEL, JACH. Formerly San Francisco-based trance medium of a "group being" entity named Lazaris. Pursel began **channeling** in 1974. He now heads Concept Synergy in Orlando, Florida. Lazaris is presented as having never embodied in our dimension of space and time. He describes himself/themselves as "a spirit of consciousness" whose purpose is simply to have fun in human realization and evolution. The Pursel/Lazaris teachings concern humanity's spiritual journey to God/Goddess/All That Is. The person who develops a proper relationship with the All is known as a "Spiritual Adult." Such a person must engage in "shadow work" in learning to deal with hidden as well as conscious agendas. Lazaris' message is that we must overcome our negative programming in order to express fully our true natures as evolving, spiritual, immortal beings. In **Shirley MacLaine**'s 1987 book, *It's All in the Playing*, she claims that Lazaris teaches that the natural proclivity of humans is to be in harmony, that nature is the ultimate teacher, and that being itself is the goal and secret to happiness. The essential Lazaris communication is to be found in *Lazaris: The Sacred Journey. You and Your Higher Self* (1988).

PYRAMID POWER. An alleged energy concentrate reputed to exist within any pyramid modeled on the outline of the Great Pyramid of Cheops at Giza. Psychic or spiritual pyramid power is that which was reputedly employed by those who constructed the Great Pyramid through levitation and/or dematerialization—ranging from divinely inspired Hebrews to Erich Von Daniken's unidentified visitors from space, but it also refers to the energies encapsulated by the shape itself. These serve to provide communications channels between earth and extraterrestrial consciousness, a means of energy storage, a locus for **healing**, an augmentation of psychic awareness, the storage of food, and as access to the **akashic records**. **Blavatsky** made the claim that the interior of the pyramid is where the rituals of the Egyptian Book of the Dead were performed, and contemporary **theosophists** accept that mysteries are connected to the stone monument but known only to initiates. Adventist Charles Taze Russell, in his book *The Divine Plan of the Ages* (1886), argued that the pyramid's measurements both explained and prophesied biblical events from the flood of Genesis to the post-millennial reign of Christ.

Edgar Cayce, through his trance readings, advised that the Great Pyramid is the storage place of all human history and prophecies up to the year 1998, which was to be the time of the second coming of Christ. For Cayce, this information is stored in the language of mathematics, geometry and **astrology**. He claimed that the structure is ten thousand years old and was built by a consortium of Egyptians, **Atlanteans** and itinerant Caucasians from southwest Russia—led by Hermes Trismegistus, an Egyptian high priest Ra Ta (a former incarnation of Cayce) and an adviser named Isis. Cayce also put forward the idea that the Giza Pyramid was a temple in which Jesus was initiated in preparation for his ministry.

The notion of "pyramid power" frequently appears throughout what could be identified as New Age theology. The pyramid shape itself is seen as a supernatural source of energy or power. The pyramidal shape is also seen as especially conducive to **meditation**—by either sitting within a pyramid or beneath one that is suspended overhead. Pyramidology refers to the study of the energies produced both inside and outside pyramids.

-Q-

QIGONG (Ch'i kung). A combination **meditation**/martial arts form of Chinese **yoga**. Qigong or "breath skill" refers to a large variety of Chinese health techniques based on the movement of *qi*/*ch'i* ("vital energy") throughout the body. Along with **acupuncture** and the use of ginseng, qigong physiotherapeutic gymnastics form a central plank in Chinese medicine. This Sinitic form of kinesiatrics seeks the curing of illness through muscular movement. Increasingly popular in the west as a New Age/**human potential** technique, qigong aims for both physical and spiritual **healing** through the practice of meditation, posturing and "soft style" movement. Dayan gong ("wild goose method") is one form of qigong that is receiving greater attention. Another is tai-chi qigong with eighteen basic movements that serve as a bridge to the more complicated practice of **tai-chi**.

QUIMBY, PHINEAS PARKHURST (1802-1866). An American experimenter with mesmerism who has developed it into a method of **healing**. Quimby had found that some diseases could be cured by suggestion rather than with medicine and concluded from this that such diseases were essentially delusions. Eventually, he decided that all disease is illusory. He came to argue that sickness is simply a malfunction of the mind caused by a false idea or error condensing into the material. For Quimby, the major sources of error are religion, reason and medicine inasmuch as they all perpetuate the idea that people are ill.

Consequently, Quimby discarded all of **Anton Mesmer**'s original theories about magnetic fluid. Instead, he attributed healing agency to mind alone. His system was variously known as the Science of Christ, the Science of Health and even as Christian science. Under Quimby's student, **Emma Curtis Hopkins**, his teachings eventually coalesced as the **New Thought** movement. For Quimby, God is Wisdom, and matter is only a condensation of the essence of Wisdom. The human being, therefore, is a creation from the most gross forms of matter who has been breathed with the essence of God or mind. Quimby's devolving sequence becomes one of Wisdom—mind—matter. He argued that once the Truth of Wisdom or science is implanted into the mind of a patient, it can operate directly on the body to heal. Another of Quimby's students was **Mary Baker Eddy** who founded Christian science.

-R-

RAËLIAN MOVEMENT, THE. Founded by Claude Vorilhon (1946-)—renamed Raël ("messenger of the Elohim"), and using typical **galactian** but **astral** and atheistic rather than **gnostic** terminology by recognizing "our fathers from space" as Elohim. According to Raël's teachings, the Elohim, through their perfect mastery of DNA, created humanity in their own image. For Raëlians, these extraterrestrials originally came to earth in spacecraft. They maintained contact with their human creations through Moses, Buddha, Jesus, Mohammed and other prophets who were specially trained by them. The Elohim's mission now is to alert the human race to the imminent danger of self-annihilation. In this task, Raël has become the prophet for the present "Age of the Apocalypse" that began with the detonation of the nuclear bomb in 1945. Although Raël has been taken aboard a flying saucer twice, he communicates with the Elohim and Yahweh, his personal teacher and Elohim president, primarily through **telepathy.** He has been instructed that a major enterprise for the Raëlians is to construct an international embassy to which the Elohim can return once more to earth to welcome the planet into a technological world of choice, infinity and pleasure. Following instructions from the Elohim, the movement would hope to establish this embassy near Jerusalem. World government is then to be established as a form of "geniocracy" or rule by geniuses. Along with this, a universal humanitarian economy will eliminate the need for inheritance.

Unlike the more typical gnostic-idealist aversion to the joys of the physical universe, there is no Raëlian rejection but rather an endorsement of pleasure. The central practice of sensual **meditation** is a set of contemplation techniques that aim for individual communication with the Elohim in order to regain control over and happiness in all areas of life (body discovery, sexuality, enjoyment through the senses, cosmic organism, etc.) Some of these methods are designed to be used by two people of the opposite sex. Nevertheless, the movement stresses complete choice in the selection of sexual partners as well as in all other aspects of life. As long as no one else is harmed, Raëlians are encouraged to be free of social mores and inhibitions.

For the Raëlians, our galaxy is simply a tiny particle of an atom of a living being on a planet revolving around a sun in some super-galaxy.

Likewise, the subatomic particles of atoms in our own world are seen by Raëlians as galaxies in themselves. The mystical union between the sub-universes and super-universes within and beyond the individual is accomplished through sensual meditation. The immortality of **reincarnation**, in turn, is to be achieved through the process of serial cloning. Consequently, and in view of the Raëlian belief that all earthly life originated artificially, Raëlians support biotechnological developments—whether concerning genetically altered foods, increased mechanization, robotized automation, space exploration, use of computers or reproduction of animal and human life through cellular cloning. By the steady advances of science as well as the assistance of the Elohim, Raëlians expect the world to enter a golden age.

RAMANA MAHARSHI (1879-1950). Vedantic teacher who stressed asking the central question: "Who am I?" He described the "most direct path" as that in which the meditator withdraws attention from all objects, both the external world and internal thought, to reverse awareness to its source. Ramana felt another direct path beside self-inquiry is unreserved surrender of one's life and world to God. This last also places one's mind into a position of detached observer of all that reputedly belongs to God: the world, one's own body, emotions and thoughts. Following in the Advaita-Vedanta tradition of non-duality, Ramana taught that the ultimate purpose of life is self-realization. The guru's teachings have been continued at the Sri Ramanasramam of south India, but other jnana **yoga** centers in the tradition of Ramana have been established worldwide: e.g., the Society of Abidance in Truth at Santa Cruz, California, the Aruachala Ashrama Centers of New York and Nova Scotia, the Associazione Italiana Ramana Maharshi, etc. While not a direct "part" of New Age, the teachings of Ramana Maharshi have introduced **Hindu** concepts and practices to many within the movement.

RAPID EYE TECHNOLOGY. *See* IRIDOLOGY.

REBIRTHING. Continuous or circular hyperventilation technique developed by **Leonard Orr** in 1974. Also known as conscious breathing and intuitive energy breathing, the process is an attempt to develop one's ability to breathe energy as well as air. It involves unraveling the birth trauma, the death urge and, ultimately, all human conditioning with the final goal of having a conscious and sustained experience of the "Eternal Spirit." Orr describes the breathing rhythm of rebirthing as the most powerful form of prana **yoga**. Its continual alteration between conscious inhaling and exhaling is believed to release physical, mental and emotional toxins. Initially, the breathing work was conducted in warm water following Orr's accidental discovery of its benefits while taking a bath. Subsequent experimentation has led to the realization that aquatic immersion is not necessary. The rebirthing experience usually lasts approximately an hour and fifteen minutes. In many respects, Orr's rebirthing breathwork is similar to **Stanislav Grof's holotropic breathwork**. In 1979, Jim Leonard modified rebirthing into a form he designated Vivation. This last deals with lower levels of emotional intensity and is based on the realization that it is not necessary to undergo the full trauma of the original emotional experience but that effectiveness is more powerful and integrating if the relived event occurs at more comfortable levels of feeling. Instead of the cathartic prenatal and perinatal experience of rebirthing, vivation is more concerned with gentle integration. Leonard and Phil Laut published *Rebirthing: The Science of Enjoying All of Your Life* in 1983.

REFLEXOLOGY. A discipline that seeks to diagnose ailments through an examination of the foot or hand. In reflexology, the foot and hand are believed to mirror the body as a whole—the large toe, for example, corresponding to the head. Treatment involves the manipulation and **massage** of the foot part or hand part that connects to the afflicted area of the body itself. Reflexology was introduced to the West in 1913 by William Fitzgerald, an American ear, nose and throat surgeon. Eunice Ingham further refined foot reflexology in the 1930s. Congestion or tension in any part of the foot is claimed to link to congestion or tension in the corresponding part of the body. Reflexology operates on the principle of unblocking vital pathways and rebalancing energies. There are many, many books on the subject including Michael Blate's *How To Heal Yourself Using Foot Acupressure (Foot Reflexology)* (1983), Kevin and Barbara Kunz' *The Complete Guide to Reflexology* (1984), Nicola Hall's *Reflexology: A Patient's Guide* (1986), Laura Norman's *The Reflexology Handbook* (1988) and Ann Gillanders' *Reflexology: The Theory and Practice* (1994).

REICH, WILHELM (1897-1957). Fomenting instigator behind much of New Age's therapeutic body-work. Focusing on his belief that orgasms lead to a healthier and more complete lifestyle, Reich claimed to have discovered a new kind of energy that he named "orgone" and which is detectable in basic units of *bions* (at a microscopic intermediate stage between the organic and non-organic). These, he argued, permeate the universe in pulsating waves but can be captured and harnessed into a special "orgone energy accumulator" and used to heal disease. Despite the opposition he engendered and his eventual imprisonment by federal authorities, his idea of a vital field of psychic bio-energy that can be accessed and employed toward the curing of cancer and other physical ailments is the foundation for the wide range of New Age alternative **healing** therapies. Along with **Abraham Maslow**, Carl Rogers, **Fritz Perls** and others, Reich is recognized as instrumental in the emergence of humanistic psychology and the **human potential movement**. He developed "character analysis" in dealing with neurosis and stressed the need for "libido stasis" to be overcome through gratification in the sexual act rather than in the sexual act alone—what he termed the increase of "orgastic potency." In developing his "science of orgonomy" that deals with the reputed functional laws of cosmic energy, Reich made three principal discoveries: the reality of the libido as a flow of energy, the orgasm's regulatory function of that energy flow, and the body's muscular armor that prevents energy regulation. He died in prison shortly before he was due to be released.

REIKI. "Universal life energy" from *rei* "free passage" or "transcendental spirit" + *ki* "vital life force energy" or "universal energy." A Japanese form of **healing** that involves the transference of energy from the practitioner to the patient to stimulate the body's natural propensity to heal itself. Reiki is a laying-on-of-hands technique that manipulates the energy field and seeks to rebalance energy within the body. It may combine spiritual healing with use of **auras**, crystals, **chakra** balancing, **meditation**, **aromatherapy**, **naturopathy** and **homeopathy**. Essentially, reiki is energy work rather than **massage**, but unlike forms of spiritual healing in which it is the healer who sends out the energy, in reiki it is the recipient who draws the energy as it is required.

Reiki possibly originated anciently in Tibet but was rediscovered by Mikao Usui (died in 1893). It was introduced into the Western world in the mid-1970s. While there are today many variations, there are two principal forms: the Usui system of natural healing that aims to balance and strengthen the body's energy—thereby promoting self-healing, and the radiant technique that employs transcendental, pure light energy as the "reiki factor." This last follows a direct lineage from Usui through Jujiro Hayashi and Mrs. Hawayo Takata (1900-1980) to Barbara Weber Ray. It focuses more on teaching the client the means to enhance his/her own healing energy. Ray's book is *The Reiki Factor* (1983). Another related work is Paula Horan's 1990 *Empowerment through Reiki: The Path to Personal and Global Transformation*.

REINCARNATION. Rebirth into a new and different physical body after the death of one's present incarnation. While the doctrine of reincarnation, metempsychosis or transmigration of the soul is an early western belief (e.g., Pythagoras), with its subsequent rejection by **Christianity**, it has largely re-entered the west through **Hinduism** and **Buddhism** and especially via **theosophy**. The eastern notion is that if a person's accounts are not settled before death, he/she returns to terrestrial life in order to complete them. The seed of **karma** is believed to become stored in the causal body, and no soul can detach itself until its karmic accounts are cleared.

For theosophists, the register of past lives is maintained as the **Akashic Records** that penetrate both the physical and spiritual worlds. In Hinduism, the law of karma as action or cause and effect is a basic tenet of belief. It is what binds one to the cycle of birth, death and rebirth from which Hindus hope to attain release. With Buddhism, it is human desire that makes the cycle of rebirth. *Nirvana* is obtained with the quenching of all desire. Sikh religion also accepts the notion of reincarnation as the route toward a love-union with God. The process of transmigration could also end when a person meets his/her "true" **guru**.

Adopted into the general "canon" of New Age belief, reincarnation is the process by which the divine and immortal soul perfects itself. Unlike contemporary western **paganism** in which rebirth is a means to continue experience of the joys of life, for New Age following in its **gnostic** and theosophical heritage, reincarnation is to be superseded by final reintegration with the divine. For many, the idea of reincarnation explains the reality of suffering and unfairness in the world. Differences in life span and fortune are understood in the light of individual progress toward perfection.

New Age figures who work with an understanding of reincarnation include **Adi Da Samraj, Asahara Shoko, Helena Blavatsy, Edgar Cayce,** Elizabeth Clare Prophet, **Benjamin Creme, Ram Dass, JZ Knight, Shirley MacLaine, Mother Meera, Ruth Montgomery, Swami Muktananda,** Chögyam Trungpa Rinpoche, **Thich Nhat Hanh, Ramana Maharshi, Sathya Sai Baba, Houston Smith,** Luc Jouret, **Rudolf Steiner, Tarthang Tulku Rinpoche, Penny Torres, George Trevelyan,** and **Paramahansa Yogananda.**

RELIGIOUS SCIENCE. Like **Divine Science,** a denomination within the **New Thought** alliance. But unlike Divine Science, the United Church of Religious Science employs a more overt form of "New Age-speak." It makes use of spiritual mind treatment structured as an affirmative five-step prayer. The basic affirmations of Religious Science include that people are made in the image of God, that they are thus one with infinite life, that all life is governed by spiritual laws, and that people create their experiences by their thoughts and beliefs. Religious Science emphasises the distinction between objective mind (waking consciousness) and subjective mind (or subconscious that is most clearly seen under hypnosis). Health is accordingly obtained when the subjective mind becomes impressed by the objective mind with images of **healing** and wholeness. In this vein, the ministry of Religious Science includes its many practitioners who have been trained both in spiritual mind treatment and in the use of the Universal Subjective Mind to bring healing to others. *See also* TERRY COLE-WHITTAKER.

ROBBINS, JOHN. Leading expert on the **dietary** link with the **environment** and health. Rejecting his Baskin-Robbins inheritance, Robbins seeks active engagement with the living world to end pollutions and extinctions. He lives ecologically and in self-sustainability and promotes a wise and compassionate stewardship of a balanced ecosystem. He has founded Y.E.S.! (Youth For Environmental Sanity) and, in 1988, EarthSave International dedicated to healthy food choices, preservation of the environment and a more compassionate world. His books include *Diet for a New America: How Your Food Choices Affect*

Your Health, Happiness, and the Future of Life on Earth (1987), *May All Be Fed: Diet for a New World* (1993), *The Awakened Heart: Meditations on Finding Harmony in a Changing World*—with Ann Mortifee (1997), *Reclaiming Our Health: Exploding the Medical Myth and Embracing the Source of True Healing*—with **Marianne Williamson** (1998) and *The Food Revolution: How Your Diet Can Help Save Your Life and the World* (2001).

RODEGAST, PAT. *Nom de plume* of Pat de Vitalis and channel of the Emmanuel material. Rodegast serves as a trustee of the Pathwork Foundation, a charity and international network dedicated to personal transformation and spiritual self-realization. For nearly three decades, Rodegast has channelled Emmanuel, described as a "Being of Light." Emmanuel's message is that separation from our true selves is the source of all human pain. Out of fear, we create prisons for ourselves, but there are unlimited possibilities that emerge when we experience our lives as love—love being the only thing that is real. The reputedly lucid insights of Emmanuel have been hailed by **Ram Dass** and edited into three *Emmanuel's Books* by Rodegast and Judith Stanton: Volume 1: *A Manuel for Living Comfortably in the Cosmos* (1985), Volume 2: *The Choice for Love* (1989), and Volume 3: *What's An Angel Doing Here?* (1994). A fourth volume is underway. The Emmanuel material concerns the interconnectedness of human divinity with daily life as well as the process of making things conscious. Emmanuel Book discussion groups are to be found in New York, Houston, New Bedford, Massachusetts, and Bonn, Germany. *See also* CHANNELING.

ROLFING or Structural Integration. A holistic somatic work method developed by Ida P. Rolf (1896-1979; Ph.D. from Columbia University in 1920) that aims to rebalance a person's structural, postural and movement patterns. Developed in the 1950s, Rolfing is a leading **human potential** technology for postural realignment, body-centered stress management, release of energy blockage and the resolution of trauma. Concerned with both deep tissue body-work and organic structural integration, it is particularly popular for the treatment of sports injuries, but it also encourages emotional freedom as an additional consequence of increased bodily comfort and flexibility. Trainers and practitioners are certified through the Rolf Institute that continues Dr. Rolf's work. Much of the **therapy** involves the gentle manipulation of the connective tissue, joint decompression and encouraging the body to find its natural alignment. Emotional and spiritual well-being are claimed as further consequences for a body freed from pain. Although originally a painful therapy, Rolfing is now a much softer and holistic focus on the whole person that is used to develop inner resilience and peaceful centeredness.

ROSICRUCIANISM. A brotherhood of mystic scholars, esoteric researchers and **alchemists** dating allegedly to the seventeenth century. The first historical appearance of the Rose-Cross fraternity dates to 1710 when Samuel Richter established the Golden Rosicrucians. Lodges were established in Great Britain and America and subsequently proliferated in the eighteenth, nineteenth and twentieth centuries. Whether actual or mythical, Rosicrucianism itself is traced to the writings of a Christian Rosencreutz (1378-1484) who had reputedly traveled from Germany to the Mediterranean mystery-schools and acquired knowledge of the fundamental harmony between the microcosm and macrocosm as well as the **magical** cure of disease. The interaction between **Freemasonry** and Rosicrucianism has been a persistent feature, and a collective symbolism for both orders draws from such eclectic sources as **Christianity**, the **Kabala** and ancient Egyptian iconography. This is reflected variously in different societies—e.g., Stanislas de Guaïta's Cabalistic Order of the Rose-Cross or the Egyptian temple of the A.M.O.R.C. with its headquarters in San Jose, California. **Theosophy**'s Ancient Wisdom tradition can itself be traced to both Freemasonry and Rosicrucianism. Like Freemasonry and the later theosophy, contemporary Rosicrucianism teaches a form of Christian **gnosticism** in which psychic development, **meditative** discipline and spiritual transformation are emphasized. Advance is made by a system of initiation through a series of degrees.

RUTHERFORD, LEO. A leading expert on **shamanism** in the United Kingdom. Rutherford has experimented with ayahuasca and trained with North American Indians. He is concerned with trance dancing, shamanic journeying and soul retrieval and employs the **medicine wheel** (a "Circle of Knowledge") as a macrocosmic/microcosmic model. He directs the Eagle's Wing Centre for Contemporary Shamanism that organizes shamanic workshops, trance dance experience, and distributes books, tapes and other materials relating to shamanism. He has written *Principles of Shamanism* (1997) and *Way of Shamanism* (2001). Rutherford teaches something more akin to traditional shamanism; he tends to be less sensational than a **Michael Harner** or a **Carlos Castaneda**.

-S-

SAI BABA, SATHYA (1926-). Controversial Indian spiritual leader—worshipped by many as an avatar of God, and deplored by others as a fraudulent trickster and pedophile. Born in the Andra Pradesh village of Puttaparthi as Satyanarayana Raju, as a youth he helped others, performed miracles and demonstrated that he was beyond pleasure and pain. With the growing recognition of his spiritual uniqueness by others, he established his ashram, Prasanthi Nilayam (Abode of Eternal Peace), as well as Brindavan, his summer residence, as his principal centers for receiving devotees. Sathya Sai Baba is believed to be a **reincarnation** of Shri Sai Baba of Shirdi, a respected Moslem holy man who dressed like a Moslem but wore the Hindu *vibhuti* ash on his forehead and died in 1918—predicting his successive incarnation as Sathya Sai Baba. The present incarnation is expected to conclude in the year 2022 and will be followed by rebirth as Prema Sai in the Mandya district of Karnataka who will teach "that not only does God reside in everybody, but everybody is God."

Sathya Sai Baba's Prema Sai Baba Organization is devoted to the social, moral and spiritual uplift of humanity through the five principal universal values of *sathya* ("truth"), *dharma* ("right conduct"), *santhi* ("peace"), *prema* ("love") and *ahimsa* ("non-violence"). Individuals are encouraged to serve humanity. Over 5,000 service groups have been established under Sai Baba's service organization, and 6,500 poverty-stricken villages of India have been adopted as part of a rural village uplift program. Sai Baba has also established three charitable hospitals and over 250 charitable medical clinics. As an educator, Sai Baba has founded a major Indian university, six colleges and twenty technical schools. In addition, emphasizing service to the community and dedication to practicing the ideals of brotherhood, 6,500 Sathya Sai Baba centers, non-sectarian spiritual groups in over 137 countries, exist to study the practice and teachings of Sai Baba and incorporate them into their daily lives.

Sai Baba claims omnipresence and says that "God is not subject to any limitation." He also insists that "miracles are [simply] my visiting cards." The production of *vibhuti*, jewelry, fruit and flowers through the wave of a hand is declared to be incidental to the spiritual discipline that is his true emphasis and core of his teachings. He reputedly restored Radhakrishna to life in 1953 and Walter Cowan in 1971. Sai Baba affirms the truth and unity of all faiths as well as the ecumenical/interfaith elements of worship. While Sai Baba practice may be described as "Neo-Hindu," in India dedication is integrated with the surrounding religious culture, and only the most devoted devotees regard membership as an ultimate or exclusive commitment. Most western devotees reject the label of "Hindu" and deny that Sai Baba is a **Hindu** figure. Instead, they emphasize the universal mission of the **guru** as a "world teacher." The ecumenical stress and spiritual practice are fully compatible with New Age ideals, and Sathya Sai Baba remains *de facto* a New Age figure.

SAMS, JAMIE (1951-). Writer and artist of Seneca and Cherokee descent. Sams promotes "Native American Wisdom" and working with sacred patterns. With David Carson, she produced in 1988 *Medicine Cards: The Discovery of Power Through the Ways of Animals.* Other books and/or audiotapes include *Earth Medicine: Ancestors' Ways of Harmony for Many Moons* (1994), *Animal Medicine: The Wisdom and Symbolism of Animals* (1997), *The Land of Enchantment*—with Meatball Fulton (1997), *Dancing the Dream: The Seven Sacred Paths to Human Transformation* (1998) and *The Woman's Book of Dreams: Dreaming as a Spiritual Practice* (1999). Two students of Sams', Julie Rivers and Dona Wilder, have established the Heyokah Center near Santa Fe to provide space for women's sweatlodge ceremonies.

SATIR, VIRGINIA (1916-1988). Designated "the Columbus of Family Therapy," Satir's goal was to improve relationships and communication within the family unit. The Satir model postulates that **therapy** involves an intense experience with the inner-self. In 1959, along with Don Jackson, Jules Ruskin and Gregory Bateson, Satir began the Mental Research Institute in Palo Alto, California, with the country's first formal program in family therapy. As a creative family therapist, she sought to help people realize their full **human potential**. This, she believed, involved both **healing** and connecting with one's inner self and focusing on personal growth and health rather than illness and pathology. Satir also stressed the development of the interconnection of all human beings as essential to world peace. In 1977, she founded Avanta: The Virginia Satir Network as a non-profit organization dedicated to training and supporting people "to be more training and supporting people "to be more fully human." Its affiliate, the Satir Institute of the Southeast, Inc., sponsors personal and professional training. Beside *Conjoint Family Therapy* (1964), Satir authored or co-authored eleven other books including *Peoplemaking* (1972) and *The New Peoplemaking* (1988).

SCIENTOLOGY. A cyber-religion with **pagan**, New Age and humanist affinities. It does not identify with or as New Age per se, but endorses self-determination and will-to-success scenarios. In opposing psychiatry and psychology as mechanistic disciplines that disregard or discount the soul (psyche), Scientology anticipates **transpersonal psychology**. Founded by L. Ron Hubbard in 1954 as an outgrowth of his earlier dianetics, or techniques for handling the unknown reactive (stimulus-response) mind that causes irrational and psychosomatic behavior, the Church of Scientology is dedicated to "the freeing of the soul by wisdom." On the community level, Scientology desires an evangelical antiseptic world as a better place to which one can return in a future life. The Church's belief in "past lives" and the ability to determine future lives is a variation on the doctrine of **reincarnation**.

SEVEN BODIES OF THE INDIVIDUAL. Theosophy's seven bodies of the individual deriving from the seven planes of existence: Divine—Adi; Monadic—Anupadaka; Spiritual—Nirvanic; Intuitional—Buddhic; Mental—Mental; **Astral**—Astral; and Physical—Physical. On the monadic level, one unites with all that exists. The seventh level is that of physical reality and, for the human being, constitutes the gross material body. In theosophical thought, the astral is considered to be a low-grade immaterial plane. In its rejection of **spiritualism**, theosophy argues that most spiritualist phenomena involve contact with the lower psychism of the astral plane—including "discarded astral shells" of beings who have moved on to higher planes of existence.

SEVEN RAYS. The **theosophical** assistants to the chief representative of the cosmic departments of Will, Love Wisdom and Intelligence. These assistants, or Seven Rays, manifest the department heads to humanity. The first three are known as the Three Aspects, or Major Rays; the remaining four, as the Four Attributes, or Minor Rays. They employ the colors of the rainbow in aiding people to free themselves from rebirth and return their spark of divinity (manifest as a trinity of spirit, intuition and mentality) to its spiritual home.

The Department Head of Will is Manu Vaivasvata, whose assistant (the First Ray) is Master Morya. The Bodhisattva **Maitreya** rules Love Wisdom and has the Master Koot Hoomi as his assistant (the Second Ray). The remaining five rays serve as assistants to the Maha Chohan, whose province is Intelligence. The Venetian Master is the Third Ray, Master Serapis the Fourth, Master Hilarion the Fifth, Master Jesus the Sixth and Master Prince Rakoczi the Seventh. All these Ascended Masters belong to the **Great White Brotherhood**. Within the Brotherhood, Morya has an assistant in Master Jupiter, who in turn has a special relationship to India. The assistant to Koot Hoomi (Kuthumi, Kut Hoomi, etc.) is Djual Khool, who has a special connection with the **Theosophical Society**.

However, the hierarchy of the Seven Rays represents positions rather than specific entities. For instance, the Bethlehem Jesus was a **reincarnation** of Sri Krishna. According to theosophy, he is now occupying the position of the Bodhisattva Maitreya. The Master Jesus position in the hierarchy is currently being filled by the person who had previously been the Greek philosopher Apollonius. Among the remaining present masters of the Seven Rays, there are Pythagoras for the position of Koot Hoomi, **Plotinus** for the Venetian, Iambichus for Hilarion and both Rosenkreutz and Roger Bacon for Prince Rakoczi. Each of the Seven Rays has one or more chief characteristics: (1) Power and Strength, (2) Wisdom, (3) Adaptability, (4) Harmony and Beauty, (5) Science, (6) Purity and Devotion and (7) Ordered Service (Ceremonial Magic).

SHAFFER, CAROLINE. Organizational coach and consultant concerned with developing and maintaining long-term commitments to partner, family, friends and community. Shaffer is a member of the non-profit owners association of Shenoa, a northern California retreat center. With Kristin Anundsen, she has published *Creating Community Anywhere: Finding Support and Connection in a Fragmented World* (1993).

SHAH, IDRIES (1924-1996). Afghan writer and foremost authority on contemporary **Sufi** spirituality and education. Raised a Sunni Moslem,

Shah as a voice for moderate and liberal Islam adapted classical Sufi spiritual thought to the modern world. He wrote more than thirty books—many as the carefully constructed stories often used in Sufism for teaching purposes: *The Sufis* (1964), *Tales of the Dervishes: Teaching-Stories of the Sufi Masters over the Past Thousand Years* (1967), *Thinkers of the East: Studies in Experientialism* (1971), *The Book of The Book* (1976), *Neglected Aspects of Sufi Study: Beginning to Begin* (1977), *Learning How to Learn: Psychology and Spirituality in the Sufi Way* (1978), *Wisdom of the Idiots* (1979), *World of the Sufi* (1979), *The Elephant in the Dark: Christianity, Islam and the Sufis* (1982), *A Perfumed Scorpion: A Way to the Way* (1982), *The Way of the Sufi* (1983), *Reflections* (1983), *Darkest England* (1987), *A Veiled Gazelle: Seeing How to See* (1988), *Caravan of Dreams* (1988), *Sufi Thought and Action: An Anthology of Important Papers* (1990), *Seeker After Truth: A Handbook of Tales and Teachings* (1992), *Oriental Magic* (1993) and *The Commanding Self* (1994).

SHAMANISM. In the narrow sense, the religious practices of the people of Siberia—particularly the Tungusic tribals. In its wider and more generally used sense, however, shamanism designates any religious system that is centered on a religious specialist whose authority derives from ecstatic experiences. In this extended sense, shamanism includes not only the shaman of the Tungus peoples, the *angakut* of the Arctic Eskimo, the *noiaidit* of the Lapps, the Yoruban *elegun* or the equivalent medicine person/"witch-doctor" of other preliterate, oral tradition ethnicities, but also the Mayan *chilan*, the Chinese *wu*, the Japanese *miko* or the Korean *mudang*. Predominantly, shamanism is not a religion per se but rather a set of techniques that are employed within the framework of a quasi-religious animistic ideology.

Shamanism, however, has developed a third application that refers to western techniques and practices involving deliberate shifts of perspective aiming to augment spiritual understanding. These techniques are variously known as "new shamanism," "New Age shamanism," "Neo-shamanism" and **Michael Harner**'s "core-shamanism." Collectively, Neo-shamanism is a polyglot, pluralistic movement that parallels the eclectic and multicultural/multiperspectival developments of contemporary western spiritual proliferation. It encompasses not only New Age but also **Neo-paganism** as well as *ayahuasca*, *San Pedro* and related explorations whether under the auspices of a Latin American *curañdero* or within the context of a western workshop. In its more New Age emphasis, the Neo-shamanic tends to deny the reality of intrinsically nefarious spirits.

While traditional shamanism is a largely rural if not indigenous tribal phenomenon, New Age and related shamanisms are increasingly urban in context. Altered states of consciousness are induced through **meditative** techniques, trance drumming, frenzied dancing, fasting, sleep deprivation and/or entheogenic ingestion. These can occur in the privacy of one's home, in a ritual group setting, in disco venues or through visits to significant and possibly ancient urban nexi and especially to the countryside. As a rule, however, New Age shamanism does not possess the intimate community support and purpose that is integral to the traditional context. Instead, it represents an adaptation of trance techniques to contemporary, largely urban, western needs. But what it does share with original concerns is a focus on **healing**, although again this healing is less something that the shaman performs on behalf of one or more members of the immediate community but rather is an effort undertaken for the physical, mental and/or spiritual welfare of the shaman himself/herself. In this sense, or at least in its present stage of development, New Age shamanism constitutes essentially a form of self- or auto-healing. It derives primarily from romantic notions established by Mircea Eliade and **Carlos Castaneda**.

Unlike indigenous shamanisms, for core shamanism knowledge becomes exoteric rather than esoteric. There is also little attempt to master spirits. In fact, its New Age aim is to give power directly back to the people and thereby eliminate the specialist altogether. Contemporary western shamanism becomes, accordingly, a spiritual discipline that enables one to contact and use the spiritual dimension of the universe directly—a practice that establishes itself on the animistic understanding that everything that exists in the physical plane contains spirit power. While some New Agers prefer to see this process as a shamanic revival rather than as "Neo-shamanism," there nevertheless remains much confusion between the peak experience as the goal rather than simply the doorway. The new shamanism retains the New Age theodicy that denies the negative as either real or evil.

Overall, New Age shamanism derives as much from Amerindian spiritual practice as it does from Harner's Eliade and Castaneda-inspired "core-shamanism" and related developments. **Sun Bear** and his Bear Tribe Medicine Society have played a key role in this derivation as well as the auxiliary fascination with the **medicine wheel** and its accompanying ceremonies. Others that belong to the Native American branch of Neo-shamanism include Castaneda, Black Elk (Oglala Sioux), **Lynn Andrews** and Britain's **Leo Rutherford** (London's Eagle's Wing Centre for Contemporary Shamanism). More in the tradition of Harner and shamanic vision quest is Jonathan Horwitz, while names associated with Latin American "power plant" practice are Alan Shoemaker and Wilfred van Dorp.

SHEARER, TONY. Lakota American Indian artist, flutist and storyteller. Shearer is credited with interpreting the Aztec sun calendar stone and conveying to **Jose Argüelles** in the late 1960s/early 1970s the "Harmonic Convergence" Earth changes dates of August 16th and 17th, 1987. At this point, the 5,720 year calendrical cycle was to complete and rebegin. Influenced by the Book of Mormon, Shearer affirmed Quetzalcoatl's prophecy of the Thirteen Heavens and Nine Hells that foretells the New Aeon. The pivotal point has been described as the "Point of Perfection" and the **"Omega Point** of vision." Shearer has written *Lord of the Dawn* (1971), *Beneath the Moon and Under the Sun* (1975) and *The Praying Flute: Song of the Earth Mother* (1975).

SHELDRAKE, RUPERT (1942-). London-based biologist and biochemist. Sheldrake explores the connections between mystical experience, spirituality, philosophy and science. He has fused a holistic philosophy of nature with **alternative medicine**, parapsychology and quantum theory. Sheldrake has been influenced by Father Bede Griffiths' attempts to bridge **Christianity** with **Eastern mystical traditions**. Nevertheless, as a scientist, his emphasis is on re-empowering the independent investigation of the scientific discipline. Sheldrake is a fellow of the San Francisco-based Institute of Noetic Sciences. He is married to Jill Purce, active in the British New Age world as a musical healer through the use of vocal sound.

Sheldrake's books are *A New Science of Life* (1981), *Presence of the Past* (1988), *The Rebirth of Nature* (1990), *Seven Experiments That Could Change the World: A Do-It-Yourself Guide to Revolutionary Science* (1994) and *Dogs That Know When Their Owners Are Coming*

Home, and Other Unexplained Powers of Animals (1999). With Ralph Abraham and Terrence McKenna, he wrote *Trialogues at the Edge of the West* (1992), and with **Matthew Fox**, two books: *Natural Grace: Dialogues on Science and Spirituality* (1996) and *The Physics of Angels* (1996).

SHIATSU. A Japanese-derived **therapy** similar to acupressure that remains a centrally popular New Age and human potential technique. Shiatsu, from *shi* "finger" + *atsu* "pressure," employs various hand pressures (using palms, fingers and/or thumbs) on specific body surface points to counteract fatigue and stimulate the natural self-curative abilities of the body. Strictly speaking, it is not a medicine but a preventative. It aims to keep the body in an optimal condition of health in order to prevent the development of symptoms that would require medical assistance. Shiatsu is based on many years of study and research into the natural response to rub a part of the body that is sore. It represents the systematization of the findings of such instinctive treatment as a therapeutic method that is applicable to a wide range of ailments. In 1940, the Namikoshi Institute of Shiatsu Therapy was the sole Japanese institution devoted to Shiatsu. In 1955, the Japanese Ministry of Health and Welfare acknowledged the validity of shiatsu within the category of Japanese **massage** (*amma*) and Western-style massage. Since receiving official governmental recognition, the Nippon Shiatsu School has continued to spread the practice throughout the world. As a therapeutic system without unpleasant or harmful side effects, shiatsu is considered to be in complete accord with nature. The points of the body surface that are important include those over muscles, bones, nerves, blood vessels, lymph nodes, and the glands of the endocrine system. *See also* ACUPUNCTURE.

SIEGEL, BERNARD (BERNIE) S. (1933-). New Haven-based pediatric and general surgeon following classical medical training at Colgate University, Cornell University Medical College, Yale New Haven Hospital and the Children's Hospital of Pittsburgh. Siegel's first book is *Love, Medicine and Miracles* (1986); his third, *Peace, Love and Healing* (1989). He emphasizes that illness, disease and suffering, as "motivators and redirectors," constitute opportunities to heal not just the disease but our lives as well. The *person* must be understood first before the disease that manifests in the body-mind can be. Any particular disease is not arbitrary or accidental but visits certain types of people as a "form of existential self-expression for a patient" and indicates a fundamental lack of balance. Siegel stresses that illness is not a signal of failure, since the only failure he accepts is not living life to the full. It is guilt alone that blocks one's innate **healing** capacities. Health and mental balance depend on the maintenance of a firm and cheerful spirit.

Siegel's views accord with those of **Louise Hay, Deepak Chopra** and **Caroline Myss**. The core contention with all these New Age healers and spokespeople is that the route to rejecting or eliminating illness from our bodies is by changing the way we think and behave. For Siegel, the approach must be individual, and healing itself may entail either a cure or at least a transformation that allows one a positive reconciliation to death. Disease, therefore, becomes a means for self-redirection. Rather than a sentence, it represents a "new beginning."

Siegel encourages those he treats to become "exceptional patients"—a central term in his philosophy. These are those who fight for themselves and challenge their doctors and health carers if they feel they are not receiving the support or information they need for recovery. But above all, these are people who "don't try not to die. They try to live until they die." Siegel has here fused traditional medical training with a **New Thought** emphasis on positive affirmation and the New Age belief that love and healing supersede the curing process itself. He pioneered talking to people under anesthesia and in 1978 began the Exceptional Cancer Patients program of individual and group **therapy**. Patients' dreams, drawings and images are used in a loving and safe confrontation to facilitate personal change and healing. Former president of the American Holistic Medical Association, Siegel has attempted to humanize medical education. Some of his other books and/or audio transcriptions include *Personal Reflections and Meditations* (1989), *Healing Images* (1990), *How to Live between Office Visits* (1993), *Healing From the Inside Out* (1997) and *Prescriptions for Living* (1999). Siegel's primary concern is self-healing through **visualization** and guided imagery. For him, the New Age represents "Let's open our eyes."

SIKH DHARMA. A western Sikh movement established by Harbhajan Singh Khalsa Yogiji (1929-), *a.k.a.* Yogi Bhajan, in Los Angeles in

1969. His followers are known by their distinctive white clothing—women with veils; men with turbans. Returning to his native India in 1971, Yogi Bhajan received the authority from Amritsar's Golden Temple to initiate his followers directly into the Sikh faith (khalsa). The headquarters of Sikh Dharma with its educational arm, the Healthy-Happy-Holy Organization, or 3HO, was transferred to Espanola, New Mexico, in the 1980s. The movement forbids use of tobacco, alcohol or recreational drugs. Members are also **vegetarian**, and bodily hygiene is emphasized. Yogi Bhajan's published works include *The Teachings of Yogi Bhajan* (1977), *The Experience of Consciousness* (1977) and *Kundalini Yoga/Sadhana Guidelines* (1978). The Sikh stricture of uncut hair is explained in New Age terms as facilitating electromagnetic fields in the body.

The movement emphasizes a form of Kundalini **Yoga** (*see* **Muktananda, Swami**). Through chanting, breathing exercises and yogic positions, the energy coiled at the base of the spine is said to be unwound and directed to the pineal gland or seventh **chakra** as the "seat of the soul." Yogi Bhajan's movement is hierarchical with the **guru** at top followed by a Khalsa Council and then regional ministers. Local centers with their ministers form the base. Members who have been baptized into the Sikh Khalsa are designated Amritdhari; the others are Sahajdhari. Women have equal status and are regarded as female aspects of divinity. They also have their own auxiliary: the Grace of God Movement of the Women of the World. Yogi Bhajan also personally teaches a form of **tantric** yoga when he visits particular congregations. The movement also operates several vegetarian restaurants. It is to be found principally in North America.

SILVA MIND CONTROL. A positive thinking, self-help, non-mystical and practical philosophy that validates all positive aspects of the individual's life including health, relationships, understanding of others and the appetite for life itself. Developed by Jose Silva (1914-1999) in the 1960s in the state of Texas, Silva Mind Control aims to create an awareness of self-responsibility for one's own life as well as a capability for controlling it. The concept and technique are usually presented through a series of weekend lecture classes. The basic premise is that fear, hate, guilt, resentment and ugliness as well as courage, love, self-forgiveness and beauty are all mental creations. Through control of one's image-making faculties, the individual seeks a bright, joyous and cheerful world through enhanced **visualization**, imagination and inner mental constructs. On a more esoteric level, the Silva Method is a particular mind-technique that is employed to orient oneself to the world of etheric vibrations in order to receive psychic information. It is broadly classed, along with **Arica**, *est*, **psychosynthesis** and **Scientology** as a "cult of man" group. Through guided imagery and visualization, one seeks to encounter "inner wisdom," a "master teacher" or his/her "higher self."

There are many spin-offs of Silva Mind Control including **mind dynamics** and Lee Lozowick's Hohm Community (founded in 1975) as well as Burt Goldman's Silva Mind Control method of mental dynamics that aims to solve family problems, develop business confidence, remove stress, decrease or eliminate fear, achieve weight control, increase desire and obtain emancipation from past mental/emotional scars. The initial text detailing this **New Thought** methodology is Jose Silva and Philip Miele's *The Silva Mind Control Method* (1978). Another basic exposition on the method is Burt Goldman's *Silva Mental Dynamics: An Introduction* (1988). The Silva Mind Control organization has centers and offices in most cities of the United States as well as branches in at least seventy-five countries throughout the world. There are approximately 450 certified Silva instructors.

SMITH, HOUSTON (1920-). Author and commentator on world religions. Houston is particularly concerned with the relationship between science and spirituality. In opposing scientific materialism and existentialism, he recognizes the importance of science but also its limitations. His own spiritual explorations have tended to focus upon **Christianity**, **Sufism**, Vedanta and **Tibetan** and **Zen Buddhism**. Houston is a member of the Advisory Board of the Agency for Human Interconnectedness through Manifestation of Spiritual Awareness or AHIMSA. In response to the attacks of September 11th, 2001, Houston argued that if life is governed by **karma**, "it is not right for one nation to possess such disproportionate power and wealth" when two-thirds of the world lives in poverty. A prolific writer, his books include *The World's Religions: Our Great Wisdom Traditions* (1958, 1992), *Forgotten Truth: The Common Vision of the World's Religions* (1976), *Beyond the Postmodern Mind* (2nd edition, 1989), *One Nation Under God: The Triumph of* *the Native American Church*—co-edited with Reuben Snake (1996), *The Eye of the Heart: Metaphysics, Cosmology, Spiritual Life*—with Frithjof Schuon (1997), *Cleansing the Doors of Perception: The Religious Significance of Entheogenic Plants and Chemicals* (2000) and *Why Religion Matters: The Fate of the Human Spirit in an Age of Disbelief* (2001).

SOLAR TEMPLE, ORDER OF THE. Belgian Luc Jouret, claiming to be a reincarnated member of the Knights Templar, founded the Order of the Solar Temple in 1977. As with **Aum Shinrikyo**, defections, loss of charisma and messianic failure played a role in the violent final denouement of the group. Chiliastic expectation led to predictions (on varying dates) of a catastrophic fire that will destroy the earth but allow Solar Temple members—as the last remnant of the "Christ Hierarchy" or reincarnated disciples of Christ—to "transit" to the next life. Solar Templists regard death itself as an illusion. While Aum Shinrikyo retains a **Buddhist-Hindu** foundation, the Solar Temple turned instead toward an eclectic mixture of Cathar, Druid, **Freemasonic**, Templar, **Rosicrucian** and alchemical symbols.

Leadership of the Solar Temple came to be shared between Jouret and French-Canadian Joseph Di Mambro, and the latter may have become the movement's de facto head. The New Age tenor of the Temple is to be found in its consideration that its members are the Star Seeds of the Universe as well as Christ's Torch that is to reanimate the Primordial Fire of Life. The Order regularly recited **Alice Bailey**'s **Great Invocation** and also spoke in terms of the New Age of the Era of the Virgin. Its **gnostic** emphasis sought the release of the "inner person" from the bonds of the world in order to return to the native realm of light. In the early 1990s, combining this impulse to escape the world with the emerging notion of "transit" Di Mambro suggested the possibility of a flying saucer that might come to find the adepts and take them to another world or dimension. But he also spoke of "transit" as something to be accomplished by a shift in consciousness. And as the group in general came to view the world increasingly as unjust, it appears that preparations for death began many months before the 1994 and 1995 events.

While the movement was certainly **apocalyptic**, like **Aum Shinrikyo** and the **Church Universal and Triumphant**, it was also survivalist. Moreover, the Order clearly subscribed to a **galactian** theology. The exact causes that led to the culminating suicides and murders are not known, but increased membership defection, loss of charismatic prestige, mounting financial debts and other difficulties may have hastened the final decision to "transit." But where Aum Shinrikyo turned to violence against outsiders, the Order of the Solar Temple turned some—if not the predominant part—of its violence against itself. In this conclusion, the **millenarian** expectation of apocalyptic change along with a gnostic devaluing of the world and life on this planet—both characteristic of a recurring theme throughout the New Age movement itself— obviously contributed to the explosive amalgam that the Order became.

SPACE CLEARING. A technique associated with **feng-shui** that seeks to remove negative energies believed to accumulate over time in rooms, one's home, office or building. New Age versions of feng-shui draw on North American Indian techniques, Hawaiian Kahuna rituals, Balinese purification rites, and the like. Two names associated primarily with "space clearing" are those of **Denise Linn** and Karen Kingston.

SPANGLER, DAVID (1945-). Leading spokesperson of the New Age whose 1976 *Revelation: The Birth of a New Age* serves as a popular statement of the movement's goals and perspectives. Spangler emphasizes New Age as an expression for transformation and cocreative spirit rather than any specific psychic, occult or spiritual particularity. For him, it is an orientation that grounds itself in holistic and planetary values. He tends to deny New Age as a "movement" or "prophecy" but sees it instead as largely a "mnemonic device" for a wide spectrum of people holding different if not contrary opinions who nevertheless support contrasting efforts for social **healing**. Like **Marilyn Ferguson** and **Baba Ram Dass**, Spangler understands the self and society as inseparable—with self-transformation becoming a chief impetus to social action (including efforts toward ecological restoration, educational reform, citizen activism and diplomacy, etc.).

Until 1973, Spangler served for three years as codirector and spokesperson of the **Findhorn Foundation**. Returning to the United States, he then became the founder-director of the Lorian Association. He lectures widely on personal and community development, spiritual philosophy, eco-theology and futures studies. Working with intuitive skills, he claims to receive information from the inner worlds. A prolific writer, he has authored numerous books including *Festivals for the New Age* (1975), *Toward a Planetary Vision* (1977), *The New Age Vision* (1980), *Emergence: The Rebirth of the Sacred* (1984), with William Irving Thompson—*Reimagination of the World: A Critique of the New Age, Science and Popular Culture* (1991), *Everyday Miracles: The Inner Art of Manifestation* (1996), *Towards a Planetary Vision* (1997), *A Pilgrim in Aquarius* (1997), *The Call* (1998), *Parent as Mystic, Mystic as Parent* (2000) and *Blessing: The Art and Practice* (2001).

SPIRITUALISM. A religious-philosophical thought and practice that studies psychic phenomena and explains them in terms of discarnate spirits that have an interest in the living. The origins of the movement are multiple, but its formal inauguration occurred with the "shenanigans" of the Fox sisters in Hydesville, New York, in 1848. Nevertheless, there is a long antecedence to contemporary psychic experience that stretches across the ancient civilizations of the Fertile Crescent and Greece to the Puritan and Wesleyan counterreactions against deism in the late 1600s that denied the validity of any intercourse with spirit entities.

Following the terminology now used for parapsychology since J. B. Rhine's experiments in the 1930s at Duke University with extrasensory perception (ESP), there are four basic types of ESP: **telepathy** or mind-to-mind (subconscious-to-subconscious) communication; **precognition** or seeing into the future; **clairvoyance** or perception of the world beyond the senses and without the aid of any other mind; and **psychokinesis** or mind over matter. Spiritual **healing** is generally understood as a subcategory of this last, that is, a form of psychokinesis. **Astral travel**, on the other hand, that is, experience of the conscious self outside the body, appears to be something not subsumed by these main four divisions of psychic activity. The general concerns of spiritualism, however, deal with mediumship, and this would appear to be clairvoyance and/or telepathic communication with beings that are not of this world. In the Bible, there are incidents of telepathy, precognition, clairvoyance and psychokinetic healing. The communication of Saul, the Israelite king, with the ghost of Samuel through the "witch" of Endor is a famous mediumistic incident. Likewise, during the transfiguration, Jesus' conversation with Moses and Elijah is another significant mediumistic event. In more recent times, the visions, angelic communications and astral travels of the Swedish physicist, **Emanuel Swedenborg** (1688-1772) became a virtual bedrock to the later developments of spiritualism, **New Thought** and **theosophy**.

But along with Swedenborg, the other significant forerunner of spiritualism and what emerged earlier as the New England transcendentalist movement is **Franz Anton Mesmer** (1734-1815). Though he was denounced by the French Academy in 1784 and died in disgrace, Mesmer's students took his philosophy of magnetic healing and hypnotism to Great Britain and the United States. In America, Andrew Jackson Davis (born 1826) came into contact with a traveling Mesmerist teacher and subsequently developed clairvoyant capabilities and a propensity to perform magnetic healing. He claimed to have had visions of both Swedenborg and the Greek physician Galen. Davis taught that the individual progresses after death through the higher spheres ("Summerland") toward God. His teachings and writings during the last thirty years of his life became formative to the development of spiritualism.

The single event that became the catalyst to American spiritualism occurred when the Margaretta, Kate and Leah Fox claimed in 1848 to be able to communicate via rapping sounds with the ghost of a murder victim in their upstate New York home (known as the "Rochester rappings"). Word spread rapidly of the Fox sisters' mediumistic talents, and soon other people who allegedly could communicate with the dead appeared rapidly across the country. As a result, the séance, the heart of spiritualism, became a popular religio-social gathering. Usually led by a medium for as many as fifty people, the séance emerged as a venue for a range of psychic activity including telepathy, materialization and the levitation of objects. The normal procedure is for a "spirit control" to speak through a medium, that is, for the medium's constant companion from the spirit realm to control the medium's vocal chords while the medium is in trance. The "scandal" that developed for the spiritualist movement occurred in 1888 when the Fox daughters confessed the fraudulency of the rapping noises. Margaretta recanted her confession the following year and was accepted back into the spiritualist fold, and the movement as a whole did not seem to suffer to any fatal degree.

The years between 1880 and 1920 are considered the era of the great mediums. Important spiritualist books appeared as supplements to the works of Swedenborg and Davis. These include John B. Newbrough's *Oahspe* (1881/2) and Levi H. Dowling's *Aquarian Gospel of Jesus Christ* (1908). The study of spiritualism from a more scientific perspective led to the formations of the Society of Psychical Research in London in 1882 as well as the American Society of Psychical Research in 1884.

The National Spiritualist Association of Churches was organized in the United States in 1893 with its headquarters in Washington, D.C. In its 1930 *Constitution and Bylaws*, spiritualism is defined as "the Science, Philosophy and Religion of a continuous life, based upon the demonstrable fact of communication by means of mediumship, with those who live in the Spirit World." It is this belief in personal survival of death, which can be demonstrated by mediumship, that distinguishes Spiritualism from other psychic groups.

In general, spiritualists accept an unending development of every individual in a glorious hereafter. They see the cosmos as friendly, and they reveal affable conversation between earth dwellers and their beloved in Summerland. Spiritualists seek guidance from the spirits of those who once lived as humans on earth. They uphold a spiritual democracy and expect salvation for everyone. Opposing any notion of morose soteriology, they understand cosmic design in terms of humanity's enjoyment of freedom, love and joy.

The New Age movement can in many respects be seen as an outgrowth of American spiritualism and especially of spiritualism's offshoot in **theosophy**. In New Age, however, spiritualism's mediumship has been replaced by **channeling**. Unlike spiritualism, whose primary focus is to prove postmortem survival, New Age has developed a greater concern with spiritualist metaphysics. In other words, its desire is to understand the spirit world itself as well as the spiritual nature of life on earth, and it seeks this knowledge through contact with evolved spirits rather than simply departed loved ones. *See also* MEDIUM CONSULTATION.

STEINER, RUDOLF (1861-1925). Hungarian architect, artist and occultist who, after becoming the secretary of the German branch of **Blavatsky's Theosophical** movement in 1902, broke away in 1913 and formed his own similar group known as anthroposophy ("a complete science of the spirit"). Steiner described his spiritual philosophy as the result of "introspective observation following the methods of natural science." Like Blavatsky and **Edgar Cayce**, Steiner claimed to be in contact with the **Akashic Records** and spirits of the otherworld. An admirer of Goethe, Steiner edited the German poet's nature writings. He was also profoundly interested in **astrology** and considered that human life consists of seven-year cycles. This understanding formed the basis of his educational program that he instituted in 1919. The Steiner Schools, or Waldorf Schools, teach students to observe rather than critically to examine or test situations, to commune with nature spirits and to involve themselves in a form of dance-movement intended to portray music known as "eurythmy." As a **therapeutic** system of rhythmical body movements and silent gestures performed to verse and prose recitation, eurythmy is considered to be an art of visible speech and song. Another significant aspect of Steiner's teachings involves what he designated as "bio-dynamic agriculture"—a nonchemical method of agriculture that aims to work actively with the health-giving forces of nature.

Waldorf Education is a holistic, creative and global program that combines innovative developmental methods with a curriculum structured on culture and the arts (dancing, singing, painting, drawing, modeling, speech and drama). It endeavors to educate "children's hearts, hands and minds." There are now over 700 independent, non-sectarian Waldorf schools worldwide. The Rudolf Steiner College maintains campuses in San Francisco and Fair Oaks (Sacramento). The Steiner emphasis on the development of enhanced perception, imagination and creativity has become a significant component of New Age concern.

Some of the more significant of Steiner's many publications are *The Theory of Knowledge Implicit in Goethe's World-Conception* (1886), *Goethe's Conception of the World* (1897), *Philosophy of Freedom* (1894), *Friedrich Nietzsche: Fighter for Freedom* (1985), *Riddles of Philosophy* (1901), *Mysticism and Modern Thought* (1901), *Christianity as Mystical Fact* (1902), *Knowledge of the Higher Worlds and Its Attainment* (1904), *Theosophy* (1904) and *Occult Science: An Outline* (1910). Steiner's uncompleted autobiography, *The Course of My Life*, was published in parts (1923-1925). In his teachings, the Christ—who Steiner claimed to have experienced directly—occupies a central place. *See also* SIR GEORGE TREVELYAN.

STRIEBER, WHITLEY (1945-). Former modern-gothic horror novelist who promotes the notion of alien encounters as a reality. Strieber's earlier works include *The Wolfen* (1978), *The Hunger* (1981) and *Black Magic* (1982). Subsequently, he moved from the horror genre into that of social conscience—promoting opposition to even limited use of nuclear exchange as a political solution to conflict. The works of this period include *Wolf of Shadows* (1985) and, coauthoring with science writer James Kinetka, *Warday* (1984) and *Nature's End: The Consequence of the Twentieth Century* (1986). Strieber's third career phase began with his autobiographical *Communion: A True Story* (1987) that described the possibility of an assault from intelligent nonhuman beings in his isolated cabin in upstate New York. Insisting that he is not **channeling**, Strieber questions whether the unknown reality he labels "the visitors" represents aliens, demons, angels, something extratemporal, mental projections or another kind of human being. He has learned, however, that thousands of other people claim to have had the same experience. Following *Transformation: The Breakthrough* (1988), Strieber speculated in *Beyond Communion* (1995) whether the physical presence of the visitors is part of a much larger continuum of being. His contact experiences essentially ended after leaving upstate New York in 1993. He has since published *Confirmation: The Hard Evidence of Aliens Among Us* (1998) and *The Key* (2001) and announced in 2001 that he was beginning work on *The Path*.

SUBUD. Developed by Bapak ("father") Subuh (Muhammed Subuh Sumohadiwidjojo, 1901-1987) from the mystical tradition of Java. Subud describes itself as not a teaching or ritual but as an open process of inner receiving. It involves the *latihan* as a group spiritual exercise designed to provide deeper insight into one's religious/spiritual beliefs for purposes of **healing**, purification and new life meaning. The *latihan* is held twice a week and lasts approximately thirty minutes. It begins with participants standing in stillness and is followed by spontaneous movement, dancing, singing and/or shouting. Subud is considered a development of **Sufism**.

SUFI ORDER INTERNATIONAL. An esoteric school that seeks awakening in life and balancing and grounding spirituality founded by Hazrat Inayat Khan (1882-1927) in London originally as the Sufi Order

(1910), renamed the Sufi movement (1916) and, finally, in Geneva, becoming the International Sufi movement (1922). The Sufi Order stresses a universal message of love, harmony and beauty and affirms the common ideals of all religious faiths. It seeks to deepen the individual's spiritual experience through working with whatever faith is meaningful. It endeavors to avoid religious opinions and theology and concentrate instead on the actual experiences of spiritual practice and their discussion. In 1926, Khan named his son **Pir Vilayat Khan** as his successor.

SUFISM (Arabic *tasawwuf*). The inner, esoteric, mystical or psychospiritual dimension of Islam. Sufism has developed its own special vocabulary and is usually transmitted directly from master to student. It seeks an awakening to the awareness of the unmanifest world and consists of spiritual journeying toward God. In Sufi thought, closeness to God is held to be possible in this life rather than to be something that is only obtainable after death. In the West, names associated within and by New Age thinking with Sufism include **Idries Shah**, Bapak Subuh (developer of **Subud**), **Pir Vilayat Inayat Khan (Sufi Order)**, **George Gurdjieff** and **Meher Baba**.

Western Sufism, sometimes referred to as Universal Sufism, is often distinguished from Islamic Sufism in that it variously incorporates mystical elements from other traditions such as **Hinduism**, **Buddhism**, **Christianity**, Hermeticism and the **Kabala**. Union with the godhead is considered to transcend all religious divisions. The person perhaps most associated with the international dimensions of Sufism is Hazrat Inayat Khan (1882-1927)—founder of the Sufi Movement that he later brought to England in 1910 as the Sufi Order of the West, now the Sufi Order International. A further spin-off from the Sufi movement is Sufism Reoriented that came to recognize Meher Baba.

SUN BEAR (Gheezis Mokwa, 1929-1992). Founder and former medicine chief of the Bear Tribe. Born into the Chippewa tribe on the White Earth reservation in Bemidji, Minnesota, and already experiencing visions by the age of three, during an acute bout of diphtheria at the age of four, an apparition of a large black bear standing on its hind legs and surrounded by a rainbow appeared to Mokwa. The bear touched the child's forehead, and from this time he was known by his spirit name of

"Sun Bear." He continued to experience visions and always felt himself guided by spirits.

Sun Bear received his initial training through his medicine men uncles. He left school in the eighth grade during the Depression when his family was forced to move in search of work. Eventually, he became a technical consultant in Hollywood for ten years where he worked on such films as "Bonanza" and "Broken Arrow." In 1961, he founded the magazine *Many Smokes* that aimed to promote communication between different Native American tribes and writers. After Hollywood, he worked as a development specialist for the Intertribal Council of Nevada. He also helped to establish the Tecumseh Indian Studies Program at the University of California, Davis.

Originally, Sun Bear's medicine work was confined to Native Americans, but after a series of powerful visions of cataclysmic **end times**, or "Earth changes," he felt impelled by the Great Spirit to expand his ministry, and, in 1970, he founded the Bear Tribe Medicine Society in Placerville, California. Relocated to Reno, Nevada, the Society moved to its present home, the renamed Medicine Mountain near Spokane, Washington, in 1991. The purpose of the tribe is to spread the spiritual teachings of the Amerindians to a wider audience. To this end, it promotes such organized activities as **medicine wheel** gatherings, wilderness retreats, vision quests, and internship and apprentice programs. The journal *Many Smokes* was renamed *Wildfire* and became the official publication.

Sun Bear has proved to be a popular and commercially successful author, but his decision to make traditional Native American knowledge internationally available has led to much criticism and division within the Amerindian community. Foremost among Sun Bear's antagonists are those from the Lakota tribe who are determined to protect their heritage from commercial and self-seeking exploitation by nonnatives. In their perspective, Sun Bear has been slated a charlatan, but beyond this, the medicine man garnered great respect by many others within the Native American world. Following his death, Sun Bear's "medicine" and position in the Bear Tribe passed to Wabun Wind, but due to health and family responsibilities, she had to relinquish her duties which, after much prayer and soul-searching, have been accepted by Wind Daughter who, in 1996, became medicine chief of the Bear Tribe. Nevertheless, the legacy of Sun Bear remains at the heart of the appropriation accusations that critics level against many of the New Age movements.

SWEDENBORG, EMANUEL (1688-1772). A Swedish scientist/visionary who allegedly communicated with angels and encountered **out-of-body experiences** and provided the initial contributions to the emerging spiritual idiom of the **American metaphysical tradition**. Through vivid dreams and paranormal experience, the scientist came to stress personal exploration of the supernatural in contrast to the insipid and non-direct spiritual knowledge taught by the mainstream churchmen of his day. Eventually he abandoned his career as a scientist in order to pursue psychic/mystical exploration and published sixteen works based on his findings. After his death, the Church of the New Jerusalem was founded in England as a systemization of his thought. It came to the United States after the American Revolution. The Church of the New Jerusalem stresses the precedence of the world of spirit over that of matter. For Swedenborgians, spirit is the ultimately real. Based on spirit's priority, Swedenborg developed the "law of correspondence" between the spiritual and the material. This allowed Swedenborg to offer what he considered a true spiritual interpretation of scripture over a mundane literal one. **Ralph Waldo Emerson** was among those who were strongly influenced by Swedenborg.

Swedenborg came to affirm an exact "law of correspondence" between the physical or phenomenal realm and that of the spiritual or what he considered reality itself. He also believed in human immortality, but for him the human soul passes directly into conscious spirit existence. He therefore denied the Lutheran doctrine of physical resurrection. He also reinterpreted the orthodox concept of the Trinity. Instead of one God in three persons, Swedenborg saw God as one in three principles—the Father being love, the Son divine wisdom, and the Holy Spirit as the consoling, inspiring and sanctifying energy operating for humanity.

-T-

TAI-CHI-CHUAN (taijiquan; literally, "supreme ultimate boxing"). A popular form of Chinese spiritual development and martial arts (*wushu*) through which the individual performs slow, graceful, stylized movements in order to align himself/herself with the vital energy (*qi/ch'i*) of the universe. The Yang style of tai-chi usually consists of sixty-six or eighty-eight steps. The "short form" has reduced the number of sequences to thirty-seven. There is also a Chen style of forty-eight steps or positions, and in the West a twenty-four-step form of tai-chi has been increasingly gaining acceptance as a gateway to the inner self. As the art of **meditational** movement, tai-chi is one of China's five traditional accomplishments along with painting, calligraphy, poetry and music. It takes a holistic approach in seeking to balance the male and female essences of *qi* (**yin and yang**) that permeate both individual and universe as an interrelated organism. Consequently, tai-chi is recognized not only as a martial art but also as a health-building activity. It may be described as involving one in a continuous series of coordinated movements centered on inner stillness. The **human potential movement**'s fascination with tai-chi arises through a western desire to keep fit. A simpler form of tai-chi exercises is known as tai-chi qigong. *See also* QIGONG.

TANTRA. One of the more esoteric Hindu schools that has influenced various New Age movements and practices. Dating from approximately the ninth century C.E. but having affinities with the original materialistic (*Lokayata*) orientations of the *Rigveda*, the magical-mystical spirituality of Tantra represents a non-conformist and often amoral if not immoral tradition within **Hinduism** as well as **Buddhism** and even Jainism. In general, the tantrist aims to achieve spiritual emancipation and, to this end, may employ various techniques—including **yoga**, **visualization**, **meditation**, chanting mantras, enhanced setting (use of candles, incense, bells, cosmic designs), the development of *siddhis* or occult powers, and such practices more usually associated with the pursuit of carnal pleasure: use of alcohol, eating of meat and sexual congress. Though associated with Shakti, the female personification of cosmic energy, the tantric godhead is typically conceived in terms of bipolar gender differentiation and may focus on such popular figures as Shiva and Parvati, or Krishna and Radha. Traditionally, tantric practice is undertaken under the auspices and instruction of a **guru**, but in the West, it can become incorporated into a more individualistic and eclectic New Age format pursued on an *ad hoc* basis and without supervision. While **Tibetan Buddhism** incorporates much of a, chiefly "right-hand," form of tantrism, tantric elements are found to range from practices and concepts promoted by **Osho/Rajneesh** and **Swami Muktananda** to those of western ceremonial **magic, Neo-paganism** and **Wicca.**

TAOISM. A Chinese religious school of thought first mentioned in 97 B.C.E. Legend has it that Taoism was established by Lao Tzu, a sixth century B.C.E. Chinese sage who wrote eighty-one poems that have been compiled as the *Tao Te Ching* ("Book of the Way"). This last is a popular New Age focus of study for spiritual development and self-centering. As a religion, Taoism seeks ultimately the state of *wu-wei* or "inaction." It opposes civilization *per se* and works instead to develop a simple and tranquil companionship with nature. Nevertheless, as a religion in China it consists of both a monastic-centered pursuit of long life through **alchemy** and a popular composite of superstitious practice involving a multitudinous pantheon. By seeking harmony with the Tao (the "way" or "path"), the practitioner hopes to gain **magical** powers. Taoism's alchemical efforts involve harnessing the polarities of **yin and yang.** In the western New Age context, Taoism tends to involve efforts to merge with the Absolute or Ultimate Void. For many, however, it is chiefly an ethical undertaking for living in balance with the earth and others. Taoist thought is also to be found in the *I Ching*.

TAROT (tarocchi). A deck of cards used for **magic,** fortune-telling and esoteric interpretation. Its major arcana cards appear to have been originally inspired by Petrarch's *Il Triompho* which in turn was modeled on the triumphs or triumphal marches of imperial Rome. The cards themselves became prominent in eighteenth century France—comprising the fifty-six minor arcana (essentially the fifty-two cards of the popular deck of playing cards plus four Knights) and the major arcana (the twenty-two pictorial trump cards). The minor cards are divided into four suits of wands (clubs), cups (hearts), swords (spades) and pentacles (diamonds) numbering from one to fourteen (the ace plus nine others and the four court cards of King, Queen, Knight and Knave). The major cards, comprising enigmatic emblems, form the divinatory kernel of the tarot. Occult scholar Antoine Comte de Gébelin (1719-1784) identified these with the twenty-two letters of the Hebrew alphabet. De Gébelin, J. F. Vaillant or "Papus" also linked the tarot with the Gypsies (reputedly but erroneously associated with Egypt). As

The Dictionary 183

a result, the tarot has become associated with the ancient schools of esoteric philosophy belonging originally to Egypt, Chaldea or even India.

Two of the surviving earlier versions of the cards are the Marseilles and Swiss decks. Under the influence of the **Hermetic Order of the Golden Dawn**, revised versions of the tarot were developed by Aleister Crowley (1875-1947) and Arthur Edward Waite (1857-1942). Crowley's commentary, *The Book of Thoth* (1944; 1969), affirms de Gebelin's belief in the cards as repositories of Egyptian magical symbolism. Waite, on the other hand, more influenced by the alleged correspondence between the major arcana and the Hebrew alphabet, develops a symbolism based on the **Kabala**. His 1910 *The Pictorial Guide to the Tarot* ensured the cards popularity throughout the English-speaking world of the twentieth century. With the emergence of the New Age movement, the number of new and innovative versions of the tarot deck has increased dramatically. The cards may be used for esoteric reflection and/or divination but are more often employed for ascertaining current conditions in terms of self-understanding and spiritual growth.

The major arcana consist of the Fool (0), the Magician or Juggler (I), the High Priestess or Juno (II), the Empress (III), the Emperor (IV), the Hierophant, Pope or Jupiter (V), the Lovers (VI), the Chariot (VII), Justice (VIII), the Hermit (IX), the Wheel of Fortune (X), Strength (XI), the Hanged Man (XII), Death (XIII), Temperance (XIV), the Devil (XV), the Tower (XVI), the Star (XVII), the Moon (XVIII), the Sun (XIX), the Last Judgment (XX) and the World (XXI). In the Waite deck as well as some other versions, Justice becomes the eleventh trump; Strength or Fortitude, the eighth.

TARTHANG TULKU RINPOCHE. Tibetan Buddhist monk who left Tibet in 1958. Tarthang Tulku recognized the urgency of saving the cultural traditions of Tibet. He came to America in 1968 and opened the Nyingma Institute in Berkeley, California, to provide for the study and practice of Buddhist teachings. He established the Tibetan Aid Project (TAP) in 1969 to provide emergency relief for Tibetan refugees. He founded Dharma Publishing in 1971 as a non-profit organization dedicated to the preservation and dissemination of books, Tibetan texts, Buddhist art and thankas of the Nyingma School of **Tibetan Buddhism**. In 1989, Tarthang Tulku established the World Peace Ceremony at Bodh Gaya, India. His books include *Sacred Art of Tibet* (1972), *Gesture of Balance: A Guide to Awareness, Self-Healing and Meditation* (1976), *Time, Space, and Knowledge: A New Vision of Re-*

ality (1979), *Hidden Mind of Freedom: Meditation for Compassion and Self-Healing* (1981), *Skillful Means: Patterns for Success* (1991), *Mastering Successful Work: Wakeup!: Mastering Successful Work* (1994), *Sacred Dimensions of Time and Space* (1997) and *Enlightenment Is a Choice* (1998).

TECHNO COSMIC MASS. A new form of worship innovated by **Matthew Fox** to invoke the sacred into the total person (body, mind, heart and soul). Fox's mass blends Western liturgical forms with Eastern and indigenous spiritual constructs as well as multimedia technical imagery, dance and ecstatic music. It is described as an "interfaith, multicultural and intergenerational celebration." The mass is a democratic communal expression that is cosmologically oriented through stress on the interconnection of all creation. In Fox's understanding, the mass seeks to augment justice and compassion in the world by praising and thanking the Creator. This is done through giving expression to the four spiritual journey pathways articulated by Creation Spirituality. The Techno Cosmic Mass is conducted and performed using the ritual circle. It endeavors to be drug-free, alcohol-free and tobacco-free.

TEILHARD DE CHARDIN, PIERRE (1881-1955). French Jesuit priest and paleontologist whose evolutionary philosophy and visionary prophecy have become fundamental ideas for the New Age movement. In a manner similar to **Ken Wilber**, Teilhard frames the history of the universe in a linear evolutionary ascent that progresses from matter into the "band of life" that, in turn, is superseded by the mental "band of consciousness." In other words, the eventualizing process consists of movement from the "geosphere" through the "biosphere" to the "noosphere." Beyond this, Teilhard's "cosmogenesis" of increasing complexity and consciousness culminates with an **Omega Point** of Christogenesis. In this development, the human becomes the turning point through which increasing differentiation shifts toward greater unity and concentration. While many within the more **pagan** orientations of both **Neo-paganism** and New Age reject the idea of a convergent end-point or "return" of the individual divine spark to its Creator or Source, for those New Agers inspired in particular by Teilhard and a doctrinal **Christianity** compatible with New Age thought, there is no conflict between universal evolution and affirmation of a personal God. Teilhard's vision of anthropogenesis comprehends a Neo-humanism that unites love of the world and love of God and centers both on the performance of earthly tasks.

TELEKINESIS. The psychic production of movement and motion over a distance. Telekinesis is a form of extrasensory perception (ESP) similar to psychokinesis, but whereas the latter refers to mental concentration as the cause of the effect, telekinesis is closer to **mediumistic channeling** in which supernatural or etheric forces use the medium's psyche as the vehicle by which objects are moved. Shamanic shape-shifting is a further form of telekinetic transformation. Apport, or the dematerialization/rematerialization of objects in new locations or to make things appear from the atmosphere, is a product of either telekinesis or psychokinesis. A well-known apport medium is **Sathya Sai Baba**.

TELEPATHY. The transmission or reception of mental thoughts or emotions from one person or extraterrestrial entity to another; psychic communication. Telepathy is the basis of both spiritualist mediumship and New Age **channeling**. Biblical examples are found at I Samuel 28 and Matthew 17:1-9.

TENSEGRITY. From "tension" (the force created by pulling or stretching an object) + "integrity" (the state of wholeness or completeness), refers to structures whose shapes are held together by tension but remain flexible and strong. Tensegrity is a science employed by visionary **Buckminster Fuller** in seeking more efficient and organic design for the future needs of humanity. Much of the social and ecological impetus of the New Age movements are indebted to Fuller's ideas of tensegrity and related concerns.

THEOSOPHICAL SOCIETY. *See* THEOSOPHY.

THEOSOPHY. A philosophical religious system that grew out of American **spiritualism**. Its chief distinctions are twofold. First, it is less interested in contacting the departed loved ones of family and friends and seeks instead to commune with Ascended Masters that collectively it terms the **Great White Brotherhood**. The second distinguishing feature of Theosophy is its rich incorporation of Eastern spiritual notions: **karma, reincarnation, akashic** world, ascended masters, etc. Theosophy, in short, becomes a spiritual tradition that combs the truths of the orient and incorporates them into a western system of thought. In many respects, it is the direct precursor of today's New Age movement and, in fact, according to Mary Farrell Bednarowski (1989), New Age is essentially an updating of theosophy and a recasting of it into the contemporary spiritual idiom.

More broadly, theosophy is part of what is often called the Ancient Wisdom tradition. By the end of the nineteenth century in both England and the United States, a number of spiritualists became less interested in making contact with the spirits of the deceased or in demonstrating "proof" of life after death and, instead, claimed to be bearers of occult wisdom ("hidden" wisdom) that they declared to have received from various teachers all descending from a long lineage dating to the obscure reaches of time. In some instances, the wisdom teachings are traced to ancient, hidden texts that have recently been found. In theosophy itself, the transmission of occult knowledge is usually made through the efforts of special people who, through spiritual training, have gained the ability to enter occult realms where they are taught directly by spiritual masters.

Theosophy itself developed with **Helena Petrovna Blavatsky**. Upon her death, the theosophical mantle passed to Annie Besant (1847-1933) who, with the guidance of Charles Leadbeater (1854-1934), came to recognize and promote **Jiddu Krishnamurti** as the physical vehicle of the Bodhisattva Avatar as world teacher. However, by the late 1920s, Krishnamurti rejected the notion that he was a spiritual messiah. Meanwhile, theosophy itself underwent a number of schisms with two rival societies (the Theosophical Society in America and the Theosophical Society of America), along with their respective European and Indian extensions, contesting for leadership.

The objectives of the original Theosophical Society founded in New York were to form a nucleus of the Universal Brotherhood of Humanity without distinction of race, creed, sex, caste or color; to encourage the study of comparative religion, philosophy and science; and to investigate the unexplained laws of nature and the powers latent within humanity. Blavatsky's cosmology forms the basis of theosophical thought. Theosophy teaches that spiritual progression comes through occult practices, reincarnation and spiritual masters. These practices include **meditation** and **yoga**. Reincarnation is understood as the presentation of repeated opportunities in which to overcome lower plane attachment. One's future life will reflect the spiritual achievements of the present life. But it is the help of the masters that is the most important for theosophists.

Theosophy remains at the center of the Wisdom Tradition. While its **gnostic** and mystical form of **Christianity** has heavily infused contemporary forms of both **Rosicrucianism** and **Freemasonry**, theosophy has also spawned a number of offshoots that themselves fall within the orbit of the modern-day New Age movement. These include **Rudolf Steiner**'s anthroposophy, the Krishnamurti Foundation, **Alice Bailey**'s Arcane School and World Goodwill, the Ballards' **"I AM" Religious Activity,** Elizabeth Clare Prophet's **Church Universal and Triumphant, Benjamin Creme**'s Tara Centre and even, to an extent, **Edgar Cayce**'s Association for Research and Enlightenment among others. *See also* DIVINE HIERARCHY.

THERAPY. Any series of actions that aim to achieve or increase health and wellness. Popular New Age therapies include **acupuncture, Alexander Technique, aromatherapy, aura-soma, biofeedback,** chiropractic manipulation, **craniosacral therapy, dream-work, Feldenkrais, Gestalt, iridology, kinesiology, massage therapy, Mind Dynamics,** osteopathy, psychological counseling, **qigong, reflexology, Reiki, Rolfing,** and **tribal dancing and drumming.** Methods of **healing** dominate virtually all New Age concerns, and its techniques are usually therapeutic in one sense or another. These can range from Dolores Krieger's Therapeutic Touch using hands to locate the body's energy field imbalances, ease and/or eliminate pain and encourage healing to such **New Thought** figures as **Terry Cole-Whittaker, Bernard Siegel, Louise Hay, Caroline Myss** and **Deepak Chopra** who use mental suggestion and the sheer will power of the mind to eradicate illness. *See also* FRITZ PERLS and VIRGINIA SATIR as well as ALTERNATIVE MEDICINE, HOMEOPATHY and NATUROPATHY.

Within New Age, other therapeutic methods include art therapy (a form of creative **visualization** used for post-traumatic stress reduction), music therapy (employing music to deal with physical, mental and emotional problems), and polarity therapy (developed by Randolph Stone as a blend of chiropractic, naturopathy, acupuncture/acupressure, **yoga** and diet to correct energy imbalances or blockages). There is also past-life therapy—a use of psychotherapeutic hypnosis to treat psychological disorders believed to stem from earlier lives. *See also* REINCARNATION and KARMA.

THICH NHAT HANH. *See* NHAT HANH, THICH.

TIBETAN BUDDHISM. The form of Buddhism traditionally centered in Tibet as a blend of **shamanism,** indigenous Bon practices, **Tantra** and the "Middle Way" of **Buddhism.** Tibetan Buddhism stresses cultivation of the virtues of wisdom and compassion. It has developed an elaborate pantheon of Tathagatā (or Cosmic) Buddhas, bodhisattvas, yi-dams or tutelary protectors, deities, consorts and attendants. These may be symbolically represented in the form of a **mandala** and used as an object of concentration. Through its tantric and shamanic incorporation along with **yoga**, Tibetan Buddhism has cultivated the development of *siddhis* (psychic or **magic** powers) as part of its **meditative** practice. These embrace such reputed supranormal abilities as **clairvoyance, clairaudience, telepathy**, the power to pass through physical matter, to walk on water, the ability to recall past lives, to cure illness, to obtain indefinite longevity, to fly, to be invisible, to project astrally and the ability to attain a state of suspended animation during which all major bodily functions are halted. Nevertheless, Tibetan Buddhism seeks to emphasize that such *siddhis* are mundane accomplishments when com-pared to the achievement of buddhahood and omniscience. Through the Tibetan diaspora, especially under the post-1959 aegis of the Dalai Lama, the Tibetan form of Buddhism has become increasingly popular in the West and as part of the New Age movement. From a traditional perspective, the relation between Tibetan Buddhism and New Age is uneasy and contentious, but from the all-accommodating stance of New Age, Tibetan practices have a welcomed place. *See also* NAROPA IN-STITUTE.

TORRES-RUBIN, PENNY. Southern Californian housewife who began to **channel** an entity named Mafu in 1986. Mafu's last physical incarnation is claimed to have been as a leper in first century Pompei. He is described as a member of the "Brotherhood of Light" and as a "highly evolved being from the seventh dimension." Like Ramtha who is channeled by **JZ Knight**, Mafu seeks to help humanity find its proper direction.

TOTEMISM. In the New Age context, the association with natural objects and, especially, with animals as spirit guides. In North America, totemic practices have been strongly influenced by **Native American spirituality** and notions of vision quest. In Australia, the Aborigines fulfill this inspirational source for its colonial descendants. For Europe itself, New Agers often share with **Neo-pagans** a quest for icono-graphic knowledge from among indigenous pre-Christian traditions—particularly the Celtic. A totemic object (rock, tree, bird, bee, deer, wolf, etc.) may become a focus for **visualization** and **psychic dream experience**. It may also be used in the individual's **meditative** practice or as a vehicle for **shamanic** journeying or vision work. Unlike primitive societies, the totem for the New Age practitioner is not an emblem of ancestral descent nor even a group unifier but functions instead for the individual specifically as an agent for mystical relationship.

TRANSPERSONAL PSYCHOLOGY. The discipline that seeks to integrate eastern spirituality and western psychology. It came about with the realization by **Abraham Maslow** and other psychologists that there are cosmic meanings and ultimate concerns beyond the boundaries of humanistic psychology. Maslow considered that the "first force" is represented by Freudian and other "depth" psychologies, the "second" by behavioralism and the "third" by humanism and European existentialism. He argued that a "fourth force" comprising a "still higher transpersonal form" exists for which humanistic psychology serves essentially as a transition. According to **Marilyn Ferguson**, transpersonal psychology, in drawing from the world's spiritual disciplines, seeks to transcend suffering rather than reduce it to "normal" dimensions. **Ken Wilber** has constructed a transpersonal model of human evolution as it moves toward what he describes as "integral Wholeness and Spirit." For Wilber, the discipline is less a psychology than a modern-day effort to create a synthesis between western psychology and eastern religion.

Transpersonal psychology is multidisciplinary and has holistic understanding as its goal. It adds authentic spirituality to the more usual psychological aims of healthy functioning. While endeavoring to maintain an empirical perspective, it encompasses the study of ultimate values and meanings, peak experiences, ecstasy or mystical experience, the soul, self-actualization, self-transcendence, cosmic oneness, interpersonal encounter, transcendental phenomena, and the familiarity with and expression of bliss, wonder and awe. Related to its concerns are the fields of parapsychology and the study of near-death experience. These last, however, are controversial, and several psychologists argue that parapsychology should be kept separate from transpersonal psychology. Nevertheless, a New Age expectation is that, with paradigm shift, the time might come in which paranormal phenomena and **near-death experience** are widely accepted. Advances in understanding transpersonal psychology are expected to lead to greater acceptance of the miracles, prophecies and visions of religious narrative. *See also* MYTHOLOGY.

TREVELYAN, SIR GEORGE (1906-1996). Visionary British orator often referred to as the "Grandfather of the New Age Movement." Influenced by the ideas of **Rudolf Steiner** concerning the spiritual nature of humanity and earthly existence as the foundation for the soul's development, in the words of Peter Dawkins, Trevelyan became the rallying point for a new initiative in spiritual awareness. From 1948 to 1971, he offered esoteric courses through Attingham Park. Upon his retirement from the college, he founded the Wrekin Trust as an educational charity promoting spiritual awareness and training. His orientation was to combine the ancient Wisdom Tradition with the findings and insights of modern science and psychology. He became an active advocate of food reform, organic horticulture and natural **healing** and maintained close ties with the **Findhorn Foundation**, the Lamplighter movement, dedicated to maintaining "ever-burning" lamps as part of a conscious network of light throughout Great Britain and the world, and the Open Gate and Gatekeeper Trusts that seek to reawaken pilgrimage to sacred places.

Trevelyan's annual "Round Table" gatherings of healers, holistic practitioners and spiritual innovators furnished much of the foundation for the New Age network in Britain. For him, the New Age is essentially a non-sectarian, scientific and mystical holistic outlook based on a compassionate, global humanitarianism. Among his books, we have *Twelve Seats at the Round Table* written with Ted Matchett (1976), *The Active Eye in Architecture* (1977) and *Magic Casements* (1983). His trilogy on the awakening of a spiritual worldview comprises *A Vision of the Aquarian Age* (1977), *Operation Redemption* (1981) and *Exploration into God* (1992). In the second of these, Trevelyan explores the meaning and role of the Christ impulse for our times. With his "absolute certainty" of the "I AM," he denies any ultimate reality to death and claims that we are all part of the "one great conscious being which is humanity."

TRIBAL DANCING AND DRUMMING. An ad hoc ritual gathering that is often a standard feature of collective New Age spiritual retreats. Tribal dancing takes much of its inspiration from indigenous traditions such as **Native American**, Aboriginal and even African spirituality. The use of drums and percussion rhythms is part of these traditions but may also be an influence that derives from **Hindu** temple worship (*pūjā*) as well as **Tibetan Buddhism**. In the New Age format, such dancing and drumming usually is conducted as part of the ritual circle and, in this sense, shares much with the ceremonial structure of contemporary Western **paganism**. Large-scale drumming and dancing circles occur during the popular **Neo-pagan** summer camps across North America, but they also are to found as smaller gatherings—whether in public venues, New Age open centers or private homes. They may be undertaken for engendering collective ecstasy, group catharsis and spiritual insight or as vehicles for individual or group **healing**. They may be used in conjunction with various **visualization** techniques, and much of their alleged source of inspiration derives from **shamanism** or Neo-shamanism.

-U-

UNITY. The largest of the **New Thought** bodies—correctly the Unity School of Christianity. This group is important in the New Age context because it uses, expresses and appears to be fully at home with the New Age idiom. Unity claims to teach "practical **Christianity**." That is, it espouses a return to what is believed to have been the primitive Christianity of Jesus and the Apostles. Unity teaches belief in one God and in Christ, the Son of God, manifest in Jesus. In other words, Jesus is believed to be divine, but in what reflects New Age in general, divinity is not considered confined to Jesus alone. Since all are created in the image of God, all are potentially divine.

Typical of New Age, at least its Christian wing if not the broader spectrum of New Age itself, Jesus is seen as the way-shower. He is not hailed as the Redeemer who saves us from original sin, but rather as the one who shows us the way *par excellence*. In other words, Jesus becomes the way-shower in the regeneration of each person. He creates "at-one-ment" between God and humanity through which each person can then regain his or her estate as a son or daughter of God. Essentially, Unity teaches that God is not a personality but a spiritual energy "force" or principle of love. Jesus is man, and Christ is divine consciousness, so that Jesus represents humanity while Christ represents God in humanity.

In Unity's teachings, the authority of the Bible is accepted, but Unity follows a metaphysical interpretation. **Reincarnation** is accepted as a step toward immortality. Humanity evolves toward Godhood through physical, mental and spiritual development and will find solutions to all problems in collective God consciousness. This process involves discovering one's innate divinity and raising consciousness into full God-realization. With the recognition that one is in perfect oneness with God, there is no need for redemption.

Unity's founder, Charles Fillmore, recommended both vegetarianism and chastity as helpful means toward eventual physical immortality. His wife, and Unity's co-founder, Myrtle (Mary Caroline Page), was healed in 1886 when she heard the noted metaphysician E. B. Weeks proclaim, "I am the child of God and therefore I do not inherit sickness." Myrtle believed that by repeating this phrase as a positive declaration, she and others would be healed. Within the larger context of New Thought metaphysics, Unity stresses a form of silent prayer as well as the use of affirmations--the repetition of positive statements affirming the presence of a hoped for condition. The Fillmores were students of **Phineas Quimby, Mary Baker Eddy** and **Emma Curtis Hopkins**. They founded Unity in 1889 and adopted the name Unity in 1895 to denote that the spiritual practice is devoted to the spiritualization of all humanity while taking the best from all religions. In 1903, it was incorporated as a church by the Unity Society of Practical Christianity in Kansas City. Its best known publication is *The Daily Word. See also* PROSPERITY CONSCIOUSNESS.

-V-

VEGETARIANISM. Restriction of nutrient intake to non-animal sources—especially if the food supply were to involve pain for sentient life forms and/or the death of the animal. In general, vegetarians will consume eggs, milk and milk products, whereas vegans avoid all ovo-lactarian consumption and eat no animal products (including, for some, honey). Demi-vegetarians are those who include fish and/or fowl in their diets but exclude the meat of mammals. While the term was coined in the 1840s, vegetarianism itself was especially promoted during the late 1960s counterculture by **gurus** such as Stephen Gaskin (*see* **The Farm**) who argued that the further away on the evolutionary scale the better in spiritual terms was the food for the individual. It has since become a practice for many who identify with the New Age movement—especially through its incorporation of ideas from **Hinduism** and **theosophy**. Consequently, while some avoid meat and/or animal products for strictly religious or moral reasons, some claim that meat consumption is detrimental to health, while others claim that livestock husbandry is an inefficient means of food production and is instead anti-ecological.

In the New Age context, vegetarianism is often part of the move toward organic and unprocessed foods—usually free of chemicals, pesticides and other synthetic factors (e.g., use of artificial fertilizers). Raw food advocates tend not to cook their food. Following the ideas of A. T. Hovannessian, an Iranian Armenian teacher, Ann Wigmore (1909-1994) established the Hippocrates Health Institute in the United States to promote the raw foods diet and use of wheatgrass. Fruitarianism is similar but restricts its choice of foods to uncooked fruits and nuts. Another popular vegetarian diet is macrobiotics, which centers on cereals as its principal food ingredient—especially brown rice. Incorporating a **Zen Buddhist** understanding of all foods being divided between **yin and yang**, macrobiotics argues for the necessity to balance consumption of "female" and "male" qualities. It also restricts the accepted range of approved vegetables and fruits. Names associated with the macrobiotic **diet** include Georges Ohsawa (1893-1966) and his student Michio Kushi (1926-), among its foremost promoters. Kushi stresses a standard diet of miso soup, cereals, fresh fruit and cooked vegetables. In general, and with the exception of lemons, foods should be regionally grown and eaten in their proper season. In more recent times, Kushi has relaxed some of the macrobiotic standards to allow cereals to comprise only fifty percent of the diet and even the occasional consumption of fish.

Indian-born Dinshah Pestanji Ghadiali (1873-1966) brought the seminal ideas of veganism teachings to the United States prior to World War II. It was Ghadiali who also helped develop the practice of **chromotherapy**. His son, H. Jay Dinshah, founded the American Vegan Society in 1960. Dinshah, moreover, in 1974, reorganized the remnants of various vegetarian groups into the North American Vegetarian Society. The Fruitarian Network and the Vegetarian Information Service were both established in 1976. As vegetarianism has been a common feature for many who identify with the New Age movement, it is typically regarded as a way of life that augments such spiritual concerns as assisting planetary consciousness, elimination of pain infliction, reduction of environmental pressure, **healing** of disease, increase of physical health, and pursuit of transcendental enlightenment.

VISUALIZATION. A form of mental imagery used toward self-healing and spiritual insight. Visualization descends from **New Thought** with its emphasis on the power of the mind over the body. The individual may picture benevolent forces consuming the afflicting physical disease. Spiritual healers may encourage their patients to amplify the **healing** process through such visualization. The process is also used, often in a group context, in which a spokesperson, therapist or facilitator leads people through a guided imagery path—working toward spiritual and euphoric renewal. In New Age gatherings, creative visualization is frequently combined with **meditation** techniques. Participants are prompted to experience unconscious **archetypal** and personal symbols. In general, they are first encouraged to relax and breathe deeply in order to enter into a passive meditative state. The prompter then supplies a suggestive outline in which the day-dreamer encounters healing and transforming images and symbols. Often, New Agers collectively concentrate on images of a peaceful or environmentally holistic world.

VOLKTUMSBEWEGUNG. Late nineteenth century German movement that integrated its call for the creation of a national German religion with popular, countercultural experiments in new ways of life: **vegetarianism**, free sex, self-sufficient farming and **pagan** festivals. The close similarity between this quasi-mystical folk movement and present day New Age raises and exacerbates the issue of **New Age controversies**. In Germany, "anti-Semitism" became popular around 1879, and thereafter the *Völkisch* movement developed the dream of a *Judenrein* **Christianity** alongside its romantic views of the peasantry and its opposition to democracy, market economy and socialism. Former linguistic concepts were now changed into purely biological ones. While Friedrich Nietzsche in his attack on belief in Christian transcendence repudiated both nationalism and anti-Semitism, the Völkisch interpretation of Nietzsche *circa* 1900 adopted his ideas of cyclic time and the Overman (*Übermensch*); from the romantic perspective, the growth of secularism, egalitarianism and industrialism was seen to represent the lowest point in the current cycle of time. As a result, the Völkisch movement, influenced by its reinterpretation of Nietzsche, sought a rebirth of the people rather than their development or evolution. While one Völkisch element sought to find pagan alternatives to Christianity, another faction attempted instead to purge Christianity of Jewish elements. *See also* ARIOSOPHIE.

VOODOO. A West Indian religion associated primarily with Haiti but part of the wider Afro-Atlantic diaspora that includes Santería, Lukumí, La Regla de Ocha, Obeah, Espiritismo, Candomblé, Umbanda and Macumba. Strictly speaking, none of these practices is New Age, but as are all world religions, they become sources for eclectic borrowing and incorporation into New Age spirituality. For instance, the commercialization of the *botannica* as a source center for African-based religious supplies (candles, incense, statues, amulets, etc.) is condemned by most traditional practitioners but allows the kind of unguided, unchecked and sporadic pick-and-mix that characterizes much of the New Age movement. The spiritism of Allan Kardec that first became popular in France in the 1850s has infused portions of Afro-Latin spirituality, and its notions of spiritual hierarchy and non-corporeal spiritual advance toward enlightenment have strong resonance with New Age orientations. Voodoo itself is perhaps best known for its use of a magically charged wax doll that can be "worked upon" to effect changes, usually negative, for the person it is designed to represent. While such "black magic" may have little to do with Haitian religion, it is suggestive of whatever more nefarious intentions are to be found within some individuals who adopt a *laissez-faire* and "I am my own authority" approach to spiritual appropriation. The Voodoo quality that is most found within New Age religions is that which motivates a contemporary search for amulets and talismans. Another feature is that which feeds into the psychic mediumship of **channeling** and **spiritualism**. A third is the assimilation of Voodoo *loas* or gods with "etheric world intelligences" and efforts to acquire spiritual guidance, prophecy and **healing** from them.

-W-

WALK-IN. A concept of soul transference presented by **Ruth Montgomery** in her 1979 book *Strangers Among Us* and again in *Threshold to Tomorrow* (1982) to describe "an entity who is not born as an infant but who takes over (always with permission) the body of one who wishes to depart." Such souls, though not perfected, are superior and have earned the privilege through the lives on earth they have already undergone to bypass childhood and return directly as adults. They inherit the memory bank of the walk-out and are expected to play a leading role through social reform work as well as in dispelling the fear of death in the establishment of the "New Age of Aquarius." Montgomery claims there are already "tens of thousands" at work on earth today. *See also* AGE OF AQUARIUS, REINCARNATION.

WEIL, ANDREW. "**Guru** of **alternative medicine**" and popularizer of New Age medical remedies. Weil graduated from the Harvard Medical School and now teaches at the University of Arizona College of Medicine. He is a physician and researcher in ethnopharmacology, a clinical professor of internal medicine, a promoter of self-**healing**, an expert on both medicinal herbs and mind-body interaction, and the director of the Program in Integrative Medicine which he founded in 1994. Weil emphasizes a perspective that considers the person to be a totality of the physical, mental and spiritual. His integrative medicine combines ideas of conventional and alternative medicine as complementary systems which together allow for the body's optimum performance of its natural healing mechanisms. Weil seeks to move the focus to health and healing rather than on disease and treatment. His approach is to address all levels of the healing process from diet, exercise, stress reduction, sleep improvement, work, relationships, etc. He also promotes the therapeutic, nutritional and practical use of Cannabis sativa ("useful hemp")—especially hemp oil.

Weil has produced a steady stream of books beginning with his controversial but popular *The Natural Mind: An Investigation of Drugs and the Higher Consciousness* (1972, 1986), *The Marriage of the Sun and Moon: A Quest for Unity in Consciousness* (1980), *From Chocolate to Morphine: Everything You Need to Know about Mind-Altering Drugs*—with Winifred Rosen (1983, 1998), *Health and Healing* (1983), *Natural Health, Natural Medicine* (1995), *Spontaneous Heal-*

ing: How to Discover and Enhance Your Body's Natural Ability to Maintain and Heal Itself (1995), *Eight Weeks to Optimum Health* (1997), *Meditations for Optimum Health* (1997), *Vitamins and Minerals* (1997), *Eating Well for Optimum Health* (2000) and *The Healthy Kitchen: Recipes for a Better Body, Life, and Spirit* (2002).

WICCA. A **pagan** magical mystery religion that recognizes Gerald Brosseau Gardner (1884-1964) as its founder. It posits a godhead that consists of male and female polarities—most often expressed as The God and The Goddess. It also tends to revere nature, while its ethics conform to the principle or "law" of the threefold return: whatever one sends out (i.e., does) returns three times or three times as strong. There are many different lineages of Wicca beside Gardnerian: including Alexandrian (a more formal version established by Gardnerian initiate Alex Sanders), Algard (Mary Nesnick), Georgian (George Patterson), Dianic (worshipping The Goddess exclusively), NROOGD (New Reformed Orthodox Order of the **Golden Dawn**), School of Wicca, a largely Celtic-based Fairy/Faery Folk tradition, etc. Most of these lineages operate through small initiatory groups known as covens. The coven tends to range in membership from four to twenty. In addition, Wicca initiates style themselves as "priest" or "priestesses."

Unlike traditional ceremonial **magic**, Wicca's ritual circle is employed to separate participants within it from the mundane world beyond rather than as a means of confining a conjured and possibly dangerous spirit or entity inside. Beyond the lineage system of Wicca, there is a wider spiritual tradition known as witchcraft that may claim to be hereditary or ethnic, preexisting and independent of Gardner, and more akin to the tradition of cunning craft. Witchcraft as a spiritual practice is as much solitary as it is coven-based or communal.

Wiccans and modern witches often have the reputation of autonomously inventing their tradition and combining elements from other traditions on an *ad hoc* and eclectic basis. To the degree that this occurs, they are frequently confused with New Age license. Theologically, New Age and paganism/**Neo-paganism** are generally distinct. On the other hand, inasmuch as they justify all behavior through self-legitimation alone, they reveal similarities.

WILBER, KEN (1949-). Contemporary philosophical, popular and prolific writer who is often identified with the New Age. While he is frequently considered a voice from within the movement that both promotes and explains New Age thought, he also clearly delineates its weaknesses. In the realm of health, Wilber has criticized influential New Age teachers who argue for direct correlations between emotional states and illness as naïve and manipulative. He feels that it is too simple to claim that all cancer has been created out of resentment. Wilber insists that the contention that thought can be applied directly to create a given reality is not found in the mystical traditions but is instead a symptom of "narcissistic and borderline pathology." For Wilber, those who teach this paradigm are in reality teaching by intimidation: recovery depends on agreeing with the teacher that reality is self-created; death is the result of non-agreement. That the mind is the sole creator and healer of disease is, according to Wilber, a misunderstanding of the principle of **karma**. He argues that while there may be illnesses that are produced by karma or the previous conditions of the individual, others are generated by external influences, by accident, by environmental factors and/or by provisional causes such as food or other combinations of circumstances.

For Wilber, disease has multiple origins. The most fundamental is physical, next emotional, then mental and finally spiritual. His approach to **healing** rests on making every effort to determine which causal level is actually operative and then using the equivalent and appropriate means of treatment. If one succeeds in understanding the levels properly, one then has the highest chance of healing. But if one gets them wrong, he or she will only generate guilt and despair. Yet, while there is a reciprocal relationship between physical illness and healing on the one hand, and emotional, mental and spiritual states on the other, he argues that the influence of thought on one's states of being is not as great as New Agers tend to believe. Nevertheless, Wilber does not discount the growing medical realization that the immune system is directly affected by thoughts and emotions, but his concern remains with the possible suffering that can result from New Age's **New Thought** belief system that each of us is totally responsible for everything.

Along with **Baba Ram Dass**, **Marilyn Ferguson** and **David Spangler**, Wilber is a leading spokesperson within the New Age movement. While remaining a significant theoretician in the field of **transpersonal psychology**, his own spiritual tradition is closest to Mahayana and Trikaya **Buddhism**, Vedanta and Neo-Platonism. This is a **gnostic** position that exalts a transcendental *a priori* that is fully commensurate with the fundamental New Age theological perspective. He admits that what he refers to as Emptiness, others might call God, Goddess, Brahman, Tao, Keter, Rigpa, Dharmakaya, Maat or Li. But in Wilber's non-dualist understanding, evolution is *always already* undone and ultimately canceled by the ground of Emptiness that is "prior to the beginning." Nevertheless, he remains a full proponent of direct religious experience.

Among the nearly two dozen books of Wilber are *The Spectrum of Consciousness* (1977), *No Boundary* (1979), *The Atman Project* (1980), *Up from Eden* (1981), *A Sociable God* (1982), *Eye to Eye* (1983), *Quantum Questions* (1985), *Grace and Grit* (1991) and *A Brief History of Everything* (1996). In this last, he explores subjective, collective, behavioral and objective evolution, and he laments the progressive reduction of traditional "I" and "we" language to empirically-based "it" language alone. In other words, art and ethics have been eliminated for objectivity/science—the Beautiful and the Good have been subsumed and forgotten in the True. In seeking to bypass the monological gaze of the modern industrial ontological grid, spiritual freedom for Wilber is attained solely through transcendence rather than in any fusion with the archaic, magical or mythical—whether God or nature. While often a contentious let alone complex thinker, Wilber is one of the primary intellectual influences within the New Age movement.

WILLIAMSON, MARIANNE. New Thought teacher and writer based in Santa Barbara, California. Now described as the "high priestess of pop religion," Williamson's turn-around from low self-esteem and an out-of-control lifestyle occurred in 1977 when she by chance came across a copy of *A Course in Miracles*. This provided her the ability to break through intellectual, emotional and psychological pain. Her subsequent teachings are based on the *Course* as a system of spiritual psychotherapy. Among her numerous books are *A Return to Love*, *A Woman's Worth* and *Illuminata*. She writes on such subjects as spiritual principles, relationships, death, grieving, abundance, handling fear and change, love and passion, mysticism, the empowerment of women and, more recently, focusing on children and principles of faith. Williamson teaches that spirit and mind are equally as important as the physical in **healing**. Like the physical body, the social (cultural, political) body comprises a currently compromised immune system. This renders our present social ills similar to opportunistic infections. The boosting of the immune system in which the individual citizen is compared to an immune cell is occurring through people's reinvention of themselves. Williamson speaks of a cultural awakening that is currently underway in which people, formerly sluggish through exclusive external focus, are rediscovering spirituality. She has founded Centers of Living as an organization dedicated to raising funds for worthy causes and to providing home-help for people with life-threatening diseases. As a healer, Williamson describes herself as a metaphysician whose work concentrates on stimulating healing forces, and she applies the same principles to social systems as to the human body.

-Y-

YIN AND YANG. The female and male principles that comprise the phenomenal universe in Chinese religio-philosophical thought. As polarities, yin and yang are complimentary and balancing forces. Yin qualities include the negative, passive, female, receptive, dark, cold, soft and wet as well as night and winter. Yang qualities are precisely the opposite: positive, active, male, creative, light, warmth, hard and dry as well as day and summer. These are meant to signify cosmic attributes rather than value judgments, but as the yin/yang framework has entered New Age discourse through the *I Ching*, the *Tao Te Ching* and **Taoism**, it is often disputed by **feminist spirituality** efforts to recast long-entrenched western stereotypes. Yin and yang are nevertheless prominent in **alternative medicine** practices based on the Chinese notion of *ch'i/qi* ("energy"). *See* ACUPUNCTURE, QIGONG, TAI-CHI-CHUAN as well as the Japanese REIKI. The foundation of **feng-shui** is also based on understanding proper balances between yin and yang dynamics.

YOGA (Sanskrit "union, harnessing," Cf. English "yoke"). Originally a training and self-discipline practice employed to enhance physical and mental abilities. Used by the Raja, or warrior caste of India, according to the *Aitareya Brâhmaña* 7.29.4, it was taught by them to the Brahmans or priests under whom it became a technique that aimed for transcendental ecstasy or self-extinction (*moksha, samadhi*, Buddhist *nirvana*, Zen *satori*). In its more recent exportation to the west, yoga has frequently become separated from its **Hindu** associations and has been reemployed by **human potential** often in ways closer to the Râjayana desire for physical strength and invincibility.

The classic understanding of yoga is associated with Patanjali, who considered four chief forms: raja, jnana, karma and bhakti. The "royal" way or *raja* yoga concentrates on the mind and will and developing mastery over the mental processes. *Jnana*, or "wisdom" yoga approaches the divine through knowledge; *karma* yoga, through good works and proper attitude. While presenting the latter two, the *Bhagavad Gita* (*c.* 300 B.C.E.) principally extols *bhakti* yoga—the path of *pûjâ*, or personal devotion to the gods. Bhakti encompasses the performance of ritual as the route toward godhead.

In his sutras, Patanjali himself expounds on *raja* yoga which he breaks down into *hatha, mantra* and *laya* forms. **Meditation** is central with each of these, while mantra yoga employs formulaic prayer and incantation as its chief technique. Laya yoga (the "yoga of latency") combines mantra and hatha procedures to arouse the **kundalini**. It is, however, hatha yoga that is most associated by westerners as yoga. It seeks to attain and preserve physical well-being through practice of posture (*asana*), breathing (*pranayama*) and sense control (*pratyahara*). For Patanjali, raja yoga can be divided into eight stages beginning with *yama* or non-violent asceticism followed by *niyama* or cleanliness and abstinence from desire, *asana*—including *mudras* or hand positions, *pranayama, pratyahara, dharana* ("undistracted concentration"), *dhyana* ("ego-less contemplation") and *samadhi* ("enlightenment, realization of unification").

In the New Age appropriation of yoga, its practice is frequently critiqued as superstitious and antirational pseudo-mysticism. Nevertheless, the yoga of human potential often has closer affinities with indigenous Indian yogis' feats concerning mental control over the body and ultimately with such supernormal abilities as walking through fire, burial alive, endurance of physical pain, achievement of a cataleptic state, levitation and flight through the air. The acquisition of **telepathic** powers may be another consequence of yogic prowess. But if such Human Potential practices are condemned as forms of "new narcissism" and "not the true purpose of yoga," the Kshatriya/Raja origins of the practice suggest that Brahmanic and Vedantic Hindu redirection of yogic techniques is itself an appropriation. In the western New Age context, the practice of yoga increasingly replaces the loss of belief in traditional religious doctrine for what yoga refers to as "witnessing," Werner Erhard's *est* calls "observation" and **Carlos Castaneda**'s Don Juan names "stopping the world." Throughout the New Age, yoga is associated with meditation as a chief means for personal development if not "ultimate enlightenment" or "spiritual release" as well. It is seen as a positive pathway toward mind-body-spirit holism.

YOGANANDA, PARAMAHANSA (1893-1952). Indian **Hindu** saint who pioneered **yoga** in the West. As a religious and philosophical innovator in education, psychology, business and medicine, Sri Yogananda combined modern educational methods with training in yoga and spiritual ideals. After founding a "how-to-live" school for boys in 1917, he left his native land for Boston three years later as India's representative to an International Congress of Religious Liberals. Here he began the Self-Realization Fellowship (known in India as the Yogoda Satsanga Society) dedicated to spiritual and humanitarian work. Following lectures in Boston, New York and Philadelphia on integrating humane and spiritual vision with human life, he began a cross-continental tour in 1924. The following year, he established the international headquarters for the Self-Realization Fellowship in Los Angeles. The society not only publishes Paramahansa Yogananda's writings and lectures but promotes Kriya Yoga **meditation** centers throughout the world. Kriya yoga is understood as an advanced technique of meditation founded on scientific principles. The society also sponsors self-realization temples and retreats as well as a Worldwide Prayer Circle that endeavors to channel healing energy for international peace and harmony. Sri Yogananda's techniques for contemplation and God-realization are considered to be a practical methodology that allows the aspirant rapid achievement in the here and now. It includes various "Energization exercises," the "Hong-Sau" technique to develop concentration, and the "Aum Technique" of meditation to experience beyond bodily and mental limits the "Divine Consciousness" that supports all of life. Yogananda's *Autobiography of a Yogi* was published in 1946 and has become a classic throughout Eastern spiritual branches of the New Age movement. His basic emphasis is on the underlying unity of the world's religions and direct personal experience of God.

YOGI BHAJAN. *See* SIKH DHARMA.

-Z-

ZEN BUDDHISM. A (chiefly Japanese) fusion of Mahayana and Chinese **Taoist** belief that has become fashionable in the Western world since the 1950s. It endeavors to experience enlightenment (*satori*) directly and, to this end, considers all actions—from the contemplative to the most mundane activities of life—to be forms of **meditation**. In essence, Zen Buddhism represents an adaptation of Indian Buddhism by Chinese Taoists to which Japan added its most essential ingredient, namely, simplicity. Inasmuch as Zen blends easily with other religious traditions, it has been readily adopted into the New Age portfolio of popular spiritualities. There is little affirmation of specific belief, and, in its Western context, Zen silent meditative practice is frequently separated from the Buddhist context per se—allowing it a compliance commensurate with the eclectic and consumeristic orientation of the Western market of spiritual assortment. Without a specific code of conduct, Zen allows that one is responsible for his/her own actions—making a perfect fit with the flexible and personal character of New Age ethics.

Zen represents perhaps the most intellectual of Buddhist offerings—one that is grounded in a complex metaphysical philosophy. Its effort is to overcome one's own spiritual pride in which the ego blocks the purpose of meditation ritual, usually performed under guidance of a Zen monk, to enter the silence of the deep state of consciousness in which the totality and oneness of all things are felt. This altered state of consciousness, the experience of euphoric well-being and mystical unity, can be achieved in the Zen context by numerous methods (e.g., running for sixty minutes), but is more often pursued as Zen-sitting (controlled posture and keeping still) in the zendo or room used for meditation in the monastery or in a special place reserved for meditation in one's home. There are special Zen retreat centers as well as monasteries throughout America and Europe, such as the Tassajara Zen Mountain Center near Big Sur in California (opened in 1967 as the first Buddhist monastery outside Asia).

ZUKAV, GARY. Consciousness theorist. Zukav distinguishes between "external power" as the ability to manipulate and control and "authentic power" as the alignment of the personality with the soul. In his concern for spiritual growth and spiritual transformation, he perceives the universe as alive, compassionate, friendly, wise and non-violent. He adopts a typically New Age attitude that argues we choose our experiences deliberately to learn and evolve. As cocreators in our own evolution, Zukav argues that we are immortal souls first and physical beings second. He hails the birth of a new humanity of new perceptions and new values.

With his "spiritual partner" Linda Francis, Zukav cofounded Genesis: The Foundation for the Universal Human as a non-profit organization that sponsors workshops and retreats for the development of the individual's authentic power and spiritual partnership. Zukav is particularly known for his 1979 *The Dancing Wu Li Masters: An Overview of the New Physics*—a lucid presentation of quantum physics. He has also published *Seat of the Soul* (1989), *Soul Stories* (1999) and, with Linda Francis, *The Heart of the Soul: Emotional Awareness* (2002). In 1997, Zukav released an audio cassette entitled *Authentic Power: Aligning Personality with Soul*.

Bibliography

Albanese, Catherine L. "The Subtle Energies of Spirit: Explorations in Metaphysical and New Age Spirituality." *Journal of the American Academy of Religion* 67, no. 2 (June 1999): 305-325.

Bacon, Francis. "The New Atlantis." *The Harvard Classics: Vol.III.* Edited by Charles W. Eliot. New York: Bartleby, 2001. (First published in 1626).

Bailey, Alice A. *Externalization of the Hierarchy.* New York: Lucis Publishing Company, 1957.

Bednarowski, Mary Farrell. *New Religions and the Theological Imagination in America.* Bloomington: Indiana University Press, 1989.

Blavatsky, Helena Petrovna. *Isis Unveiled.* Wheaton, IL: Theosophical Publishing House, 1972.

———. *The Secret Doctrine: The Synthesis of Science, Religion, and Philosophy*, Vol. II — *Anthropogenesis* (reprint of 1889 original). Pasadena, CA: Theosophical University Press, 1970.

Bloch, Jon P. *New Spirituality, Self, and Belonging: How New Agers and Neo-Pagans Talk about Themselves.* Westport, CT: Praeger, 1998.

Bloom, William, ed. *The New Age: An Anthology of Essential Writings.* London: Rider, 1991.

Bruce, Steve. "Good Intentions and Bad Sociology: New Age Authenticity and Social Roles." *Journal of Contemporary Religion* 13, no.1 (January 1998): 23-35.

Bochinger, Christoph. *"New Age" und moderne Religion.* Guiterskiger: Chr. Kaiser Verlaghaus, 1994

209

Bowman, Marion. "The Noble Savage and the Global Village: Cultural Evolution in New Age and Neo-Pagan Thought." *Journal of Contemporary Religion* 10, no. 2 (May 1995): 139-149.

Brown, Michael. *The Channeling Zone: American Spirituality in an Anxious Age.* London: Harvard University Press, 1997.

Campion, Nicholas. *The Book of World Horoscopes: An Annotated Sourcebook of Mundane Charts.* Bristol: Cinnabar Books, 1996.

Chryssides, George. "New Age, Witchcraft and Paganism." *Exploring New Religions.* London: Cassell, 1999.

Cornille, Catherine. "Different Forms of Spirit Mediation in Mahakiri and Shinnyo-en: Shamanism East and West." *Syzygy* 1, no. 4 (1992): 355-366.

Cumbey, Constance. *The Hidden Dangers of the Rainbow.* Shreveport, LA: Huntington House, 1983.

Cush, Denise. "British Buddhism and the New Age." *Journal of Contemporary Religion* 11, no. 2 (May 1996): 195-208.

Davies, Christie. "The Fragmentation of the Religious Tradition of the Creation, After-life and Morality: Modernity not Post-Modernity." *Journal of Contemporary Religion* 14, no. 3 (October 1999): 339-60.

Eller, Cynthia. "New Religious Movements and Social Change: The Case of Feminist Spirituality." *Syzygy* 2, nos. 1-2 (1993): 97-106.

Faber, M. D. *New Age Thinking: A Psychoanalytic Critique.* Ottawa: University of Ottawa Press, 1996.

Gardner, Martin. *The New Age: Notes of a Fringe Watcher.* Buffalo, NY: Prometheus Books, 1991.

Greer, Paul. "The Aquarian Confusion: Conflicting Theologies of the New Age." *Journal of Contemporary Religion* 10, no. 2 (May 1995): 151-66.

Guthrie, Stewart. "McClenon's 'Shamanic Healing, Human Evolution, and the Origin of Religion': A Critique." *Journal for the Scientific Study of Religion* 36, no. 3 (September 1997): 355-57.

Hanegraaff, Wouter. *New Age Religion and Western Culture.* Leiden: Brill, 1997.

Heelas, Paul. "New Age Authenticity and Social Roles: A Response to Steve Bruce." *Journal of Contemporary Religion* 13, no. 2 (May 1998): 257-64.

———. *The New Age Movement: The Celebration of the Self and the Sacralization of Modernity.* Oxford: Blackwell, 1996.

Kemp, Daren. "The Christaquarians? A Sociology of Christians in the New Age." 2000. http://www.christaquarian.net/default.shtml (14 September 2002).

Lewis, James R., and J. Gordon Melton. *Perspectives on the New Age.* Albany: SUNY, 1992.

McClenon, James. "Shamanic Healing, Human Evolution, and the Origin of Religion." *Journal for the Scientific Study of Religion* 36, no. 3 (September 1997): 345-54.

McDermott, Rachel Fell. "New Age Hinduism, New Age Orientalism, and the Second-Generation South Asian." *Journal of the American Academy of Religion* 68, no. 4 (December 2000): 721-31.

Melton, J. Gordon. *Encyclopedic Handbook of Cults in America.* New York: Garland Publishing, 1986.

Melton, J. Gordon, Jerome Clark, and Aidan A. Kelly. *New Age Encyclopedia.* Detroit: Gale Research, 1990.

Newport, John P. *The New Age Movement and the Biblical Worldview.* Grand Rapids, MI: Eerdmans, 1998.

Olson, Roger E. "Rudolf Steiner, Esoteric Christianity, and the New Age Movement." *Syzygy* 1, no. 4 (1992): 341-53.

Partridge, Christopher H. "Truth, Authority and Epistemological Individualism in New Age Thought." *Journal of Contemporary Religion* 14, no. 1 (January 1999): 77-95.

Pearson, Jo, ed. "Assumed Affinities: Wicca and the New Age." In *Nature Religion Today: Paganism in the Modern World*, edited by J. Pearson, R.H. Roberts and G. Samuel. Edinburgh: Edinburgh University Press, 1998: 45-56.

———. *Belief Beyond Boundaries: Wicca, Celtic Spirituality and the New Age.* Burlington, VT/Milton Keynes: Ashgate/The Open University, 2002.

Porter, Jennifer E. "Spiritualists, Aliens and UFOs: Extraterrestrials as Spirit Guides." *Journal of Contemporary Religion* 11, no. 3 (October 1996): 337-53.

Raphael, Melissa. "Goddess Religion, Postmodern Jewish Feminism, and the Complexity of Alternative Religious Identities." *Nova Religio* 1, no. 2 (April 1998): 198-215.

Rose, Stuart. "An Examination of the New Age Movement: Who Is Involved and What Constitutes Its Spirituality." *Journal of Contemporary Religion* 13, no. 1 (January 1998): 5-22.

Simmons, John F. "The Forgotten Contribution of Annie Rix Militz to the Unity School of Christianity." *Nova Religio* 1, no. 2 (October 1998): 76-92.

Spangler, David. 1981. *Reflections on the Christ*, Findhorn Lecture Series, 3rd ed. Forres, Scotland: Findhorn Foundation.

Spink, Peter. *A Christian in the New Age*. London: Darton Longman & Todd, 1991.

Steyn, Chrissie. *Worldviews in Transition: An Investigation of the New Age Movement in South Africa*. Pretoria: University of South Africa Press, 1994.

Streiker, Lowell D. *New Age Comes to Main Street: What Worried Christians Must Know*. Nashville: Abingdon, 1990.

Susumu, Shimazono. "New Age and New Spiritual Movements: The Role of Spiritual Intellectuals." *Syzygy* 1, nos.1-2 (1993): 9-22.

Sutcliffe, Steven. "The Authority of the Self in New Age Religiosity: the Example of the Findhorn Community." *Diskus* 3.2 (1995): 23-42.

———. "A Colony of Seekers: Findhorn in the 1990s." *Journal of Contemporary Religion* 15, vol. 2 (May 2000): 215-31.

Sutcliffe, Steven, and Marion Bowman. *Beyond New Age: Exploring Alternative Spirituality*. Edinburgh: Edinburgh University Press, 2000.

Tacey, David. *Jung and the New Age*. Sussex: Brunner-Routledge, 2001.

Van Hove, Hildegard. "Higher Realities and the Inner Self: One Quest? Transcendence and the Significance of the Body in the New Age Circuit." *Journal of Contemporary Religion* 11, no. 2 (May 1996): 185-94.

Waterhouse, Helen. "Reincarnation Belief in Britain: New Age Orientation or Mainstream Option?" *Journal of Contemporary Religion* 14, no.1 (January 1999): 97-109.

York, Michael. "Emergentism and Some Post-Big Bang Perspectives." *Journal of Contemporary Religion* 14, no. 2 (1999): 291-97.

———. *The Emerging Network: A Sociology of the New Age and Neo-pagan Movements*. Lanham, MD: Rowman & Littlefield, 1995.

———. "New Age and Paganism," pp. 157-65 in *Paganism Today: Wiccans, Druids, The Goddess and Ancient Earth Traditions for the Twenty-first Century*, edited by Charlotte Hardman and Graham Harvey. London: Thorsons, 1996.

———. "New Age and the Late Twentieth Century." *Journal of Contemporary Religion* 12, no. 3 (1997): 401-19.

———. "New Age in Britain: An Overview." *Religion Today* 9, no. 3 (1994): 14-22.

———. "The New Age Movement in Great Britain." *Syzygy* 1, nos. 2-3 (1992): 147-58.

———. "Postmodernity, Architecture, Society and Religion: 'A heap of broken images' or 'a change of heart'." pp. 48-63 in *Postmodernity, Sociology and Religion*, edited by Kieran Flanagan and Peter Jupp. London: Macmillan/New York: St. Martin's Press, 1996.

Index

Abraham, Ralph, 167
Academy of Religion and Psychical Research, xxvii
Actualizations, 121
acupressure, 11, 38
acupuncture, xix, 11, 17, 22, 28, 38, 103, 104, 131, 150, 167, 187, 187, 203
Adi Da Samraj, xxvii, xxx, 11-12, 64, 91, 156
Aetherius Society, xxiv, xxv, 12-14, 57, 58, 79, 81
Age of Aquarius, xv, 7, 14-15, 19, 21, 25, 30, 47, 50, 52, 57, 66, 67, 73, 114-15, 120, 145, 190
age of information, 1, 7
ahimsa, 160
Aihara, Herman, xxv
aikido, 95
Akashic Records, 15, 27, 41, 44, 63, 149, 155, 176, 185
Albigenses, 82
alchemy, 15-17, 21, 137, 158, 171, 182
Alcott, Amos Bronson, 2, 65

Alexander Technique, 17, 131, 187
alternative medicine, 11, 14, 17, 48, 60, 124, 130, 166, 187, 198, 203
Alternatives Programme, xxxi, 37, 47
American Academy of Kinesiology and Physical Education, xxii, 103
American Astrological Society, xxii
American Federation of Astrology, xxiii
American Holistic Medical Association, xxix, 168
American metaphysical tradition, 2, 7, 17-18, 66, 71, 119, 180
American Society of Psychical Research, xx, 175
American transcendentalist movement, 2, 65, 66
American Vegan Society, xxv, 195
Ampère, André-Marie, 58

homoeopathy, 17, 90, 93, 154,
187
Hopkins, Emma Curtis, xx, 65,
71, 74, 90, 93, 133, 150,
193
Horwitz, Jonathan, xxx, 94,
166
Houston, Jean, 108
Hovannessian, A. T., 194
Howard, Mike, 67
Hubbard, Barbara Marx, xxxi,
33, 72, 90, 94
Hubbard, L. Ron, xxiv, 79, 86,
162
human potential, xv, 2, 14, 60,
68, 73, 86, 89, 95, 103,
112, 113, 115, 121, 128,
143, 147, 150, 154, 157,
161, 167, 181, 203, 204
Hunt, Roland, 48
Hurtak, James Jacob, 19, 28,
79, 80
Huxley, Aldous, 59, 68, 95,
109
hydrotherapy, 131

"I AM" Religious Activity,
xxiii, 49, 51, 55, 62, 79,
96-97, 187
Ichazo, Oscar, xxvi, 21, 67, 87,
97-98, 109, 128
I Ching, 97, 98, 137, 182, 203
Iglehart, Hallie, 71
Illich, Ivan, 36
Ingham, Eunice, 155
Insight Transformational
Seminars, xxix, 123
Institute for the Harmonic De-
velopment of Man, 86

Institute in Culture and Creation Spirituality, xxix, 75
Institute of Noetic Sciences,
73, 166
integral yoga , 32
Integral Yoga Institute, xxvi
integrative medicine, xxxi, 198
International New Thought
Alliance, xxi, xxiv, 133
International Vegetarian Union, xxi
iridology, 98-99, 131, 187
Islam, 21, 55, 82, 103, 164,
178

Jackson, Don, xxv, 161
James, William, 95, 114, 140
Jampolsky, Gerald, 100, 108
Jefferson, Thomas, 114
Jensen, Bernard, 98, 99
Jesus, xxi, 3, 13, 14, 41, 46,
49, 50, 51, 58, 63, 65, 70,
74, 87, 93, 96, 97, 113,
119, 135, 140, 149, 151,
163, 173, 175, 192
Jones, Franklin Albert, xxvii,
11
Jouret, Luc, xxix, 156, 171
Judaism, 53, 54, 55, 82, 83,
101, 122, 135, 143, 196
Judge, W. Q., xix, xxi
Jung, Carl Gustav, 16, 19, 20,
82, 88

Kabala, xxi, 21, 83, 97, 101-2,
135, 158, 178, 183
Kardec, Allan, 196
karma, 3, 21, 29, 30, 35, 38,
48, 50, 51, 102-3, 111,

Ray, Sondra, xxix, 138
rebirthing, xxviii, xxix, 138,
    139, 152-53
reflexology, xxi, 153, 187
Reich, Wilhelm, 143, 154
Reiki, xxx, 90, 95, 154-55,
    187, 203
reincarnation, 3, 13, 22, 35, 38,
    41, 51, 55, 62, 85, 102,
    105, 110, 111, 112, 122,
    139, 152, 155-56, 160,
    162, 163, 171, 185, 186,
    187, 192, 198
Religious Science, 53, 133,
    134, 135, 156
Rhine, J. B., 173
ritual healing, 17
Rivers, Julie, 161
Robbins, John, xxxi, 156-57
Roberts, Jane, xxv, xxvii, 43,
    44
Rodegast, Pat, 44, 72, 157
Rogers, Carl, 143, 154
Rolfing, xxvii, 38, 69, 157-
    158, 187
Roosevelt, Eleanor, 114
Rosenbleuth, Arturo, xxiv, 58
Rosicrucianism, xix, xxi, 7, 21,
    48, 76, 82, 83, 93, 121,
    158, 171, 186
Rossi, Andrew, 92
Rudrananda, Swami, 11
Ruether, Rosemary Radford,
    71
Ruhani Satsang, 64, 123
Ruskin, Jules, xxv, 161
Russell, Charles Taze, 149
Russell, Peter, 138

Rutherford, Leo, xxxii, 131,
    158-59, 166

Sai Baba, 87, 91, 156, 160-61,
    185
Saint Germain, Comte de, 49,
    50, 96, 97
Saint Germain Foundation,
    xxiii
Sams, Jamie, xxxi, 130, 161
San Mat, 55, 112, 123
Satchidananda, Swami, xxvi
Satin, Mark, xxix
Satir, Virginia, xxv, xxix, 72,
    161-62, 187
School of Enlightenment, 105,
    106
School of T'ai Chi Chuan, 98
Schucman, Helen, xxv, 9, 10
Scientology, xvi, xxiv, 68, 79,
    86, 95, 123, 162, 170
Seicho-No-Ie, 134
self-actualization, 68, 114
Self Realization Fellowship
    Society, xxii, 64, 205
Selver, Charlotte, 115
Seva Foundation, 59
seven bodies of the individual,
    61, 162
Seven Rays, 34, 43, 49 62, 85,
    96, 162-163
Shaffer, Caroline, 72, 163
Shah, Idries, xxv, 128, 163-64,
    178
Shaivism, 123, 124
shamanism, xxx, xxxii, 17, 18,
    21, 24, 40, 52, 63, 67, 71,
    73, 88, 90, 93, 94, 116,

230   Index

Twitchell, John Paul, 123

UFOs (flying saucers), xxiv, 8,
13, 14, 44, 57, 78, 79, 171
Unarius, 79
Unification Church, 74, 80
Unitarianism, 2
United Nations, xxxii, 74
United Nations Oslo Confer-
ence on Religion and Be-
lief, xxxii, 37
Unity, xx, xxx, 11, 62, 121,
133, 134, 192-93
University of Creation Spiritu-
ality, 75
Upledger, John, 56
Urantia, xxiv, 44, 79, 80
Usui, Mikao, 154, 155

Vajradhatu Foundation, xxvi,
128, 129
Vatican, the, xxxi, 75
Vedanta, xxi, 11, 12, 170, 200,
204
Vegan Society, xxiii
Vegetarian Information Service, 195
vegetarianism, 3, 17, 21, 60,
118, 131, 169, 192, 194-
95, 196
Vegetarian Society of New
York, xxiii
Vishnu, 12, 50, 90, 91
visualization, 17, 24, 34, 35,
45, 81, 84, 88, 90, 95, 101,
102, 114, 116, 130, 142,
146, 168, 170, 181, 187,
188, 191, 195
vivation, 153

Vivekananda, Swami, xxi, 12,
32
Volktumsbewegen, 21, 54, 195-
96
voodoo, 51, 196-97
Vorilhon, Claude, 79, 151

Wabun Wind, 116, 179
Waite, A. E., xxi, 83, 183
Waldman, Anne, 129
Waldorf Schools, xxii, 176
Walker, Barbara, 71
walk-in, xxix, 122, 198
Ward, Barbara, 77
Watcher Angels, 28, 80
Watson, Lyall, xxix
Watson, Patrick, xxviii, 98
Watts, Alan, 68, 95, 109
Weber, Max, xvii
Weeks, E. B., 192
Weil, Andrew, xxxi, 198-99
Westcott, William Wynn, xx,
83
White Eagle Lodge, xxiii
Whitten, Ivah Bergh, 48
Wicca, xvi, xxiii, 72, 132, 182,
199
Wiener, Norbert, xxiv, 36,
58
Wigmore, Ann, xxv, 194
Wilber, Ken, xxix, 81, 184,
189, 199-201
Wilder, Dona, 161
Williamson, Marianne, xxix,
72, 157, 201-2
Wilson, Steve, 101
World Fellowship of Relig-
ions, xxiv
World Future Society, 94

World Peace Ceremony, xxxi,
  183
World's Parliament of Religions, xx, xxxi, xxxii

Yahweh, 151
Yeats, William Butler, 83
Yin and Yang, 16, 72, 98, 111,
  181, 182, 194, 203
yoga, xxii, xxvi, 4, 12, 13, 14,
  22, 28, 29, 32, 35, 36, 38,
  39, 42, 64, 68, 69, 73, 83,
  91, 92, 101, 107, 117, 123,
  124, 131, 169, 181, 186,
  187, 188, 203-4, 205; Chinese, 150; jnana, 153; ki-

palu, xxvi/xxvii; kriya,
  205; kundalini, 123, 124,
  169, 204; prana, 153
Yoga Institute, xxii, xxvi
Yogananda, Paramahansa, xxii,
  xxiv, 64, 91, 156, 204-5
Yogendra, Sri, xxii
Yogi Amrit Desai, xxvi
Yogi Bhajan, xxvii, 64, 168,
  169

Zarathustra/Zoroaster, 70, 119
Zen Buddhism, 39, 68, 80, 95,
  97, 117, 135, 139, 170,
  194, 203, 206
Zukav, Gary, xxix, 206-7

About the Author

Michael York is principal lecturer for the Sophia Centre for the Study of Cultural Astronomy and Astrology at Bath Spa University College in Britain. He is director of the Bath Archive for Contemporary Religious Affairs, as well as codirector of the Academy for Cultural and Educational Studies in London and director of the Netherlands-based Amsterdam Center for Eurindic Studies. Books by Michael York include *The Roman Festival Calendar of Numa Pompilius*, *The Divine versus the Asurian: An Interpretation of Indo-European Cult and Myth*, *The Emerging Network: A Sociology of the New Age and Neo-pagan Movements* and *Pagan Theology: Paganism as a World Religion*. He is an associate editor for the *Encyclopedia of Religion and Nature*, to which he has contributed articles on the New Age Movement, shamanism, magic, New Religious Movements, pantheism, polytheism, UFOs, and channeling. Michael York has trained in the Sociology of Religion with particular emphasis on the Sociology of New Religious Movements. He has pursued an interest in alternative forms of spirituality for many years, has studied astrology since the 1960s, and retains a first-hand encounter and understanding of the San Francisco counterculture from its Haight-Ashbury heyday to the present. His interest in New Age religiosity has taken him across North America, Britain, continental Europe and the subcontinent of India.